[To] Know You

"Even though I'm known for writing nonfiction, fiction is what I love to read—and Shannon has created a storyline with more twists and turns than a mountain road. But more important than the twists is the way this story explores love and sacrifice and the effects of our decisions. This book will grab you and not let go. Anyone who reads Shannon's nonfiction books knows she hooks you with her narrative, and now she's put that skill to great use in her first novel!"

—Shaunti Feldhahn, best-selling author of *For Women Only* and *The Veritas Conflict*

"Can you ever truly escape your past? Shannon Ethridge weaves a gripping story of a respected Christian woman who has to dig up the past she thought buried in order to save her son's life. And amazingly, sometimes even the things we hoped we could forget end up being the things God uses to bring real wholeness to our lives. A no-holds-barred realistic portrayal of a messy life that finds peace when we confront our pasts, not try to ignore them."

—Sheila Wray Gregoire, author of *The Good Girl's Guide to Great Sex*

"*To Know You* is one of the best emotional roller coasters I have been on! Who knew it was possible to interweave so many powerful sexual, emotional, and relational themes into one story and so seamlessly? This novel is what other Christian fiction needs to be: refreshingly honest, grace-inducing, and the opposite of 'preachy.' A work well done!"

—Michelle N. Onuorah, author and screenwriter

"In *To Know You*, Shannon Ethridge does a brilliant job of turning the truths she is known for teaching into a dynamic, page-turning narrative that will touch your heart and stir your soul. She takes the reader on a very real journey of temptation and redemption along with the characters, crafting a story you do not want to miss."

—Leigh Congdon, freelance writer

"I literally read *To Know You* in one night. I couldn't put it down. Everything about the characters is so real. There is no sugar-coating their struggles and temptations, and it made the entire book very relatable. But most of all, I loved the story of how the redeeming power of God's grace transformed them one by one. Such a great example of God's unconditional love! The world needs more books like *To Know You*!"

—Amber P.

"*To Know You* offered an exhilarating escape each time I picked it up, and I felt so spiritually uplifted each time I put it down. I recommend this book to anyone looking for a riveting yet wholesome story that gets your heart racing and your blood boiling at the same time!"

—Michele A.

"I picked up the pre-released version of *To Know You* while on vacation. The first chapter totally hooked me and I couldn't stop. I did not expect to identify so closely with some of the characters, and more particularly with some of the characters' personal struggles. It helped me realize that I am *not alone*, and that no temptation seizes us but what is common to man (and woman!). I'm so grateful for gripping stories like this, and the power they have to transform the heart and mind—especially *my* heart and mind."

—Gretchen E.

Veil of Secrets

Veil of *Secrets*

SHANNON ETHRIDGE
and KATHRYN MACKEL

NASHVILLE MEXICO CITY RIO DE JANEIRO

Published in Nashville, Tennessee, by Thomas Nelson. Thomas Nelson is a registered trademark of HarperCollins Christian Publishing, Inc.

Author is represented by the literary agency of Alive Communications, Inc., 7860 Goddard Street, Suite 200, Colorado Springs, CO 80920. www.alivecommunications.com

Thomas Nelson, Inc., titles may be purchased in bulk for educational, business, fund-raising, or sales promotional use. For information, please e-mail SpecialMarkets@ThomasNelson.com.

Library of Congress Cataloging-in-Publication Data

Library of Congress Cataloging-in-Publication Data
Ethridge, Shannon.
Veil of secrets / Shannon Ethridge and Kathryn Mackel.
pages cm
ISBN 978-1-4016-8867-7 (trade paper)
1. Married people--Fiction. 2. Man-woman relationships--Fiction. 3. Daughters--Fiction. 4. Family secrets--Fiction. 5. Domestic fiction. I. Mackel, Kathryn, 1950- II. Title.
PS3605.T48V46 2014
813'.6--dc23

2014002838-

Printed in the United States of America

14 15 16 17 18 RRD 6 5 4 3 2 1

Dedicated to the
moms, daughters, sisters, friends
who help each other find joy
through life's unexpected journeys.

Third Week of November

Presidential Primary Season

one

Monday afternoon

PIZZA RUNS.

Melanie Connors knew all about pizza runs. She needed to make it clear to Sophie that there would be no more pizza runs.

She sat in stalled traffic on the Everett Turnpike, staring at a sea of brake lights. To her right, she could see the Merrimack River, laced with ice. The wind surged, rattling the windows of the rental car. Even with the heat blasting, frigid air snaked down Melanie's back.

November was New Hampshire's ugly secret. The brochures boasted about the state's sparkling lakes, flaming autumns, and serene snows. No one talked about trees ripped raw and skies tarnished to soot.

The flight from Nashville had been poorly heated with blankets nowhere to be found. The wait for the shuttle bus was endless. By the time Melanie took possession of the SUV in Boston, her icy fingers could barely wrestle the key into the ignition.

It never should have come to this. Why wouldn't Will listen to reason?

She scrolled through her phone, clicked on Will's private number.

Will answered on the first ring. "Hey, sweetheart. Can I call you back in a whi—"

"No."

"No? Are you all right?"

I'm here, she should say. I'm here and I can't wait to see you. "You told me she'd only be in New Hampshire for two weeks."

He sighed. "Not this again."

The traffic bucked forward. "A couple is two, Will. Weeks—not months."

"Honestly, Lanie. You're being irrational about this."

Melanie tugged at her scarf, trying to release the sudden heat under her collar. Talk about irrational. Flying all the way from Nashville to wrestle her daughter away from a loving father—who was deep in the weeds of a presidential primary. "Is she with you?"

"No, she's at the call center."

"Doing what?"

"Campaigning for the best candidate this country has seen in years. How old were you when you started for your father—fourteen? Our daughter is living her heritage."

"I cherish Dave Dawson as deeply as you do, Will."

"And if Sophie's not with me, she's with the Dawsons. Or with Caroline."

"Carrie? And that's supposed to make me feel better?"

At twenty-eight, Will's half sister was bright and politically savvy. But she was untamed, a live wire shooting sparks.

Melanie riffled her fingernails on the steering wheel. When was this traffic going to move? She was so close to the exit for downtown Manchester—twenty cars at the most—and yet the distance might as well put her back in Tennessee.

"Carrie is showing her the ropes," Will said, "like I did for her when she was Sophie's age. So whatever your problem is with this, we'll have to talk about it later."

"Pizza runs."

"What?"

"Sophie told me that she does pizza runs."

He laughed. "Bless her heart, on occasion she does."

"I don't like you letting her drive in a place she's not familiar with."

"She knows all the roads, Lanie. She's got an innate sense of direction."

"She's barely sixteen years old. She doesn't have an innate sense of anything."

Melanie shivered at the thought of Sophie caught in this cold mass of steel and insane drivers.

"Lanie, please. I really need to go."

Will clicked off before she could tell him she was less than a mile away.

Inching now. Close enough to see the roof of the Radisson in the city center. Close enough to wrap her arms around Will and feel his heart beat and remind him about how tricky pizza runs can be.

You make four or five campaign stops in one day. You can't eat because everyone wants to talk to you when they can't get to the candidate. You need to make them think you've promised them the world when you've made no commitment whatsoever.

Even though your hunger makes you cranky and light-headed, you don't dare shovel something down fast. Everyone has seen the YouTube video of the governor who choked on a buffalo wing and coughed it out with a chaser of vomit.

You can save the economy and soothe the soul of a nation, but throwing up on camera can dump a candidate faster than a boatload of mistresses.

So you get back to the hotel around midnight, ready to chew the wallpaper. If you're on a grassroots candidacy, some lower-level functionary grabs you to get the pizza because in Manchester they only deliver on weekends, and don't forget the gum, breath mints, and NoDoz.

The run itself is a shared experience; exhausted laughter as you and a stray pal unravel the day and poke gentle fun at the chanting crowds or narrow-eyed reporters. You arrive back as a conquering hero. The feast becomes a grand communal experience, cheese and crust the great equalizer of candidate, staffers, and you—the kid who literally brought home the bacon. There's no big world pressing down, no victories to be won, only the four walls of a hotel suite that smells like pizza and beer and microwave popcorn.

And sometimes, when you're the one left cleaning up the mess, someone senior will stay and help. Quick glances and spilled secrets fill the late-night vacuum until the sun rises and caffeine bubbles and you're climbing in the thick of the action all over again.

"Stop it," Melanie told herself. She scrolled through her phone, found Will's itinerary. An interview with a local ABC affiliate. The spin: Dave Dawson, shoe-leather candidate.

Dave and Will were due in Concord in less than an hour for the next event. Before Melanie even got to the downtown exit, they would be heading north. They'd know to use the back roads because that's what grassroots was all about—shaking hands, driving the dirt roads, making people believe things could be better.

When Melanie worked for her father, she knew every back road in New Hampshire, Iowa, and South Carolina. And she knew every twenty-four-hour pizza joint.

Traffic stopped again.

Melanie gave the driver next to her a pleading look. He shook his head and crept forward into the gap. Behind him, the UPS truck waved her into the breakdown lane. She nosed onto the shoulder, chiding herself because the ticket she was about to earn would cost a fortune, and the rental car company would not be amused at their SUV getting towed.

Some things just had to take priority.

She grabbed the keys and her suitcase, locked the car, and started walking.

An angry wind roared off the river. So much for global warming. She wheeled her suitcase up the exit ramp, breathing in exhaust fumes. Stoplights cycled through three times and still no cars moved.

On River Street, the traffic continued its chaos. Everyone was stuck in a red-tailed, honking morass that seemed to have its origin on Manchester's main thoroughfare. Even small cities could have big traffic issues.

Dragging her suitcase, Melanie headed for the Radisson. Her feet were numb with the cold, her face flushed with worry. Will would be upset that she didn't tell him about this trip. Dave Dawson and his wife, Miranda, would beg her to stay, join the campaign because she had the experience and the passion.

Melanie turned the corner. A mob of people crowded the little park across from the Radisson.

She ran, because all she could think was, *Dear God, don't let this be something bad.* She pushed into the crowd, asking, "What's wrong?" until she heard the *thwap-thwap* of heavy tarps flapping in the wind.

She caught her breath and let her heart settle. So they were here now.

They were called MoveIn, a protest group made up of former Occupiers, hippies, and do-gooders. Activists scurrying out of their tents right before rush hour so they could cause a ruckus and make the evening news cycle.

Will should have told her that they'd set up a camp across from headquarters. Instead, he had gone on and on about the documentary Sophie was developing for her college portfolio. *Standing witness as history is being made,* he had said. So many things Will claimed their daughter was experiencing. Things Sophie would never forget.

Yet he missed the danger of pizza runs.

And the allure of powerful men who could turn the head of an impressionable young girl even faster than a vomit video gone viral could sway a public-opinion poll.

—

Monday evening

Melanie checked into the Radisson and left a keycard for Will at the front desk. She unpacked, then climbed into a hot bath. Sophie wouldn't be back until late this evening. So close and still so out of reach.

That Sophie and Hannah Dawson were like sisters was no reason for Sophie to be this close to a presidential campaign. Waters got murky when the prize was so precious.

Melanie watched the local news as she soaked in the hot water. A television in the bathroom—when would the public's obsession with media ever end?

The local news had a promo clip from Dave's upcoming interview. Hopefully this would stir some attention to Dave's candidacy. He was the perfect man for a hurting nation.

"They call you 'the General' in the war on families," the interviewer said.

Dave smiled, showing jowls that hadn't been there three months ago. Hurried meals and junk food on the bus did not make for a healthy lifestyle. The added bulk actually suited him, though. With his salt-and-pepper hair and calm demeanor, he projected confidence and accessibility.

"I wear that title proudly," Dave said.

"Really?" The interviewer raised his left eyebrow while simultaneously leaning forward on his right elbow. This guy must have been practicing that quizzical gesture for the last four years, waiting for primary season to roll around again.

"The truth is," Dave said, "I want to tear back the veil and show the *true* war on families. The schools, pushing birth control on our children from elementary school. The culture, telling our daughters that anything you want to do is fine as long as you do it safely. Preaching to our sons that they can't be men unless they have a chip on their shoulder and a gun in their hand. We never measure emotional or spiritual safety, do we? The barrage is constant. The music. The clothing. The video games. Movies and television. When was the last time you or your station took a critical look at your own programming?"

"Are you"—the interviewer sat back, as if stunned—"talking censorship?"

Dave leaned into the space that the interviewer had vacated. "I'm talking responsibility. Turn a mirror on yourself and see if you are proud of what's there."

The local anchor cut in with the promo. "The interview airs Sunday night at 6 p.m. The senator's comments will raise some eyebrows," the anchor said. "And some hackles," his female counterpart responded.

"Lanie?"

Melanie gasped, instinctively covering her breasts with crossed arms.

Will came into the bathroom. "Hey, hey. I didn't mean to scare you."

"Just startled, that's all. Let me get a towel," she said. She reached past him for the towel and wrapped herself tight.

Will touched her cheek. "Let's move your stuff up to my suite."

"I'm already settled in here."

"Okay," he said. "I'll stay here." He unbuttoned the top button on his dress shirt and pulled it over his head.

"Sophie . . ."

"She's in Concord overnight, with the Dawsons. They're doing an early-morning diner stop." Will unfastened his belt buckle. "Miranda is so grateful that Hannah has her for companionship."

"Stop selling that to me." Melanie grabbed her suitcase, found her flannel pajamas.

"Selling what?" Will said.

"Our daughter as campaigner in chief."

"You had the book tour, Lanie. And then that conference in Dallas, and that other deadline. So it was either have Sophie come here or ship her off to Destiny. And we know how that would've turned out. In a week, she'd have a ring through her nose and a butterfly tattoo on her bicep."

"I didn't expect her to get so involved up here."

"She's sixteen," Will said, all pretense of humor gone. "Lanie, please. It's late. Let's just go to bed."

The crease next to Will's right eyebrow was new, and the gray in his sideburns had advanced into his hairline. He needed a haircut. His sandy-brown curls were rowdy, showing track marks where he had worried his fingers. His blue eyes were shadowed.

He had lost weight. While Dave endured pancake breakfasts and chicken dinners, Will kept an eye on everything in the campaign—except his own well-being. She should stay and watch out for him.

If she stayed, Sophie would have to stay.

Will undid the button she had just fastened. "The years pass and yet . . ." He pressed his mouth to her throat. "You are as beautiful as the day we met."

"Will, please." She buttoned her shirt.

"Don't. Don't hide from me."

"I'm not hiding. I'm just cold."

"Then come to bed with me."

"I told you, not until we discuss Sophie being here. It's time to come home."

Will stepped back, frowned. "You. Me. That's what we need to talk about."

"Don't avoid the topic, Will."

"And don't you reframe the argument, Lanie. This isn't about Sophie." Will grabbed the duvet from the bed and in a quick swoop draped it over Melanie's shoulders. "Happy now? You're all wrapped up—and I can't get to you."

"I flew all the way up here, Will, so we can talk about Sophie."

"No. We are the primary topic here, Melanie. You and me."

"This *me* is exhausted. Can't we sort this out tomorrow?"

He grasped the edge of the duvet and pulled it around his shoulders so they were both covered by it. He smelled like coffee and sweat.

"Do you love me, Lanie?"

"I do. Of course I do."

"Kiss me. Kiss me so I know."

Melanie leaned into him, aiming for his lips, but at the last split second the heat of his breath made her turn—ever so slightly—and she kissed the corner of his mouth.

Will gently tipped her head back. "Let's not lie anymore."

"I'm not lying."

His gaze traveled slowly from her head to her feet. She felt naked even with her pajamas on and the duvet wrapped around her.

"I've been seeing a therapist," he said. "Sorting things out. The truth is I can't live like a monk anymore. When the campaign runs its course—or God willing, Dave becomes president—we need to talk about a divorce."

Melanie willed her knees to keep her upright. None of what

Will said was unexpected, and yet she had persuaded herself that things would go on as they always had.

"I don't want that," she said.

"Something needs to change. I'd like you to meet my therapist," Will said. "Can you do that for me? For Sophie?"

She touched his cheek. "I don't know."

"Think about it. I'll see you at breakfast." Will left the room, pulling the door shut with a bang.

two

Tuesday early morning

FOUR O'CLOCK IN THE MORNING. EACH MINUTE HAD passed like drips of hot wax as Melanie waited for Will to come back and tell her that he had overreacted. That he hadn't meant to use the word *divorce*.

If he wouldn't come to her, she would go to him. Melanie put on her jacket and flip-flops, found the keycard he had left for her, and went to the elevator.

Campaigns were tough, and a presidential campaign was relentless. Will would make himself a cup of black coffee, stretch out on the sofa, and sift through priorities. Identifying key people they'd meet later that morning. Reading the revised draft of Dave's stump speech to ensure the narrative had been honed to fit the occasion. Checking any overnight polls for New Hampshire and Iowa. Worrying about Iowa and New Hampshire and South Carolina and Florida and praying they'd chosen the best strategy they could afford.

Melanie slipped the keycard in the slot for Will's suite. The lock flashed green. She opened the door. The sitting room had been converted into the campaign's "situation room." Papers, soda cans, and coffee cups littered the tables. Sofas and chairs were pushed against the wall. Power cords and chargers snaked haphazardly to surge protectors on the floor.

Her father would have loved the instant news and social media. Bobby Joe Fallon would have wielded the new technology like a conductor's baton. What trick of nature had condemned one of the greatest political minds in history to a haze of Alzheimer's?

Melanie worked her way around the tables, avoiding extension cords and take-out boxes. The bedroom to her right—Sophie's room—was empty. How did she study or sleep next to the situation room with activity going deep into the night?

The room on the far side had to be Will's bedroom.

Melanie clutched the doorknob. Go in or go away? Seconds passed, then a minute. Go in, go away.

The knob turned in her hand. She yelped.

"Lanie?" Will turned on the light. The bed was empty, sheets tossed as if in violent sleep.

"What do you want?" he said.

Melanie wrapped her arms around him. "You."

Will tipped her head up, his eyes groggily trying to focus on her face. "I don't understand."

"I want to fight *for* you." She brushed his lips with hers. His were cold.

She wanted to pull away. She wanted to dive into him. She didn't know *what* she wanted.

She needed her marriage *not* to end. But there was a big difference in it not ending and in it thriving. Melanie kissed Will harder, felt his heart thump against her ribs. She pushed him toward the bed.

Lord, let my flesh cleave unto his.

His breath against her throat was hot. Too hot. She pulled away, just a little.

He stepped back. "That's what I thought."

She pressed her hands to his face. "You can't make love to me?"

"I want to. You're the one who isn't willing."

"I'm here. I'm willing." She pressed her face to his shoulder. "Of course I'm willing."

"You're forcing yourself, Lanie. And it makes me feel . . . like I'm forcing you. Like I am raping my own wife."

"No. Don't say that. That's a terrible thing to say."

"It's a terrible thing to feel." Will kissed the back of her hand. "I've got a crowded day. Might as well grab my shower now. Go back upstairs and get some sleep." He kissed her cheek and went into the bathroom.

Melanie collapsed on the bed and buried herself in a pillow. The pipes clunked as the shower ran. She rolled over and stared at the ceiling. Better hot wax than cold ashes.

She wrote a note, left it on his iPad.

Text me the name and # of your therapist. I'll make an appt today.

Tuesday morning

What a terrible time to have a bashful bladder, Carrie Connors thought.

Her stomach was in open revolt, and she was huddled in a stall, trying to pee on a stick. The bathroom door opened.

"You okay in there?"

"Sophie!" Carrie yelled. "I asked you to stay in the hall."

"Why?" her niece said. "I feel like an idiot standing out here."

"Just give me a minute in here, Soph. Please?" In theory, no one would wander down this hall to use this bathroom because the pool didn't open for two more hours. Even so, Sophie was a fail-safe.

The logical thing would be to take the test in her hotel room. Carrie shared the room with Victoria Peters, her brother's assistant. The last thing she needed was this getting back to Will. And sweet Victoria would do anything to climb over Carrie's back to advance in the Dawson organization.

"What if someone needs to use the bathroom?" Sophie's voice echoed on the tile.

"That's the point of you being out there. Tell them to use the one in the lobby. Now can you please let me pee in peace?"

"Why not use the one in the situation room?"

"I just need some privacy."

There was no more privacy in the situation room than in her hotel room. This restroom offered anonymity. Maybe she should have come alone, but she wanted the comfort of someone nearby. Even if that someone didn't know what Carrie was doing.

"But what if someone wants to come in?"

"Tell them I'm sick and I need the bathroom to myself for a few minutes. You can do that, right, Sophie? For me?"

"Of course. It's just that . . . this is creepy. So can you please hurry up?"

Sixteen years old, her niece had been a lamb when she came to Manchester in September. Will was so adept at navigating shark-infested waters. Sophie had blossomed quickly, showing the fire in her blood. A real Connors.

"Are you almost done?" Sophie said.

"No. It's just a little bladder infection. Makes it hard to pee, that's all. And I can't relax if you're bugging me about it."

"Sorry. Want me to, like . . . pray about it?"

"Just close the door and give me some privacy. Can you do that?"

"Sure. Try and hurry up." The door closed.

Like Carrie wanted to rush through the next two minutes? Waiting for the stick to determine if she'd been lucky or an absolute idiot. She'd been celibate since college, a hard-won battle.

So careful until that hazy afternoon last month.

The trees were aflame with yellow and orange and red and the sun was warm on her back and she ran into some guy at a fund-raising picnic. Good-looking in a woodsy kind of way. Young and funny, he wanted her to experience New Hampshire in all its October glory. So he walked her along the river and then into the woods and she kissed him because she had to do something or she'd just burst from the beauty. Before she knew it, she was kicking the leaves into a fragrant pile and then . . .

Cold November arrived but her period did not.

Finally, a stream of urine. Carrie followed the instructions on the box. She left the stall and set the stick on the vanity so she could wash her hands.

"Hey," Sophie said, swinging through the door. "I heard the flush—"

"No!" Carrie said. Before she could shoo Sophie out, the girl spotted the stick.

"What's that?"

"Get out! I'm not done in here."

Sophie held it up to the light. "Carrie, are you pregnant?"

"No. Of course not."

"That's not what this says." Sophie shoved the stick in her face. "See?"

Carrie washed her hands. "And if I am, how is that any of your business?"

"What are you going to do?"

"I'm going to take care of it."

"How?"

How? Oh dear Lord—how? "I'm going to consider my options. And I don't want your father involved. So forget you ever saw that."

Sophie sniffed back tears. "I'm sorry."

"Put that down. You do realize I peed on it."

Sophie squealed, dropped the stick onto the counter. "What about the baby's father? You have to tell him, Carrie. He has the right to know."

The baby's father. Jeremy something or other. How shameful that she couldn't even remember his name. Carrie could go through the donor list, get his contact info, give him a call. Hey, man. Remember that little roll in the leaves we had?

"Sophie, I'll deal with this." She had the right to decide what was best for her own body. Her baby. No, certainly not a baby. Not at five weeks. Just an unfortunate lapse in judgment that Carrie would deal with.

Period, end of story.

Two hours later Carrie leaned against the Dumpster and lit up a cigarette. She had stopped smoking eight years ago—but she needed something to calm her nerves and it was way too early for a glass of wine.

Thankfully, Sophie had been summoned to see her mother. Carrie swore her to utter silence. As hard as Will would ride Carrie if he knew about this, Melanie would be a storm trooper. Her sister-in-law was known nationally for her championing children's safety through her Lord's Heritage ministry. "Children are a heritage from the Lord, offspring a reward from him."

Not always.

The cold air snaked around her ankles. She should have grabbed her coat before she came outside. This was going to be a two-smoke break, at least. She had to get past this distraction so she could attend to her job. Thousands of details passed through her hands, and if she let anything slip, it could rebound on her candidate.

Carrie had been smoke-free and man-free for all these years.

If a puff a couple times a day would keep her calm, so be it. She did her best thinking here, in the Dumpster bay outside the hotel's kitchen. And now the nicotine kicked in, helping her focus.

Pregnant. What an epic mess. Options, options . . . were there any that didn't result in making more of a mess?

Have the baby, go single-parent with it. Bad option for the baby.

Have the baby, surrender it for adoption. Bad option for Carrie because once she had her hands on something, it was impossible to pry them off. Her talent was her curse.

A simple D & C. Clean the uterus of its scrap of tissue, be back to work that afternoon.

Oh God, please . . . blink. Just for this moment. Just for the moments to come—the only thing that makes sense is for this baby not to be.

Carrie would find the closest clinic out of state and use a fake name so it couldn't bounce back to the Dawson campaign. Get it done, get back to work.

Will would freak if he knew about the pregnancy. Their father's only son, Will had twenty-plus years on Carrie. He was the son of Mark Connors's first marriage; she was the product of the second marriage. Her brother detested Carrie's mother for disrupting his own mother's happiness. Even so, when Papa died, Will stepped in as father and role model for his baby sister.

He had helped her get into Princeton, got her an internship with Dave. After graduation, gave her a job on the senatorial staff. Carrie loved the drama and the personalities, the shaping of perception, the wooing of minds, the nailing of votes.

"You're smoking that thing like you mean it."

Carrie jumped. "Geez, don't sneak up on a body like that."

The intruder was a young guy, maybe thirty or so. His thick red hair was pulled back into a ponytail. He had lively eyes, a brownish scuff of beard, full lips, straight nose.

He heaved a couple of bags into the Dumpster, wiped his hands on his jeans. "My humblest apologies," he said. "It's my daily trash run."

"Ah, you're one of them," she said. "A Mover."

He nodded. "And I'm guessing you're a Dawsonite."

"You make it sound like a disease." Carrie ground her cigarette out with the tip of her high heel. "How do you know I'm not a hotel guest or on staff?"

"Guests smoke on their balconies or in the smoking gazebo. If you were hotel staff, you'd be wearing a name tag. And besides, I've seen you with the entourage."

Carrie laughed. "The campaign doesn't have enough money to qualify as entourage-worthy. But yes, I am an object of your derision."

"I prefer to think of you as a worthy opponent. Or better yet, a heart still to be won."

"Politically speaking, you mean."

"I don't separate politics from life." He grinned, offered his hand. "I'm Jared. Jared O'Dea."

"Caroline Connors. Carrie," she said, accepting his handshake. His fingers were warm, despite his being gloveless.

"You're freezing. Take this." Jared pulled off his sweatshirt. Underneath, he wore a long-sleeved thermal shirt. Tight enough to show that in between shouting slogans and blocking traffic, he must be lifting some serious weights.

She recognized his name, had done some quick research on the group. He was an activist out of Seattle, one of the original Occupiers of Wall Street. Despite huge media support, that movement had collapsed under bad behavior and poor messaging. MoveIn was their new incarnation, establishing camps at every candidate's field headquarters as well as selected businesses, city halls, and the like.

"Take it," he said. "I insist."

"No, thanks," she said. "I need to get back inside."

"So soon? I was just going to bum a smoke."

"How eco-wicked of you."

"I have my vices." Jared grinned again. "Like I'm sure Senator Dawson has."

"Are you pumping me for info?"

"Just trying to be interesting enough to get you to keep me company."

"Gotta go." Carrie handed him the pack. "Keep them."

"I don't like smoking alone, Carrie. I promise I won't rant."

Smoking is bad for babies. Then again, what did it really matter? And it had helped to settle her stomach. "Sure," she said. "Only because you promised a truce."

"Put this on." He held the sweatshirt out. "So I won't feel guilty."

Carrie tugged the sweatshirt over her blouse. It smelled like citrus and wood smoke. She wore a skirt and heels today for a donor meeting. She loved field events when they all wore jeans and sneakers to prove that Dave Dawson was "just like you."

Jared lit a cigarette for her and then one for himself. They smoked the first minute in silence, drawing in deep breaths, exhaling with contentment. She thought about the lore of World War I when Germans and Brits shared a smoke before going back into the trenches.

"So, are you from Tennessee like the senator?"

"DC, born and bred," she said. "You?"

"Seattle. Are you a volunteer or paid staff?"

"Six years on staff. What about you?" Carrie eyed him through the smoke. "Volunteer or paid staff?"

Jared laughed. He had great teeth, a strong jaw, and was

clearly comfortable in his skin. "I wish. A paycheck would let me rent a room, grab a nice hot shower. Street work gets rather ripe, even in this weather."

"I'd ask you why you do it," Carrie said, "but I don't want to listen to a harangue."

"No harangue necessary. I can tell you in two words. If I may?"

"Sure. But if you go beyond two, I'm going to punch you."

"I believe."

"That I'll whack you?"

He stared at her. "I believe."

"Oh." She shivered under his sweatshirt. "So do I. I believe in lots of things."

"You're paid to believe."

"Not at all. Because *I believe*, I found a place where I could be productive. Dawson is a good guy. A really good guy."

Jared stubbed out his cigarette. "That's what makes him so dangerous."

Carrie laughed. "The senator is a softie. He pays people like me to supply the claws."

He picked up the butt, examined it, and tossed it into the Dumpster. "I'll get yours for you," he said. "You don't want to bend down in a skirt and heels."

"Do you have something against how I'm dressed?"

"Not at all." Jared gave her a dramatic sigh. "It's a nice change from flannel shirts and woolen caps. Sometimes I can't even tell the guys from the gals in our camp."

She tugged the sweatshirt off. "I've got to get inside."

"Stop by sometime," he said. "See what it's like for us. Close up, not from your balcony."

"My balcony?"

"You stand outside and stare down at us while you brush your hair."

Her skin flushed. "A Peeping Tom, eh?"

"An observer of human nature."

"And what do you observe?"

"A beautiful woman who wants to kick off her high heels." Jared wrapped the sweatshirt around her shoulders. "Keep it."

This was how these guys operated. One part rhetoric and nine parts personal charisma. She knew this and yet—maybe because of the strange hormones flooding her blood or maybe because of his vibrant counterculture cred—she couldn't free herself from his gaze.

"You'll be cold," she said.

"Someone will give me another one. That's what we do. Check us out. We don't bite."

"You don't bite—maybe I do." She keyed open the door to the back hall.

"Wait," he said. "Tonight, when you're looking down on us from your balcony, remember that there are two sides to every street."

Carrie yanked off his sweatshirt and, with a mighty heave, tossed it at him.

three

Tuesday morning

TUCKER KEYES HAD TO STOP DOING THIS. DROPPING this, snorting that, smoking this *and* that. Rocking the night with some woman he couldn't possibly live without. Until the sun rose and he didn't even remember her name.

Tousled hair, delicate feet, legs that went on forever—that Tuck did remember. Karen? No. Courtney. No, that wasn't it.

He scratched his face and said, "Hi there, pretty lady."

"Morning, sleepy eyes," she said as she opened the refrigerator. The gleaming Sub-Zero was the focal point of the chef's kitchen. Overkill, because Tuck had no use for the six-burner stove, prep sink, and massive black granite island.

Host some fabulous DC parties, his mother had said when she designed this townhouse for him. *Network, my darling. Find something that suits you.*

He had tried veganism and Catholicism, yoga and Pilates, Madison Avenue and Wall Street, faith and cynicism, fine arts and day trades. And still the emptiness echoed inside him like an existential tinnitus.

"No food?" the woman said.

"Sorry. Cupboards are bare, I'm afraid. I'm never here." Tuck laid on the British accent, a vestige from the boarding school Mother had sent him to. Though he was as red-blooded as any American, a touch of Oxford in his speech and a sheepish tilt to his head usually absolved him of most faux pas.

Including not feeding the woman he had seduced the night before.

Kara—or whatever her name was—leaned on the island. She held up rather marvelously to morning sunlight.

He could tell her to leave. Call her by the wrong name and humiliate her enough to make her storm out the door. Offer her money and insult her into leaving.

Mother had raised him better than to display outright boorishness. Though Blair Reynolds Keyes had little respect for the family, she cherished his paternal surname and insisted Tuck—as the Keyes lineage—do the same.

The woman rubbed his earlobe between her thumb and index finger. "So where are you when you're not here?"

"Pardon me?"

"To quote: 'I'm afraid I'm never here.' Unquote."

Egad, she did the accent better than he did.

What story did he tell her last night? *I'm the key aide to Senator Blah-blah* or *I'm an entrepreneur, working on nanotechnology to cure brain cancer.* Or maybe he told her the truth—Tucker Reynolds Keyes was a trust-fund baby who didn't know how to save himself.

No, never the truth. *You can't handle the truth, Tucker.*

"I've got things in process I need to attend to," he said. "Around town. Appointments and the like."

"You never told me what you did."

Small talk—such a bother. Why hadn't he shuffled her away last night? Given her a good-bye hug and cab fare and he'd be alone with his sorry self when the sun rose.

She leaned against him, still with a death grip on his ear. "Can you reschedule your appointment? It would be fun just to hang for a while."

"I'm sorry, I really can't. I've got to meet someone in less than an hour," Tuck said.

"Your grandfather?"

So she knew who he was. The Beltway was narrow and he was expansive in his activities. "How about I buy you a coffee and croissant on our way out?"

She frowned. "I don't do fat. Or caffeine. We had that discussion last night."

"Maybe we could do dinner sometime, if you'd give me your number."

"I programmed it into your phone. Remember?"

Last night was a pounding blur and she was becoming the same. "Sure. Of course."

She manufactured a pout. Like her hair, her teeth, her body—it wasn't totally real. But like the total package, it was alluring. "You will call?"

Tuck nuzzled her neck. Her skin smelled like roses, her hair held a lingering scent of fine cigars. If they had gotten into the Cubans, it must have been a glorious night.

"Of course," he said. And maybe he would—if he could remember her name.

—

Tuesday midday

"In my time, it was all about the Pulitzer," John Larter Keyes said.

The old man rambled on, dropping occasional words as if he

heard the ticking of time and needed to abridge to the *Reader's Digest* version.

Though Tuck was *The Journal*'s film critic, his main responsibility was to witness his grandfather's daily wallow in self-indulgent melancholy. He could almost recite the Pulitzer lecture by heart.

The sanctity of the First Amendment. The sacred duty of the press. Integrity trumped acclaim every time. Woodward and Bernstein, Huntley and Brinkley, and where was Walter Cronkite and what was journalism coming to in the age of Anderson Cooper and Bill O'Reilly?

"Of course, I eschewed chasing after trophies," J.L. said. "The story was the prize. Getting it right. Getting it first. And the writing. Succinct, precise, and powerful. Now you young folks don't want to shed any shoe leather. You aspire to be talking heads."

Somewhere in the paper's mainframe was a copy of his grandfather's obituary. It was standard practice to have prewritten obituaries so the weekend desk wouldn't have to scramble when the latest Hollywood stud drove his Ferrari into the Pacific.

It might not be all about the Pulitzer, but J.L. Keyes had made sure his Pulitzer Prize was in the first line of his obit. Since he turned ninety-three, he ended his workdays with a reading of his obituary. On good days, he'd dictate a word change or phrase placement. On befuddled days, he'd rewrite the whole thing longhand.

Last week he had added the phrase: Keyes was considered the patriarch of investigative journalism. True—the old man had earned that title by uncovering conspiracies and scandals for sixty years.

"The jabbering class." J.L. pointed a crooked finger at the television set that had never been turned on. "Bombastic. Snide. Tools of the party apparatchiks." The names changed but the verdict was still the same. Cable news would be the end of journalism.

Mother laughed when Tuck started at the newspaper, said this jaunt into journalism was *wish-fulfillment, don't you know, dear boy?* A sad attempt to gain some approbation from the great John Larter Keyes since her husband—who was J.L.'s wandering son—had disappeared off a South American waterfall.

Tuck wandered the office, gazing at the photos that served as his grandfather's trophies. Pictures of J.L. with presidents from Dwight Eisenhower to Barack Obama. Ted Kennedy, Tip O'Neil, Bobby Joe Fallon.

Tuck's baby photo and nothing more, as if he became a disappointment from kindergarten on. None of his father. Tuck was a kid when it happened, barely remembered the man now. Grandfather had stepped into the patriarchal role. That consisted of a generous allowance and frequent lectures on the sanctity of the Keyes name.

The old man droned on. Tuck stared out the window, haze blanketing the Capitol. This was one of the best views in the city.

He had seen pictures from the good old days. The curling smoke, the angle of the hat, the furrowed brow—his grandfather had reveled in the full-on Edward R. Murrow pose. Now the old man was the captain of a sinking ship.

The Journal had been too much of a dinosaur to adapt to modern times. The editorial staff had tried to explain to J.L. that reading was archaic, that the hip consumer streamed CNN and the *New York Times* on their smartphones.

That news wasn't just reported in Tweets and scrolls, it was *made* that way.

Social media and three cable news outlets needed a constant supply to feed their hungry consumers. Tuck had taken a boatload of computer courses in college, his attempt at persuading the old man that change was coming.

Instead of adapting, *The Journal* lumbered on with its publisher, dreaming of past glory and taking the slow dance to death.

The old man pounded his two arthritic fists together, the

gesture for another lecture splendidly delivered. He leaned forward, his elbows looking like stork legs on the old cherry desk. "What can I do for you today, Tucker?"

He could say, "Nothing, thank you, sir—it was nice seeing you." But he had promised Caroline Connors he'd do this. A drinking buddy from their Princeton years, Carrie was impossible to say no to.

"We need someone to cover our candidate," she told him. "We're going to do great things. If you could put in a word with your grandfather . . . I'd be so grateful."

Strange how Tucker had been the idealist in college and she had been the pragmatist. Now Carrie worked for the Don Quixote of politics with a fervor he could barely imagine. She had gone into politics and never looked back while Tuck had shuffled along.

"I want to cover Senator Dawson," Tuck said.

"What?" J.L. squinted, adjusted his rimless glasses. "Dark Ages Dave? There's no story there."

"There will be. Gallup's got him at seven."

Dawson's campaign was the last gasp of Superman nation. Truth, justice, and the American way had become like faded newsprint, good for lining cat boxes or flower beds. Voters were fatigued. Tuck shared that fatigue, that moral exhaustion. Sometimes he was so sick of himself he wanted to just get high one last time and dissolve into the travertine tile of his empty home.

"AP ran the numbers today. We need to at least do some follow-up," Tuck said.

"What is this *we* all of a sudden? You have no interest in anything except movies."

"Underdog stories sell well. There could be something here."

"Waste of time," J.L. said. "Dawson's holed up in New Hampshire, knocking on doors because he's got no money. And he's got no national press."

"He'll have some money soon."

"That's his people, trying to drive the story."

"Word is major backers are starting to look for an alternative to Governor Sanders. They're sick of the old-boy network."

"So what do you want, Tucker?"

"Will you credential me?"

"You can't just jump on the bus and dig out a story. You're no reporter."

"How do you know what I can do?"

"I know *what* you do," J.L. said. "You're a pinball, bouncing at all the bright lights. I gave you the entertainment desk because frivolity suits you, Tucker."

"Then help me, sir. I want to make a change," Tuck said.

J.L. ruffled his white hair, sighed. "Stay where you are, son. You do clever reviews. That's a gift."

"Please. Send me to New Hampshire."

"New Hampshire? That state is a pittance," J.L. said. "A woman to be wooed with roses, candy, and promises. Buy her, win her, and then it's off to South Carolina and beyond. Abandoned the instant she says yes, that state is more prostitute than bride."

"Which is why I want to go now. While there's still a fight to be had."

J.L. pursed his lips with a *pfft*. "Why not go with one of the others, then? With the incumbent finishing his eight years, both parties are free-for-alls. We could get you in with someone polling in double digits. Maybe Hal Sanders—despite what your friend claims, Dawson's not going to catch up to him. I could get you in with the vice president, if you want to trail around that old hack."

"I'd be lost in a crowd. Dawson is there for the taking."

"You don't know what you're asking for, Tucker." His eagle gaze softened. "You don't want to tromp up to New Hampshire with its endless loop of chicken dinners. Mayors of eighty-people townships clinging onto your sleeve with their donut-stained paws. Frostbitten functionaries who don't give a hoot if your name is John Larter Keyes or John Philip Sousa. You'll be begging to come back to the film desk after a week."

"Please, sir. I'd like to give this a try. Before it's too late." Tuck admired Carrie Connors for her dedication and fervency. If he jumped into this campaign, perhaps he would discover the same career passion. And maybe—a long shot *maybe*—he and Carrie would find something they shared besides a DC upbringing and Ivy League education.

J.L. buried his face in his hands. His hair was a mere wisp, his scalp spotted with age. For all his bluster, he understood the shift in the paradigm. The devolution of journalism meant that the "truth" that was fit to print had become the stories that were fit to spin.

"One month," the old man said. "And I swear, you bring even a whisper of disgrace to this paper, I'll disown you."

"I'll make you proud."

"Don't think I won't disavow you, Tucker. I am a man of my word."

"That you are, sir." Tuck shook his grandfather's hand. "That you are."

four

Tuesday afternoon

THE SITUATION ROOM—THE HEART OF EVERY campaign.

From the time Melanie was a little girl, she thrived on the electricity of it all. Coffee and half-finished muffins. Everyone with something to say. Clock ticking because the candidate always needed more time, more money, more voters.

Will harnessed the urgency of the room with a calm that her father would have appreciated. Balanced on the back of the chair, he stretched one leg to the floor in a fight-or-flight posture and ran through the day's events.

For the rest of the nation, New Hampshire meant woodstoves, maple syrup, fast rivers, snowy mountains, homespun politicos. Every four years, the Live Free or Die state transformed into First in the Nation. The state wrapped its hands around presidential hopefuls and said, "Flirt with 'em all, but you gotta get by me first." Iowa had its caucuses but little New Hampshire had balloting, preceded by months of media attention and the requirement of candidates to look voters in the eye when they made promises.

Miranda Dawson slipped into the room, found the seat next to Melanie. "I prayed," she said, kissing Melanie's cheek. "And you came."

"I would have come sooner," Melanie said, returning Miranda's hug. "But I had the book tour and speaking engagements to fulfill."

"We're glad to have you now," Miranda said. "We have been so grateful we have Sophie to keep Hannah company. Both girls have blossomed."

Blossomed. Melanie's elder daughter, Destiny, hadn't blossomed so much as erupted. Will joked that she had been born an adolescent. Ten years younger than her sister, Sophie had always been Melanie's little girl, a function of her protectiveness and Will's increasing absence from Nashville.

Melanie glanced up at Will. A woman whispered something in his ear. She was dark-haired, somehow prim and yet voluptuous in her royal blue blouse and black pencil skirt.

"Who is that?" Melanie asked.

"Victoria Peters," Miranda said. "Will's assistant."

"Where's Carrie?" Melanie said.

"When Will promoted her, he transferred Victoria in from the Senate staff. Surely he's mentioned her?"

Melanie twisted her wedding ring. "It's hard to keep everyone straight until I put a face to the name." She watched as Victoria's hair brushed Will's shoulder, like Boaz spreading his cloak over Ruth. A sign of possession.

"You *really* need to be here." Miranda stared at Victoria Peters.

"I don't know how much I could add," Melanie said.

"We need your experience, Lanie. And your platform."

Melanie was political royalty—almost on par with the Kennedys or Bushes—because the Fallon blood ran in her veins. The name of Robert Joseph Fallon—Bobby Joe—still provided a ready access into any local conversation.

Now he was in the late stages of Alzheimer's, comfortable in Nashville and living in a dream where he was still Speaker of the House.

Melanie had started with her father when she was old enough to hold a sign. By the time she hit college, she was as savvy as any political operative.

Hannah Dawson came into the room, gave Melanie a warm hug. Fifteen years old, she was sweet as strawberries with her auburn curls, freckled cheeks, and quick smile. “Mom told me you were here.”

“How are you holding up, sweetheart?”

“Peachy. Sophie had to run over to the call center. She asked me to ask you if you could catch up with her there.”

Melanie raised her eyebrows.

Hannah reddened. “She thinks you’re here to bring her home. She’s mustering her arguments.”

“Don’t worry about it.”

“So you’re letting her stay?” Hannah squeezed Melanie’s hands. “Please. I don’t want to be the only kid here.”

“It’s under discussion,” Melanie said.

“Good. I—” Hannah dropped her hands. “Oh, excuse me. Mike’s here. I have to catch up with him. See you in a while.”

Though Melanie knew Mike McGregor by sight, she had never met him. In his early thirties, he carried energy like a mantle. His eyes were a startling blue, his dark hair carefree.

Last spring Will had called her in the middle of the night to tell her the news. “McGregor’s coming on board, bringing his people.”

Mike McGregor was reputed to be the next great kingmaker, an amalgam of David Axelrod and Karl Rove. “You roped in the wunderkind. Congratulations.”

“Lanie.” That night Will’s voice—normally a rich baritone—had a creaky edge to it over the phone. “This is really going to happen.”

“You sound nervous.”

“Not nervous.” He had laughed. “Downright terrified. Can you pray with me?”

She had instinctively slid her hand to his side of the bed, as if he were there and not hundreds of miles away.

"Of course," she had said. She remembered thanking God for His provision, His encouragement, His protection of Dave and his family and staff. Now she was in the middle of Dave's inner sanctum, watching Victoria Peters glue herself to Will.

You really need to be here, Miranda Dawson had said.

Please, dear Father, don't let me be too late.

—

Tuesday afternoon

Carrie was exhausted. The pregnancy test. Dealing with Sophie. The encounter with the MoveIn guy. Countless phone calls and one live session with an event planner who couldn't plan a picnic for ants, let alone a black-tie cocktail party for potential donors. Dealing with the Nashville office on fund-raising nuts-and-bolts because Victoria—for all her MIT and Georgetown education—couldn't seem to attend to routine calls that even Sophie or Hannah could handle.

Now she had to hike to the Manchester call center. Her heels clicked as she walked, her legs cold from the east wind blowing through the buildings.

Manchester was a low-rise city with the old, brick mills on the river and the small banks, stores, shops, and restaurants on Elm Street. The business center stretched four blocks from the river to the clapboard two-family houses and corner stores.

She deliberately went out of her way to avoid Veteran's Park. That the mayor and governor had given an imprimatur to MoveIn's illegal trespass showed the type of partisan politics that choked the Northeast.

Carrie pushed through the door of the call center, spotted Sophie immediately. Eyes glued to her laptop, she must be doing the email scan. Donation emails went to the Nashville office. Generic emails ran through a special program, and any keywords implying threat got kicked over to Jason Polke and his security people.

Sophie waved her over. "You look drained. Are you all right?"

Carrie sat next to her. "You were supposed to meet your mother over at the hotel."

"She's going to take me home. I don't want to go."

"Then tell her that. Be a grown-up about it, and tell her you are in the middle of everything and we need you here."

"That's true, right?" Sophie leaned against Carrie's arm. "You can't live without me. Especially when you need to pee in private."

"Shush." Carrie pulled Sophie's head into a mock bear hug and whispered, "That never happened. You need to put it totally out of your mind."

"Of course. If you negotiate for me to stay." Sophie yanked away, banged her keyboard. "Hey, I'm crashing. Oh my goodness! Carrie, look. Something's happening."

Sophie's laptop flashed red, white, and blue.

In her hand, Carrie's phone came live, flashing the same colors. The red dripped like blood over the white while the blue threaded through the tableau like razor wire.

"What the heck?" The intern who manned the reception desk turned his laptop so Carrie could see it. All the computers flashed the same colors, the pulsing accentuated with the sound of *thrum thrum thrum*. Her phone seemed to vibrate with each beat and the room came alive.

Anyone with a smartphone thumbed their screens or shook the phone. Sophie pushed away from the table, hands on her head as if expecting the room to flash red. Carrie watched as an image formed out of the red-white-and-blue blotches.

Uncle Sam, with a skull for his face. Stick arms, a marionette on strings.

How was this happening? Hijacking phones and computers was a massive security breach and everyone in the call center knew it. Their communication network had firewalls upon firewalls. Nothing should be able to get through.

"Hey!" The intern had turned on cable television, where the same image stared back. Empty eye sockets, a joker smile on its face.

Had the nation's satellite system been compromised? What else—other than cyberterrorism—would explain this simultaneous hijack?

The marionette spoke in a raspy, deep voice. Like something out of a horror movie. "Every four years, the citizens of the United States of America elect the leader of the so-called free world. You punch the chad, pull the lever, blacken the box. When you step out of the voting booth, you believe that this act is the Jordan you will cross to the promised land."

"This is creepy," Sophie said. "Can't we just turn everything off?"

"Shush, let me listen," Carrie said, arm linked through Sophie's. "We're okay."

The marionette raised a skeletal finger at the screen. "You are drowning and you don't even know it. Special interests and seductive foreign money. The sated majority and the hungry minority. Archaic unions and obese corporations. Expansive promises and dirty tricks.

"You all want what *you* want.

"The arrogance and appetite of the ruling class is prodigious. It is its own cancer, this relentless and vast pursuit of power. And you people follow blindly.

"For you—the citizens, the voters, the sightless *sheep* of this unhallowed land—I have become Joshua."

The marionette leaned forward, skull filling the screen, the jaw flapping.

"I am Joshua. I invite you to become Jericho. Today, we speak in whispers," it said. "Soon, we will shout."

All the screens in the room went dark and then began to reboot.

Carrie's phone lit up with texts. Will wanting to know if they saw it at the call center. Melanie wanting to know if Sophie was okay. A friend in the Bresler campaign telling Carrie their call center had been taken over. Breaking news feeding into her phone. Multiple reports that the image had been seen in multiple cities. Within two minutes Homeland Security declared the Jericho incident a "prank" and promised an audit of their cybersecurity.

Some prank. The video itself was crude, the language ridiculously elevated. The ability to override cable news, personal computers, and phones simultaneously was terrifying. China, Russia, even Al-Qaeda organizations routinely hacked into corporate and governmental systems. Anyone with half a brain understood the greatest threat to this nation—other than its people losing heart—was to information networks.

Let the experts figure that out. Carrie had work to do and this silly cartoon was not going to stop her.

—

Tuesday late afternoon

"Sophie." Melanie pulled her daughter close. She smelled like bubble gum, felt like heaven.

"Ah, Mom." Sophie wiggled out of the hug. "Everyone's watching."

"Everyone" was a disparate group of young and retired people in heated conversation about the Jericho hijack. A gawky young man with a video camera filmed the action, stopping to ask a question. The kid looked vaguely familiar. Melanie thought wryly how he had just captured her hug and Sophie's disengagement for posterity.

Folding tables and chairs lined the room. Phone cables snaked everywhere. Half the phones were in use; the rest were scattered about, waiting for the evening rush of volunteers.

By nature of their transience, call centers were set up in empty buildings. Night came early this time of year. By five o'clock, it was dark. Melanie had walked the half mile from the hotel. The wind was sharp, nasty. The MoveIn people huddled in jackets without enough energy to even shout a slogan.

Hopefully the Jericho video was simply a stunt. Some group like Al-Qaeda, other Muslim extremists, or anarchist hackers could destroy this election. Or worse.

"I missed you," Melanie said, dabbing her eyes.

"I missed you too. But don't cry."

"Did you walk here?" Melanie asked. "How are you?"

"I'm fine." Sophie glanced over her shoulder at the callers, then gave Melanie a proper hug. "Dad said you got a little psycho about wanting me to leave the campaign."

"Did he actually use the word *psycho*?"

"Of course not. He said you expressed some concerns. And then I got more than a little psycho until he agreed with me that I'm in for the duration."

Melanie brushed back Sophie's bangs. Her daughter was small boned, light on her feet, quick-witted with people she trusted. She had Will's blue eyes, Melanie's dark hair, a wide smile from Grandpa Bobby Joe.

"That Jericho thing was disturbing," Melanie said. "We can't take security lightly."

"It was a stupid cartoon. You know those geeks," Sophie said. "Every once in a while they peek out of their mother's basements and make a statement."

Melanie laughed. "You got that from Carrie, didn't you?"

"Take a look, Mom. I'm in one piece. Warmly dressed. Not starving. No tattoos. Gainfully employed. So far ahead in my schoolwork, I'll finish this year before February. Poor Hannah is in the back room right now studying. She didn't get her trig work done."

The front door swung open, bringing with it a sudden chill.

Sophie's face lit up. "Oh, good. Mike's here."

"Mr. McGregor, you mean." The man moved with the confidence and energy of a college student, shaking hands with or fist-bumping volunteers, kissing the cheeks of the girls.

"He wants us to call him Mike. He's not stuffy like . . ." Sophie waved her hand in a dismissive motion.

". . . like the rest of us old folks who insist on courtesy?" Melanie said.

"It's your job to be stuffy. Mike, on the other hand, gets along with everyone. There are days when the senator and Dad don't take a breath unless Mike approves it."

"You sound like your grandfather."

"Finally, a compliment."

"What do you do here?"

"The usual. Make calls, hand out street signs, and that stuff. Mike calls us the Instant Response Team. We monitor the Twitter and Facebook feeds for him. If we see something that needs a response, we forward it to Tori."

"Tori?"

"Tori Peters. She's got programs to scan verbiage. Someone's got to actually read that garbage. That's me and Hannah."

"Oh, honey, that's not a good idea. In the heat of a campaign, people can be vile."

Sophie grinned, showing the dimple in her right cheek. "Yes, some people are downright disgusting. But everyone says the senator is about to break out. And we're seeing it, me and Hannah. We're here to witness history. And, Mom?"

"Yes, sweetheart?"

"There is no bigger kick than this."

Tuesday evening

Melanie cyberchatted with her elder daughter. "Your sister says it's a kick."

Destiny peered into the screen. "I love Dave and Miranda. You know they believed in me when no one else did. But I'd sooner stick needles in my eyeballs than trudge through a campaign."

Destiny was in her late twenties, married to a wonderful guy, living too far away in Los Angeles, and working in the film business. The consummate rebel, she had left home at eighteen, hitchhiked to Los Angeles, built a career, fallen in love with a good man, found faith.

"They've always had a soft spot for you," Melanie said.

"Ditto on that. But I'd rather have a root canal than all that talk-talk-talk stuff. By the way, I know Dave is a big boy and all, but can you tell him it's not cool to take on the entertainment establishment single-handedly?"

"Ah, the local interview," Melanie said. "I thought he went too far on that."

"First Amendment right and all that. But I'm getting the business from my colleagues who think Dave is going to slap PG stickers on every movie."

"That might not be a bad idea," Melanie said. "Speaking of entertainment, or lack thereof, did the Joshua video run out there?"

"Bad production value, terrible dialogue. Just a stupid stunt."

"Oh."

"Oh what, Mom? What's up? I can see it in your eyes."

Melanie clutched her throat as if she needed to yank the words out. "Your father is talking about . . . you know."

"Maybe I do, and maybe I don't." Her daughter frowned. "Just say it."

"A divorce."

"Hmm. Okay."

"You don't sound surprised. Did he say something to you?"

Destiny had inherited her expressive dark eyes from her birth mother. Though Will and Melanie loved their daughter desperately, the cadence of her thinking and the hues of her spirit were something with which God had blessed her and challenged them.

Her daughter studied her fingernails. "Did you know Dillon is in New Hampshire?"

"No. Wait. I saw him." The kid with the camera at the call center—he'd grown a lot since Destiny and Luke's wedding.

Dillon Whittaker was the son of Destiny's birth mother. He had been close to death a couple years ago before receiving a lobe of a liver from a living donor. Melanie had met him a year ago at Destiny's wedding.

"Dil finished high school early because of all that homeschooling when he was sick. He got accepted to UCLA Film School. Only sixteen, imagine that? He could have stayed here with Luke and me and taken classes. Julia freaked. I mean, *really* freaked. She and Matt get that he needs some independence because he was so dependent for so long.

"So they compromised. He's doing a postgrad year up at Prescott Academy in Merrimack with some dual classes at Rivier

University. His godmother keeps an eye on his well-being, and I volunteer to kick his butt via Skype every couple days."

"What a bounce-back," Melanie said. "He's a remarkable kid."

Destiny smiled. "That he is. Anyway, he approached Dad on his own, asked if he could do some videography around the campaign. Your communications guru . . . ?"

"Eli DuPont."

"Yeah. Eli DuPont has actually used some of Dillon's film. For a kid who balanced on the edge of death for so long, he's got a living lens."

"I'm glad to hear he's doing so well, Destiny. I pray for him. Though I'm not sure how we got from Dad and me to Dillon?"

Destiny tugged at the silver hoop earring. "Dil sends us stuff he's edited and also raw footage so Luke or I can give him feedback on angles, cuts, the whole thing. He's been given a lot of access. Those horrid chicken dinners. Campus visits with Carrie and the girls. And Dad lets him shoot Dave every once in a while. By the way, tell Dave to slow down on the pizza—he's turning into an oinker."

"You're still not telling me, Destiny."

Her daughter looked straight into the screen. "Dad's got this smokin' hot woman who works for him. Thick dark hair, sleepy eyes, great bod, the whole Mediterranean package."

Victoria Peters. As if Melanie should be surprised. "And?"

"The way that woman looks at Dad—it's not good, Mom. And she's smug because he's starting to look back. Starting to think about it." Destiny lowered her voice. "You'd better do something about this. Before it's too late."

five

Wednesday morning

DOCTOR ELIZABETH SIERRA RETURNED MELANIE'S phone call within an hour.

Melanie had expected a delay of several weeks to get onto the therapist's schedule. She needed time to gather her thoughts, work up her courage, prepare her defense. God had provided. Now Melanie had to obey.

"Before we meet," Dr. Sierra said, "I'd like you to write me a letter about what you think is not working in your marriage, and what you'd like to gain from our time together."

"Is it confidential?"

"Yes," Dr. Sierra said. "You will decide what you'd like—and what you need—him to know. I do want you to be aware, however, that he would like me to share his letter with you."

"Why doesn't he just give it to me?"

"He could do that. As of now, Will has expressed his preference that you be in a safe place when you consider his perspective."

"That bad, huh?" Melanie said.

"Not at all. These letters are tools, that's all. Get it on paper and we take it from there."

Commit it to paper, Melanie thought as she bent over her

laptop. Commit my absolute failure as a wife to paper. *Gracious Holy Spirit,* she prayed. *Help me share my heart.* She began to write.

Frigid.

Such an old-fashioned word. And what stigma used to be attached to it, though now the term has gone out of vogue. Sixty or seventy years ago it was a valid psychological diagnosis, almost always applied to the female gender.

I expect that Will has told you this is all about sex or lack thereof, even though he is too kind a man to apply *frigid* to me.

For the sake of openness, I am willing to start there, though I think the term *dislocation* is a better descriptor. I have dislocated my body from his in terms of lovemaking. He has dislocated his body from mine in terms of making a home together. In other words, our sex life has decreased proportionately to the time my husband has spent in DC.

It is the classic "chicken or egg" situation. We have agreed to leave the answer to that riddle up to you, Dr. Sierra. Here's the bottom line: I don't want Will to leave.

But—if I am to be honest—I don't want him to stay.

Will is a good man. A vibrant man. His intellectual energy and his physical presence are so compelling that he commands any room he enters. He is sexy. I know this, I see this.

I suppose there is something wrong with me because I don't feel this.

I will not be surprised to hear that Will has said his need to be almost full time in the District was the excuse I needed to stop pretending in the bedroom.

He will not be surprised to hear my contention that if he really loved me, he would have moved back to Tennessee.

And now he's in the midst of primary season. His work for

Dave is very important. Even so, there are younger politicians in Tennessee who would delight in having Will step in as senior advisor.

Will would say my argument is pro forma, that I really don't care to save our marriage. I worry that this therapy is pro forma and he has already decided divorce.

I am sorry it has come to this. I believe you, Dr. Sierra, are trustworthy and spiritually mature. But I cannot anticipate anything other than humiliation and recrimination in opening our lives to you.

And yet here I am, because I love my husband. I am sorry that I cannot love him like he wants.

Thank you for your assurance that this note is confidential. Will has probably told you that we have almost a hundred thousand subscribers to Lord's Heritage, families who depend on my ministry to guide them through this culture.

Given my work, there is a bitter irony in admitting that I have been insufficient as a wife and—in the view of my husband—potentially damaging to our daughter Sophie.

May the Lord bless you, Dr. Sierra. And please know that I really am sorry.

Thursday midday

Beth Sierra shook Melanie's hand. "Grab a seat, make yourself comfortable."

She glanced around, feet like cement. Even her choice of chair—Queen Anne or leather recliner—might tell Beth something about her.

Melanie kicked her shoes off and sat in the Queen Anne. If she had worn jeans, she might be tempted to throw her legs over the arm as if to say, "Despite what Will might have told you, I am perfectly comfortable in my own skin."

Beth's office was on the first floor of an old New England mansion, lovingly reclaimed from the ash heap of the Great Depression. The office had a stone fireplace with an ornately carved mahogany mantel. The ceilings were adorned with plaster crown molding that looked original.

The double set of French doors let in whatever light was available this time of year. Outside, the barren trees, brown lawn, and cold wind stirring dead leaves proved November to be merciless.

"I'd like to get to know you a bit," Beth said.

"You have my letter. I emailed it last night."

"You were honest. That's a great place to start. Shall we chat a little? I understand you were literally raised in politics. Maybe you could tell me about that?"

Will had been seeing Beth Sierra for five weeks. So did that put this woman in Will's "camp"? In politics you had to know where someone's self-interest lay to protect yourself.

A dark-eyed woman, Beth's thick brown hair was laced with silver. She had deep smile lines and a small scar across her nose. Her black slacks and heather-gray pullover were accented by a heavy necklace of silver and garnets. She wore black ballet shoes and striped crimson-and-gray stockings.

Okay, there's some give in this woman.

There was a picture frame on the sturdy oak desk of a man with thick gray hair and a shy smile. "Are you married?" Melanie said.

"I'm widowed. Tony was a great guy." Beth smiled. "Pancreatic cancer, out of the blue four years ago. As the days dwindled and the pain increased, he found comfort in his faith. And remarkably—because that was the kind of guy he was—he gave comfort."

"Do you have children?"

"Two sons, their early twenties. Jeffrey is in the marines and Max is in college. He comes home to do his laundry and to consume the entire contents of my refrigerator. And you have two daughters?"

"Yes." Melanie picked at a piece of lint. "How did Will choose you?"

"He's been coming to our church in downtown Manchester most Sundays. We met at coffee hour, discovered that we knew someone in common. Destiny's birth mother. She and I worked together decades ago."

The wind rattled the French doors, making Melanie jump. It was all she could do not to run from the room. She was a strong advocate of coaching and therapy to help couples and families under stress. Funny how skittish she was, now that it applied to her.

"This whole therapy thing. It's about communication, correct? With each other?"

"That's a big part of it," Beth said. "But it's also about communicating with yourself."

"That sounds a little too new-agey for me."

"Are you always clear on why you think a certain way or act a certain way?"

"I suppose not," Melanie said. "What I don't understand is how improving communication with Will and myself will make me . . . you know."

"Let's pretend I don't," Beth said. "Tell me."

"Want to have hot, steamy sex."

"Is that what you think Will wants? Hot, steamy sex?"

"I don't know what Will wants. Perhaps if I could read his letter now? I need to know if there's any hope."

Beth gave her another warm smile. "Your husband wouldn't be doing this if there wasn't."

"Will Connors is an expert at crafting perception. That's what he lives for." Melanie leaned forward. "I need to know if he means this."

"You may find his letter unsettling without us easing into it."

"It's more unsettling *not* to know. Please. You promised I could read it."

"I did." Beth riffled through her notes, then handed Melanie a piece of paper.

"Maybe if I go outside for a few minutes," Melanie said. "To read this in private."

"I'd rather you didn't," Beth said. "I'd like you close by so I can be helpful. But if you insist on being outside, I have a bench under my grape arbor."

Melanie went to the waiting room, grabbed her coat and scarf. Beth opened the door to the garden. "I can go to another room," she said. "Give you privacy so you won't freeze."

"That's no big deal." Melanie forced a laugh. "Not when you're frigid."

The six seconds it took her to get to the bench felt like a lifetime. Her lifetime with Will. Trapped on two pieces of paper. She began to read, grateful for the cold wind on her face.

> I love my wife. I respect her and admire her. And yet, the past twenty years with Melanie have felt like a Band-Aid being inched away from a wound.
>
> It's a blessing to have someone to speak to, Beth. I hope Melanie will be blessed as well. I'm proud of her for taking this step. It's difficult for her; difficult for both of us, because we guard our privacy. Unfortunately, that privacy has extended to each other.
>
> I don't know what she is thinking except to turtle deeper into her shell.

She doesn't know what I am thinking—how desperate I am to have a normal relationship. How I would like that relationship to be with her.

As per your instruction, I will do my best to capture where I believe my wife and I are today. I will resist the temptation to speak for Melanie, though I'll be as clear as I can with my perception of her feelings.

My guess is that she will say we arrived at this place because of my inattention to her. If that is true, I am so sorry. There was a time when we couldn't get enough of each other. And then something changed.

Melanie made occasional gestures of affection. It began to feel like she was doing her duty and nothing more. Sex became a hurried affair, usually because I was so starved for that aspect of marriage, and she was so anxious to have it over with.

Yet, she's been a loving wife in every other way. It seems as if removing sex makes our marriage better for her. I don't know what I've done wrong so I can't fix it.

You hear people talk about "putting on a great show but being dead on the inside." My wife is the opposite of that cliché—she is fully alive on the inside. I see it in her work. I see it in how she relates to people. I see it in her eyes—I swear I do—when she looks at me.

But the outside is dead. The question is: Is Melanie Fallon Connors dead only to me? Or is this hardened shell what she has become and will always be?

I am still alive. I am passionate. And I am starving.

The apostle Paul said it is better to marry than to burn.

I am married. And I am burning.

six

Friday evening

Carrie kissed Melanie's cheek, not surprised to find her sister-in-law at the call center. Sophie had already texted her three times, complaining her mother "stifled" her. In a couple more days, they'd have events set up for Melanie, and Sophie would have her freedom again.

"How're you settling in?" Carrie asked.

Her sister-in-law tugged at her sweater. "I forgot my mukluks back home."

"No kidding. I wore thermal underwear until June and dragged it back out by September."

"I still don't get how November can be so glum," Melanie said. "October in New Hampshire is gorgeous."

Too gorgeous. Time to change the subject. "Are the kids here?"

"They're digging around in the storeroom with Mike McGregor. Something about yard signs. The man is like a pied piper. He walks in and he's everyone's best friend."

"He's good with the kids," Carrie said. "We've got a nice collegiate thing going on. The girls are a big part of it. Honestly, I'm not even thirty but I feel out of touch with the younger generation."

Melanie laughed. "Caroline, you were *born* thirty."

Sophie and Hannah came into the main room on Mike McGregor's heels. They had their arms filled with yard signs.

"They shouldn't be pestering him like that," Melanie said.

"Fifteen years ago," Carrie said, "I followed Eli DuPont around, hanging on his every word. It's no big deal."

"Did I say it was a big deal?"

"No. Sorry. I just . . . wanted to let you know things are fine here. Crazy, but good." Carrie waved at the girls. "Hey, guys. We've got to get over to the arena. Puck drops in two hours."

"What's in the arena?" Melanie asked.

"A college hockey jamboree. Teams from UNH, Keane State, Southern New Hampshire, Rivier, a couple teams from Massachusetts. They're bringing in busloads of students to rock the place. We'll have water bottles, bracelets, vouchers for free nachos at the concession stands. And of course voter registration cards."

Melanie peered at her. "You're looking drawn, Caroline. Sleeping well?"

"Not really. I have a roommate. Tori Peters. She's always on her laptop. *Tap tap tap.* There are some nights I want to flush that stupid computer. When she finally gets to sleep, she sighs all night. Honestly, snoring would be an upgrade. I begged Will to let me room solo. He said no, he couldn't show nepotism. We argued about it for three weeks too long and the hotel booked up. Except for the luxury rooms and condos on the top floor. And that would be bad for perception."

"Oh," Melanie said. "So Sophie's helping out?"

Back to Sophie? Helicopter parents had nothing on Melanie Connors. She had come into camp as a fully armed Blackhawk. Carrie's mother had taken the European view of child rearing. By the time Carrie was thirteen, she took the train to Manhattan for shopping, concerts, the theater. Her mother encouraged intellectual curiosity.

"They've been great. They are savvier than I was at their age."

"That's not necessarily a good thing." Melanie frowned, erased it quickly. "Sophie texted me that congratulations are due."

"What?" Carrie's stomach dropped. "What did Sophie say?"

"That you got promoted. And this Victoria Peters took your place."

"Victoria Peters is a climber. She's glommed onto Will like a second skin. And before you beat around that bush for ten minutes, Will is too focused—too *Will*—to let anything distract him."

"Would you tell me if there was?"

"Will's a big boy. I leave him to his own business."

"We're family," Melanie said. "That makes it your business. Just promise that you would tell me if there's something I need to be concerned about. Please. Promise me."

"On my Girl Scout honor." Not that Carrie had ever been a scout. For Melanie's sake, she'd try.

Friday night

Carrie loved ice hockey. The *slick slick* sound of skates on the ice, the *pop* of a slap shot, the bursts of speed, the exhaustion after a shift, and the adrenaline flooding back when it was her turn to hop the boards and skate again.

She had starred in the sport at prep school and played wing for the women's team at Princeton. Her mother had started her in figure skating when she was three. When she was five, Carrie had earned enough money from recycling Will's water bottles and soda cans to buy her own hockey skates.

Her decision to switch from the grace of figure skating to the raw power of hockey created a minor family crisis. When Mother refused to sign her permission slip and give her the five hundred bucks needed for pads and ice time, Carrie ran away.

She walked out the front door with a backpack full of toys, her skates in one hand and a juice box in the other. Will found her two hours later. She had managed to hike the twenty blocks to the rink without getting lost or kidnapped. He signed her permission slip and took care of the fees.

The lesson was a lifelong one. Talent and training were helpful and good to have. Doggedness was essential. The other lesson was that her brother, Will—*Billy*—had her back.

Carrie stood on the ramp to the stands, listening to the razor-slick steel on ice, the steady hum of the crowd, the clamor of the pep bands. The rink smelled of hot dogs, French fries, and Zamboni fumes.

Sophie and Hannah were under the stands in the concession area, festive in bright blue T-shirts and ponytails. They had instructions not to stray more than five feet from each other. The Dawson Youth Team members were sprinkled throughout the arena, passing out water bottles with brochures and voter registration cards. Anyone who filled out a card was given a ticket for cheese nachos.

The college kids were starting to listen. They measured their college debt against the weak prospects for employment and had begun to think soberly about the albatross of debt hung on them by a wasteful generation.

Someone grabbed Carrie from behind and made a loud raspberry on her neck. She whirled around, fists clenched until she realized who it was. "You fool. People get tased for less."

Tucker Keyes lifted her off the floor, gave her a huge hug. Carrie smacked him on one cheek and kissed the other. "I could have pepper sprayed you."

"Promises, promises." Tuck kissed both her cheeks.

"What are you doing here? You don't like hockey."

"I had a craving for a sausage sub and this cheap slop they call beer. Join me?" He grinned and she reminded herself *not* to melt. Women who dissolved for him were always sorry soon after, when he disappeared into the sunrise.

"I'd love to," Carrie said. "I'm babysitting the troops. Rain check?"

"Sure thing." He kissed her on the lips—innocuously enough—then pushed through a gang of UNH kids on his way to the concession stand.

"Whoa, Auntie!" Sophie grabbed her arm. "Who is he?"

"Tucker Keyes. We went to Princeton together. Which makes him far too old for you."

She slapped Carrie on the butt. "I like senior citizens."

"Where's Hannah?"

"Looking for Mike. We had someone who wanted to make a big donation. She didn't want to take the check."

"I was right here, peanut. You should have brought them to me."

"With some guy kissing your neck? When do I get the intro to your friend? Hannah and I decided we like mature men. Forget high school kids."

"Go back down to your station. Those water bottles cost the campaign good money. We don't need Sanders's or Bresler's people stealing them while you leave them unattended. I'll call Mike, see if Hannah's found him."

Sophie skipped down the ramp and into the crowd. She had matured in the past two months and was quick-witted—when she wasn't obsessing about the opposite sex.

Dillon wandered up the ramp, camera in hand. He stopped and chatted with Sophie. Carrie hadn't realized he would be here. He wore a blue Dawson shirt. Did Sophie even realize he had a crush on her?

The arena lights flashed, strobe-like. A unanimous cry went up from the stands.

The scoreboard above the ice darkened. The referee blew his whistle, sent the two teams to their benches where they all stared up at the scoreboard.

The marionette spoke. “Take a look around. I offer you disaffected youth. Like stinking sheep, you sway with the herd. Television, social media, a whisper *here* and a mocking *there* and you know to follow.

“Let there not be light, people. Let there *not* be light.”

And suddenly, there wasn’t.

The scoreboard blacked out, taking with it every light in the stadium. Carrie turned left, then right, suddenly unsure of where she was. Her heart rattled like a snare drum. She pressed her hand to her stomach, as if that would keep her from falling.

The crowd fell silent, waiting for the *whomp* of emergency lighting to come on. Nothing. The hum of voices resumed, first as a whisper and then as a steady drumbeat of obscene insults and halfhearted jokes.

Someone brushed up against Carrie and cupped her backside. She swore, swatted the guy, flashed her iPhone so she could catch a look. He’d already disappeared. Pig.

Where were the emergency lights? She felt along the railing until she found a solid wall. The decline under her feet meant she was on the ramp.

“Sophie,” she yelled.

“Here,” a voice rang out. Wrong Sophie. Too common a name now.

“You’re okay,” Carrie said. “Stay in your seat.”

A commanding voice shouted out, “Don’t leave your seats. They are working on the problem.”

“What if someone has a gun?” another girl asked.

Carrie felt the panic taking hold. Someone said, "Like the Aurora shooting," and she felt air move as people in the section next to the ramp stood up, crouched down, looked for safety.

"No," she said in her best crowd-control voice. "You'll start a panic and people will get hurt. Just stay in your seats."

"Carrie, I'm here." Sophie looked like a ghost in the light of her cell phone. Dillon was with her.

"Where's Hannah?"

"I don't know."

"Stay right there. Dillon, do not let her move."

The arena gave a collective gasp as the scoreboard lit up again.

"Dillon," she shouted but he had already aimed his camera. His instinct matched hers. Something was coming. Something they needed to see.

The scoreboard flashed blood red. Carrie's stomach soured. This was just so wrong, so bizarre. *God, please no guns in here, please.*

Letters began to form on the scoreboard. The murmuring grew, some kids laughing, one girl crying.

Hypocrites!

How is it you know how to interpret the appearance of the earth and the sky?

How is it that you don't know how to interpret this present time?

Dillon turned to Carrie. "That's Scripture."

"Luke," she said, surprising herself. "Not sure which chapter."

The message scrolled over and over, picking up speed as it went until the letters became a red blur. Some guy yelled an obscenity and the crowd picked it up. Typical college hockey stuff—obscene and meaningless.

Someone threw a water bottle onto the ice.

Carrie had no time to worry about scriptural admonitions because Dawson water bottles began to rain down from every corner of the arena. The rebellion swept through the stands. She could feel it, a tangible energy that made her want to throw something too.

Disaffected youth could make a mighty army. Right now, their only weapons were Dawson water bottles, turned into missiles. *So this is how the world ends,* Carrie thought. *Not with a bang but with a pile of cheap plastic.*

A horn sounded. "What's that?" Dillon said, his voice tinged with panic.

"The timer's horn." Carrie breathed a sigh of relief as the lights glowed yellow and then white. The scoreboard flashed its normal display: the teams, the score, the period, the time.

The ice was littered with water bottles. "Should we pick them up?" Dillon asked. "They're, like . . . our responsibility."

"We didn't throw them," Carrie said. "They are the responsibility of all the jerks who threw them."

"They don't know that," Dillon said. "Someone needs to tell them."

"That's what Dave Dawson is trying to tell them."

"Then you have to try louder," Dillon said. "Before they listen to this Joshua creep."

Thanksgiving Week, November

Presidential Primary Season

seven

Monday morning

THE GUY'S GOT A GOOD BEDSIDE MANNER, TUCK thought.

David Dawson worked his way up the aisle of the bus, schmoozing volunteers. The media sat toward the back with poker faces. Impress me, they were thinking. Cultivate me. Remember me when you come into your kingdom. Or remember me when I destroy you.

Tuck rubbed his hands on his trousers. He had been a bona fide journalist for a few days and already he smelled blood in the air. The scent of the story, J.L. would say.

It felt good to flex his intellectual muscles. It took little horsepower to bemoan that Hollywood was now churning out prequels to its sequels.

Carrie Connors followed Dawson. Her fair hair was wind tossed, her cheeks pink. She wore jeans, leather boots, a red down jacket. Her eyes were so blue that he could see them from here. She spotted Tuck, raised her index finger.

The local reporters worked their laptops, probably prewriting their articles. Candidates made the same stump speech four times a day. It was the Q&A that could produce a sound bite, even when those were also premanufactured by the campaigns.

Nothing new under the sun. Ecclesiastes, correct? David Dawson would know. The senator had been raised in the church and still held to the traditional values he had inherited from his parents.

Sarah Dawson had been a nurse-midwife and Peter Dawson had been spectacularly successful as a manufacturer of plumbing fittings. They had left their only son a fortune somewhere in the nine-digit range. Who knew that faucets, drains, and pipes could be worth so much? More than *The Journal* was worth now.

Maybe Tuck should have been born a Dawson instead of a Keyes.

At ritzy cocktail parties in DC—the sort that the saintly Dawson would never attend—the senator was jokingly referred to as the "Toilet King."

He watched Dawson work the bus, touching a shoulder, squeezing a forearm.

Tuck heard the stories about when J.L. rode the bus with Lyndon Johnson and Richard Nixon. On Sunday mornings, the candidate made sure the photographers snapped him going into or coming out of church. The press scurried to brunch, happy for a couple hours off.

One downed communion wine, the other mimosas and bloody marys.

At Princeton, Caroline Connors had been the ultimate mimosa—bubbly with a little bite. At school, she had been quiet about her faith and claimed her Sunday evening absences to be study sessions.

Now look at her. The right hand of a man who could be president of the United States.

Tuck scrolled his phone, found the latest poll from a week earlier. Governor Hal Sanders still held a commanding lead. And—by the way he spent money—Hal's organization had a blank check for advertising and staff. Staying power in a primary fight was more about a steady stream of fund-raising than position papers and speeches. Woo the donors and the voter would follow.

Carrie slid into the seat next to him. "Lose the tie," she said. "This is New Hampshire, not DC."

He kissed her cheek. "Hello to you too. What's the word on the arena blackout?"

"Off the record? The feds are sticking with 'stunt.' They want to keep people from panicking and hitting up Home Depot for generators. You're the computer guy. What do you think happened?"

"I hacked around, helped make some games. This is beyond hacking. It's sophisticated," Tuck said. "Kind of a waste to have the ability to take over networks and yet throw a cartoon on the screen."

"Is there anything we can do to protect ourselves? I mean, here on the campaign?"

Tuck smiled. "Have plenty of flashlights."

Carrie got up so Dave Dawson could take her place. "Nice to have you join us, Tucker," he said, extending his hand. The candidate looked younger in person, with less gravitas and more good cheer. His suit jacket was snug; photos had shown a weight gain over the past six months.

"I'm happy to be here," Tuck said. "Though I am not exactly sure where *here* is going to be today."

Dawson laughed. "I know the feeling. We'll spend some time together later, but right now I've got sixty seconds, if you need a quick comment."

Tuck wasn't prepared. He cast about for a question, came up with J.L.'s old standby. "One word. If you had to describe yourself in one word, what would it be?"

"Good question." Dawson squeezed his eyes shut. "One word, one word . . ."

Christian was too parochial and would turn off too many

voters. *Conservative* was treacherous because the media had made it synonymous with racist. *Persistent*, *impatient*, *hopeful*, *honest*, *determined*—these adjectives were traps waiting to be sprung.

Dawson opened his eyes. "Grieved," he said.

"Grieved. Why?"

"You said *one* word."

"Can I have a couple more?"

Dawson rested his hand on Tuck's shoulder. "My wife and I grieve for this nation. Look at us. We would rather buy oil from oppressive nations in the Mideast than make sober decisions to find our own energy sources. We would rather borrow from our enemies and put a massive yoke of debt on our unborn grandchildren than try to rein in our own spending." He stood, his jaw tight. "And we would rather go our own way and lead this world into an abyss rather than acknowledge an almighty God."

He squeezed Tuck's arm. "God bless you. I've got to run."

Tuck had gone his own way his entire life. He was on the bus now. Who knew where it might lead?

Monday morning

Dave Dawson was everything Carrie admired. Kind, funny, perceptive. Bobby Joe Fallon—before the Alzheimer's—said Dave could talk a snake out of its skin.

Will was the anti-Dave. Sharp, relentless, cynical. Carrie was far more Will than Dave.

If he knew about the pregnancy, Dave would say, "We'll help you make a good home," or "Find it a good home, but this child shouldn't suffer because you had a moment of weakness." Will would say, "We're in the middle of a presidential campaign," and "How could you be so stupid?"

The desperation inside her was simply saying, "Fix this."

As they left the bus Dave whispered, "You're looking hazy. You okay?"

"The fumes. We need to stop idling, get on the road. We can't afford to get off schedule today."

Dave had already been to some backwoods diner, driving himself without staff to prove he was a man of the people. They now headed to Greer's Machine Shop with enough of a contingent to make a good photo and throw out a sound bite or two. After that, they had a luncheon with the Concord Chamber of Commerce. Two afternoon rallies.

The day would top off at the annual Daniel Webster dinner, hosted by the *Union Leader* newspaper. Word was Sanders was a pass, which meant Ted Rancic, Sheryl Bresler, and Dave could all go after him without return fire.

Dave's head of security, Jason Polke, had the Suburban waiting for them. Carrie climbed in the way-back next to Mike.

Will reached over the seat and laid his hand on her forehead. "You okay, pumpkin?"

I'm pregnant and scared, Billy. "I'm fine, really."

Her brother gave Carrie's hand a squeeze before addressing Jason. "Any word on this Jericho thing?"

"Power was not lost to the arena," Jason said. "It simply was selectively turned off to every device except the scoreboard. In regard to emergency lighting, that's more basic. Wires were cut, batteries removed, and the like. Well designed and well coordinated."

"Which means that someone was on the inside and had access to the arena before the crowd arrived," Will said. "Did the security cameras show anything?"

"Wiped clean. And it wasn't just us who had an incident,"

Jason continued. "There are scattered reports about road signs reprogrammed in Iowa so that Sanders's entourage would pass them on their way back from their event. One of Haines's guys said they had the same video scrolling on their Internet in the hotel. All with the same 'hypocrite' message. We have to take this seriously, though it seems purposeless."

"Purposeless?" Carrie said. "It scared the salsa out of me. And those water bottles all over the ice made a mockery of our promotion."

"The lights are nothing. It's the communications networks that have us all freaked. And with good reason." Jason pulled the SUV onto the highway. The bus followed. "My guy said it was high-level hacking. CalTech- or MIT-type."

"Victoria said it would involve more than one hacker," Will said.

"What?" Carrie said. "She's an expert on this now?"

"She went to MIT."

"Whoop-di-do. She was a communications major, right?"

"She has lots of friends," Will said, "in the tech community."

"Stop defending her. Or should I say promoting her?"

"Children, children," Dave said. "Let's leave the personalities to the talking heads. How about the NSA? It's not like we are anyone's favorite son. Maybe they've gone rogue."

"Haines is," Carrie said. "They went after him too. The FBI is on it. We'll all have to be interviewed."

"Fantastic," Will said with a snort.

"Okay. So we'll be watchful," Dave said. "I'd feel better if the girls stayed a little closer than they're used to. Last night in the dark—anything could have happened."

"We'll schedule them in-house," Will said. "If they go to an event, Jason can get us extra security. At some point we have to ask for Secret Service."

"No," Dave said. "Not unless there's an overt threat." He turned to the backseat. "So, Mike. How're we looking today?"

Mike McGregor smelled of expensive cologne and breath mints. He was an attractive man, sexy in his confidence.

Carrie stifled a sigh, thinking about Tucker Keyes. With his connections and personality, Tuck could have been a Beltway talent like Mike McGregor. Or, with his amazing brain, he could have been another Steve Jobs. He majored in art history to tick off his grandfather but took programming courses because he loved video games. For a full year, he dreamed of becoming the next Mark Zuckerberg.

"The traditional voting blocs are scattering to weird places," Mike said. "The lefties are disenchanted with all the military involvement and diplomatic messes in the Middle East. The libertarians are folding their arms and pouting about foreign entanglements, saying we told you so."

"Find me a way to talk to these people," Dave said. "We need them."

"Tweak your stance on the medical marijuana and they might listen," Will said.

"Don't ask me to do something I can't do. That's not an issue for a national campaign."

"Pull a Hillary," Carrie said. "Say you're opening the conversation on the failed war on drugs. That you'll instruct your attorney general to take a long look at current law."

"Weak," Will said.

"What else can we do when our guy wears too white a hat?"

Dave raised an eyebrow at her. "That halo will be off after we send out that press release tonight."

Will gave him a sharp look. "Second thoughts, bro? We can try to suppress the story."

"Common sense says be honest and leave it up to the goodwill of the New Hampshire and Iowa voters." Dave smiled. "So forward, march."

Carrie's stomach recoiled at the anticipation of what would

go down tonight after the Daniel Webster dinner. She was the one who suggested they release the damaging report about Dave to Tucker Keyes. That way, they could try to manipulate the outcome.

"We've got to get a little out-of-the-box," Mike said.

"What about the MoveIn people?" Carrie said.

Will burst into laughter. "What've you been smoking, Caroline? Stick to the subject."

"They hate business as usual and they want a change. So do we. I'm not saying pander to them," Carrie said. "I'm just saying pull a Hillary on them too."

"Wow, look who's got the Hillary bug," Mike said.

"If we're going to be grassroots, let's *be* grassroots," Carrie said. "If MoveIn can verbalize one or two issues reasonably, we could open a dialogue."

"The press will see it as desperation. The evangelicals will see it as a betrayal." Will glared at Carrie. "And you, Caroline, are wasting valuable time. So let's move on."

"Maybe," Dave said. "Probably. Just in case—Carrie, have Sophie or Hannah do some research on them. That'll stop their complaints that we don't trust them with anything vital."

Carrie settled back in her seat, listened to Mike's briefing on whom they needed to schmooze today during the various events. Poor Sophie was back at the hotel, in Melanie prison. Carrie leaned against the window, texted her niece:

not 1 word. I trust U

Her return text was immediate.

no worries, auntie. wish I was there.

"Senator," Jason said from the driver's seat. "We're stopping here." *Here* was an ice-cream stand, shuttered for the winter. They pulled into the empty parking lot. The bus came to a stop behind them. Dave would get on the bus so he could arrive with his supporters, keep the energy up, and maintain his image as "just another guy." All candidates did this.

"Are we all set for tonight?" Mike asked. "The release?"

"Absolutely," Dave said.

"I'm still voting against this," Will said.

Carrie's stomach tightened. They were about to send Dave high wiring without a net. "Dave's arrest is coming out whether we like it or not. This way we can manage it."

"We tell the truth and pray for redemption," Dave said. He squeezed Carrie's hand, then got out of the car.

Mike climbed out behind him, stared back at Carrie. "Drop the MoveIn stuff," he said.

Will watched them get on the bus. Dave went down the aisle, high-fiving and fist-bumping. Mike sat down next to Hannah, in what had become the "good luck" seat.

"Okay, pumpkin," Will said. "Show me what you've got on Sanders."

Carrie scrolled to the video. "This is all courtesy of Bresler's people, remember. She wanted clean hands. I'll make sure ours are clean too."

Will watched for a few seconds, then burst out laughing. "What an absolute fool. Did you get verification?"

"I've got the affidavit from the guy who taped it," Carrie said.

"What did he get in return?"

"A Bresler supporter gave him a cushy job. This is a win-win. It will get Sanders out and wash away the news on Dave. The congresswoman never would have given this to us if she knew Dave was about to stumble into trouble. But we've got it. This picture is worth a thousand words and all that."

Will kissed her cheek. "And all that, baby sister. All that."

eight

Monday afternoon

THE SUN BROKE THROUGH THE NOVEMBER GLOOM in one last gasp of Indian summer. Something about the smell of dead leaves and the brush of gentle sunshine made Melanie want to believe that hope was imminent.

Beth Sierra was the only sunshine in the room, wearing a burnt orange top and a bright yellow shawl. The socks peeking over her suede boots featured turkeys and pilgrim hats.

"So what's your diagnosis?" Melanie said. "Is it the sex, or lack thereof? And if we fix me, will it fix us?"

"Lack of sexual intimacy is just a symptom of deeper issues," Beth said. "Perhaps we could back up a little, noodle some of the root causes for the disconnection."

"It's going to hurt, isn't it?"

"Consider this like a workshop and not emotional surgery. We use whatever we have to work with and cast aside anything that doesn't serve the higher purpose."

"Okay, ask away," Melanie said. "I'll blush and stammer. But ask away."

"When you first met Will, you were fifteen. Were you physically attracted to him then?"

"I was in the throes of hormones. Smelling lilacs could make me crazy. Like . . . I just wanted to be in someone's arms and feel cherished and— Shoot, this is hard."

"What's hard?" Beth said.

"Sophie is a year older than I was back then. And campaigns—they kind of make you horny because of the intensity. It's such a relief to kick back with someone, mess around."

Beth popped the top of her Diet Coke, took a long sip. "It didn't take us long to get from you and Will to Sophie."

"Can you blame me? Look at what this culture has done to our children."

"Let's try something." Beth dug into the drawer of the end table, came up with a knotted rope. A dog's pull toy. "Grab an end."

Melanie wrapped her hand around the knot. "My daughter Destiny always wanted a dog," she said. "I knew I'd be the one taking care of it."

"We're talking about what *you* want," Beth said. "I'd like you to pull on this rope and show me how much energy you have to invest in this marital counseling process."

Destiny and her dog. Sophie growing up. Will—still electric but Melanie feared the sparks.

Dear Lord, I don't want to be afraid. So much to be afraid of, so please, Father, please give me strength.

She yanked the rope right out of Beth's hand.

"Wow, I'm pretty strong but look at you!"

"Did you do this with Will?" Melanie asked.

Beth gave her a Cheshire cat smile. "Will did say I could tell you, if you asked."

"Tell me."

"He pulled so hard the rope went flying out of both our hands. Knocked over a vase, making a perfectly wonderful mess."

An hour later they had discussed the early attraction to Will, how they lost touch through college, how when they got together again they married quickly.

"Let's back up," Beth said, "and leave Will out for a little while. Did you have previous sexual relationships prior to dating him?"

"We're talking thirty-odd years ago." Cold settled in Melanie's chest. She glanced out the window, surprised to see that the sun still shone. Beth had cracked open the French doors and a sweet breeze wafted in. All she could smell was the decay of the fallen leaves.

"Who you were," Beth said, "is still part of who you are."

"Why talk about it now? Will knows I . . . did things. Why do *you* think I'm so fixated on Sophie?"

"You're deflecting, Melanie."

"No. What I'm trying to say is that I know what campaigns are like. Daddy ran clean ships, but things could get a little down and dirty, you know? Things happen. Will knows that. What is past, is past, he says. So is it really healthy to dig all that up?"

"Let's play this again." Beth held out the knotted rope.

Melanie rolled her eyes, took an end.

"How sincerely do you believe that the past doesn't matter?" Beth asked.

The rope became the albatross, knotted around her marriage. Too heavy to even bear.

Melanie let it drop.

Monday night

Stunning, Tuck thought.

Caroline Connors wore a red dress that somehow flowed and clung at the same time. The hint of cleavage was enough to entice, yet not enough to seduce. She had traded in hiking boots for high heels and her wool scarf for an ornate gold necklace. Her blond hair shone. Even her skin shimmered.

This was vintage Carrie—you know, the girl in sneakers and then she changes to stilettos and you need to discover her all over again.

"Bored yet?" she said.

Tuck opened his arms for a hug. "Captivated, now that you're here."

Carrie stepped back. "We can't do that in public. Press and operatives are adversaries, remember?"

Tuck had watched her all day fielding phone calls, shuffling people, separating important locals from the pack and chatting them up. She was good at her job and thrived on the buzz.

Governor Sanders was sitting this event out. His people had concluded that New Hampshire was his plum, so he focused his time on Iowa. A bipartisan event, the state's majority leader speaking for the vice president. Haines was also in Iowa, sweeping out the chaff so he could have a clear path to the candidacy.

During the speeches, Congresswoman Sheryl Bresler had knocked Sanders with glee. Dave Dawson used his time to promote his "Common Sense for America" agenda. His wife looked up at him adoringly. Even their daughter got into the act, working the tables with strategist Mike McGregor as if she were hosting the event. Governor Rancic took aim at the current administration, working up some howling good zings with little content.

J.L. hadn't exaggerated the boredom factor. New faces, same old bull. Grandfather would say the heart doesn't change. Just the window dressing.

"Hey," Tuck said. "Any news on this Joshua character?"

"Put that jaw-crunching migraine of a weirdo aside, Tucker." Carrie leaned on the wall next to him. Press were invited into the room but not seated. "Something's coming down, something that's going to be a tiff for the senator."

"What kind of a tiff?"

"Not here. Find a quiet place. Text me your location and I'll join you."

Tuck listened to another minute of Rancic's disembowelment of Vice President Haines and then made his way through the lobby and out of the hall.

Smokers lined the front sidewalk. Sign holders for all four candidates stood behind large cones. They chatted amiably because it was too cold to shout each other down. A Bresler volunteer spotted him. "Hey, man. It's time for a straight talker. Congresswoman Bresler tells it like it is. Can I give you a brochure?"

Tuck waved, kept walking. They all claimed to be straight talkers. Honest Abes with private planes, cell phones, and costly agendas.

Half a block from the hotel, Tuck found a twenty-four-hour convenience store. He texted Carrie and a few minutes later she joined him.

She handed him her iPad. "We're issuing this press release tomorrow. I'll give it to you now so you can have a half-day lead on the story. Assuming you're interested."

"Are you kidding? All this secrecy—of course I'm interested." He read the document, smiled at the delightful turn of events.

For Immediate Release:

The office of the Honorable David M. Dawson

At 6:40 p.m. this evening, District of Columbia police arrested Paige Bowers, 31, and Shane Dodd, 37, for attempted extortion of Senator David Dawson (Tennessee). Senator

Dawson cooperated fully with the police department, recording Bowers and Dodd on wire as they demanded one hundred thousand dollars to ensure their silence about a traffic accident Ms. Bowers had in 2007. Senator Dawson confirmed that he was the passenger in the car. The accident followed a gathering hosted by a healthcare lobbyist. Ms. Bowers, who was also in attendance at the gathering, crashed her car into a wall and was charged at the scene with driving under the influence. The official report did not name the senator but described the passenger as "under the influence and belligerent."

"This was a onetime failure on my part," Senator Dawson said. "I ordinarily do not drink but I did that night. I knew I could not drive home so I accepted Ms. Bowers's offer of a ride without understanding that she also had been drinking. I was not charged in the incident and was pleased that no one was injured. My wife and I dealt with this in 2007, and it is a shame that it must become public now. However, Miranda and I decided not to extend my wrongdoing by submitting to criminal extortion. We're grateful to the Washington, DC, police force and to the FBI for ensuring this episode would not be compounded."

"Wow," Tuck said. "So who's Ms. Bowers?"

"She is a prostitute."

"Whoa! I'm not sure the word *tiff* is an apt noun for this."

"We've got you penciled in with Dave and Miranda right after this event."

"Tonight?" Tuck's mind raced in a hundred directions. What an opportunity and he wasn't prepared.

"I've got a conference room booked. You can have as long as you need with them. We won't issue the press release until you're ready to file. You'll be at least twenty-four hours ahead of the rest of the media."

"Is this why you asked me to come to New Hampshire?" Tuck said. "To get out front with this story?"

She wrapped her arms around his neck. "We knew this arrest was in the works and wanted to roll out Senator Dawson's part in it with someone we like."

"Do you expect me to play favorites with Dawson? I'm not going to, just because you're giving me access."

"Be fair and be accurate. That's all we're asking, Tuck. And in return?" Carrie kissed his cheek. "You'll see far bigger stories than this little dustup. Trust me on that."

—

Tuck sat with the senator and his wife in the conference room that Carrie had reserved.

"I know your mother," Miranda Dawson said. "Blair and I volunteered together on the Library Initiative. She's out of the country now?"

"London," Tuck said. "We lived there when I was a kid, and she goes back every couple years to hobnob with the royals."

"Nothing like democracy." Dawson smiled but his shifting glance betrayed his nervousness. This interview would be like a root canal for the couple. "Shall we get started?"

Tuck thumbed on his recorder. "How do you know Paige Bowers?"

"I encountered her in 2007 in Washington," Dawson said. "She is a paid escort."

"A prostitute," Tuck said. "That's . . . out of character, isn't it?"

"I want to make something clear up front." Dawson pointed his index finger at Tuck, reminiscent of a former president insisting, *I never had sex with that woman.* "When anyone gets caught in this kind of situation, they talk about a rough patch in their marriage. As if that justifies an affair or—in my case—drinking too much and inappropriately accepting a ride with Ms. Bowers. Miranda and I were *not* going through a rough patch. Miranda is and has always been the best of partners."

"And was it just a ride home?" Tuck asked.

Dawson's jovial face darkened. "Yes. She offered, I accepted."

"Why her? Why not ask one of your colleagues?"

"I was only thinking clearly enough to know I was in bad shape. I don't drink, Mr. Keyes. I learned in college that alcohol and I are not compatible. For the week leading up to this incident, my colleagues and I were staring down the threat of a government shutdown. After a nonproductive day of conferencing and caucusing, a friend suggested we stop in at this party, get a quick bite to eat. We hadn't eaten all day. I was thirsty so I just grabbed a drink from a tray. Just something while we made our way to the buffet."

He's misdirecting. The slight shift of the eyes, the tightening of the throat as you try to smooth out your words and slide sideways from the topic.

"What friend?" Tuck said.

"A colleague. That person is not relevant."

"Is this person still *friendly* with you today?"

"A friend, that's all I am saying."

"And why didn't that friend give you a ride? Or counsel you to slow down on the drinking. Given you were . . . *incompatible* with what they were serving."

"My judgment was impaired after having too much to drink," Dawson said.

"How much is too much?"

"A glass of wine and then a few beers."

"And that impaired your judgment?" A couple drinks wouldn't even register on Tuck's Richter scale. "You can't expect me to believe that, sir."

"He said he doesn't drink," Miranda said. "And he said he'd tell you the truth. Or is there some scale of inebriation that is suitable for this kind of folly?"

"Just trying to clarify." Tuck had underestimated the woman, consigned her to the role of dutiful wife and image with shining smile. "Why was Ms. Bowers at this gathering?"

"My understanding now is that Ms. Bowers and some other women were available as perks. I didn't realize her . . . role . . . on that night. I certainly do now."

"I picked David up at the scene of the accident," Miranda said. "He knew he had compromised his judgment, both with the drinking and by accepting a ride with someone he didn't know."

"And were you going to Ms. Bowers's . . . residence when the accident occurred?" Tuck asked.

"No," Mrs. Dawson said with the energy of a hard slap. "He was not. He told you that."

"So where were you going?"

"How is that relevant?"

"Miranda, it's okay." Dawson's gaze lingered on his wife. "I just wanted to go to my office, shower, drink some coffee. I didn't want to come home to Miranda like that."

It's real, Tuck thought with a flutter in his gut. Dawson might be dancing around the identity of his "friend," but the connection between him and his wife was genuine.

"Did you know Ms. Bowers was a prostitute when you left with her?"

"Of course not."

"When did you learn that she was?"

"When I sobered up. I was ashamed because I had embarrassed my wife. And I was sad for Ms. Bowers."

"You believe in free markets," Tuck said, "supply and demand.

So, according to your political philosophy, why shouldn't a woman offer a service if there's a demand?"

"Because that demeans the woman."

"Even if she enters the encounter willingly?"

"She is still God's child. Cherished and loved. And by getting into the car with Ms. Bowers, I betrayed my wife."

"Don't say that," Mrs. Dawson said. "You made a mistake."

"Why extort you now instead of all those years ago?"

"I assume it's because of the presidential campaign," Dawson said.

"There's more to it," his wife said. "David's high visibility explains why he made a good target. But clearly, there is more to it."

Tuck turned to her. "And what would that be?"

Dawson grasped her hand. "No. I'm not going there."

"I will, and you may note this as my opinion only," she said. "It is not a stretch to consider that Ms. Bowers may have been . . . encouraged by one of my husband's opponents to flush out this story."

"I won't even consider that," Dawson said, "because that kind of assumption diminishes all of us."

"Why didn't you pay the money and be done with this?" Tuck asked.

"We're doing our best to be honest with the voters," Dawson said. "Warts and all. We didn't have any meetings with strategists or lawyers. We didn't do focus groups. We called in the DC police who—by the way—are to be praised for their professionalism and for their discretion."

Mrs. Dawson smiled. "We both wore wires. Like on television."

Her husband pulled her close. "We set up a meeting and recorded the demands Ms. Bowers and the man she works with—"

"Her pimp?" Tuck said.

"Let's say her business partner, shall we?"

"If I could be honest," Tuck said. "How are you going to handle the mess this country is in if you can't even say the word *pimp*?"

Dawson glared. "Is there anything else we can help you with, Mr. Keyes? I did something stupid and am so blessed that my wife forgave me." He kissed his wife on the forehead. "We have prayed for Ms. Bowers since that night."

"Really?" Tuck raised his eyebrows. "That's hard to believe."

"Really," Mrs. Dawson said. "Do you have any other questions?"

"Will this revelation derail your husband's campaign?"

"Absolutely not. David has always been clear about who we are. He makes mistakes. I make mistakes. We try to own up to them and then look for redemption."

"Redemption is another one of those code words, isn't it?" Tuck said.

Miranda Dawson grabbed his hand. Hers was hot, dry. "It's a reality, Mr. Keyes."

"It is what this country is about," Dawson said. "We do the best we can to uphold our principles, and when we fall, we make amends and stand back up. Now, if you'll excuse us? I need to get back to the hotel, make some phone calls."

Tuck glanced at his watch. Ten o'clock. Maybe he could pull rank and get this on the front page of tomorrow's edition. Get a camera to the arraignment tomorrow to get a photo of Paige Bowers. Have someone on the Metro desk try to ferret out her police record.

A scandal was always a good remedy for boredom—especially one that might involve sex. Who was the *friend* who brought Dawson to this party? It wasn't more than a baby step to suspect it was Carrie's brother. Will Connors and Dave Dawson had been best buddies since grade school.

Was there more to the story? Carrie might expect friendly treatment for the Dawsons, but she couldn't expect Tuck not to dig around a little.

The Dawsons stood, and Tuck stood with them. "Mr. Keyes," Mrs. Dawson said. "Thank you for hearing us out."

"Why aren't you angry?" Tuck said. "The recorder's off so you can tell me. Why aren't you ripping mad?"

"I was. Trust me, I was. God's mercy is vast. It extends to my husband and Ms. Bowers and you and me." Miranda grasped his hand again. "I am going to pray *for you*, Mr. Keyes. That you will share in God's grace and mercy."

"What a terrifying thought," he said.

Dawson laughed. "Watch out, man. My wife is merciless in her mercy."

Tuck nodded, wished them a good evening, and wondered how in blazes anything good could come out of this for the Dawsons.

Prostitutes. Pimps. Blackmail. A senator who wore a wire. A wife who forgave—or at least claimed to. A sterling reputation about to be folded and spindled. Let the readers and voters form their own opinions. Tuck would report what he knew, hoped the access to the Dawsons would continue to be this productive.

Carrie poked her head into the room. "You need anything?"

"Can I talk to them tomorrow, get their reactions to *the* reaction?"

"Absolutely. The bus is leaving so I had the hotel drop off a car for you. You probably want to stay here and write so you can get something in tonight." She handed him a valet ticket, turned to leave.

"Carrie." He grabbed her arm, pulled her back. "Why me?"

"Because you came when we asked. The networks, major outlets have ignored Dave—except to brand him a misogynist or a reactionary. You came, so you get the story." She kissed his forehead. She smelled like hazelnut and cream. "And this is just the beginning, Tucker, I can promise you that."

In the two seconds it took for her to leave the room, Tuck

staggered under a wave of yearning. *Focus.* He had an article to submit.

Tuck dialed his grandfather's house phone and asked the housekeeper to find the old man. Heaven forbid the old coot come out of the dark ages and use a cell phone. And that mausoleum was too big for someone his age. Another relic he had refused to surrender too long past the sell-by date.

"I read about the record low temperatures in New England," the old man growled. "You better not be calling me to ask if you can leave."

"On the contrary—I'm glad to be here."

"So what do you want at this time of night?"

"I hate to use a cliché, sir," Tuck said. "But hold the presses. We've got a story to tell."

nine

Tuesday midnight

Carrie hugged Tuck and said, "I owe you a drink."

They met at Martha's Exchange, three blocks from the Radisson. She had been on the phone for a steady two hours after the event. Donors had to be notified—and not by the morning paper. She needed an hour at the Exchange to unwind the day.

Tuck's online blurb appeared on *The Journal* website an hour ago. Drudge picked up the link almost immediately and, if CNN and FOX News were really the twenty-four-hour networks they claimed to be, it would pop up there in the next hour.

The online alert promised the interview with the senator and his wife would appear in the morning's paper.

PLAYING HARDBALL WITH A HOOKER

Presidential candidate wears wire in blackmail plot.

In an exclusive interview, Senator David Dawson explained his part in foiling an extortion scheme.

The senator admitted to getting drunk at a 2007 party and leaving with an admitted prostitute . . .

Tucker slid out a stool for Carrie, then slid onto the one next to her. "What're we drinking?"

Pregnant women weren't supposed to drink. In a few more days, that would be moot.

Next week Dave was making a swing through Iowa, South Carolina, and Pennsylvania. Will might add Florida to the trip—making the apology tour, keeping the few troops they had on the ground interested. Will had booked Victoria to travel with them, said he wanted Carrie to manage New Hampshire while they were gone.

Their absence would be a perfect time for her to have the procedure. No worse than a bad period, she'd heard.

God, just don't look. Just for one morning.

"Earth to Carrie," Tuck said. "What can I get you?"

"Cranberry juice and Grey Goose," she said.

"Finally gave up the Bud Light?"

"Can't stay young forever."

"I'll drink to that." Tuck motioned for the bartender, giving the order for two glasses. He had an empty glass in front of him, had clearly started without her.

All the advantages in the world and he was still drowning his discontent in alcohol. Tucker Keyes never had to work for anything. At school, he whizzed through math, physics, computer science, Greek philosophy, early English poets, and that silly art history degree that he picked up just to prove he could. The guy would drink all night, solve complex programming problems or philosophical conundrums during the day, catch a short nap, and start on the sauce all over again.

Pushing six three and still looking athletic, Tuck wore a blue button-down shirt with a navy sport coat. His sun-streaked hair curled over his collar. Nonchalance didn't come cheaply. He had a trainer, a stylist, and a tailor.

Even slightly soused, Tuck looked adorable.

The famous John Larter Keyes was a towering intellect with a homely face. When you wielded as much power as J.L. had, you didn't need good looks to get what you wanted. Would that power and influence die with the old man?

A dissolute wanderer, Tuck's father had vanished from his life before the kid even knew what he was missing. In college, he had been the life of the party. By all accounts, he still was.

Carrie studiously avoided DC parties. She guarded her privacy, was careful and discreet. Will had drummed that into her. In this instance, her brother was absolutely correct. Except for that afternoon a month ago.

Flaming oak trees, the breeze a caress off the river, wood smoke in the air—and suddenly she couldn't get enough of some guy she'd probably never see again. His eyes were the same color as the sky and his breath was so sweet that she had to kiss him. The lovemaking drifted over her, like a leaf dancing on the wind.

Tuck lifted his glass to toast her. "Glad you could join me to celebrate."

Carrie ruffled his hair. "By the way, we're off the record now. Unless I say differently."

Tuck rested his arm on the back of his stool. "Is this Paige Bowers story going to derail you?"

"It's fifty-fifty odds which way it will go. America hates hypocrites and loves repentance. And I'll tell you, Tuck, Dave Dawson is every bit as good as he seems."

"From what I hear, the National Party is not happy with your guy."

The boozy sheen on his cheeks made her sad. "Stop talking shop. Just tell me how you are, Tuck."

"I'm okay." Tuck stared into his glass.

"Just okay?"

"Hmm." He drank in silence for a little while. It worried her to see him downcast. Especially after his first big story as a political reporter.

"Tuck. Are you okay?"

He touched his finger to her chin. "What did you want to be when you were at school? Like a marine biologist or child psychologist or ballerina? Or maybe go to the Olympics with the women's hockey team. You were really good."

"I wanted to be what I am," Carrie said. "The person who makes things happen. Who knows everyone and understands how to move them around to one's advantage. I'm sure that sounds bloody cynical, but someone's got to be the grease on the wheels."

"So you're happy keeping . . . the axle from squeaking?"

"I know what needs to be done, and I do it. There's great satisfaction in that."

"But does it mean anything?"

"Of course it does," she said. "Otherwise I'd do something else. What about you? What did you want to be?"

He emptied his glass, set it on the bar. "I've never had a clue."

"You've got lots of options. Like the all the programming stuff you've done with your gaming friends. Have you ever thought about writing a book?"

"Like what? *Nerds for Dummies*?" Tuck rested his head on her shoulder. "I've been chasing after the wind, Carrie. Do you ever get like that? Where you think it's always going to be like this and you can't bear another minute of *always*."

What was with these existential questions? She could only pray that Tucker Keyes—and his apparent endless thirst—didn't screw this up.

"Should I be worried for you?" she whispered into his shoulder.

He pressed her finger to his lips. "I've caught a touch of the Keyes melancholy. The old man gets mawkish every evening over a glass of brandy and it's my job to sit and listen. Aren't you tired of it, Carrie? You've been on the merry-go-round your whole life. Your mother was . . . secretary of commerce?"

"Something like that." Carrie's mother had served as treasury secretary while they were at Princeton. Her signature was on four years' worth of currency, for Pete's sake. Typical Tuck, not doing his homework.

Tuck signaled for the bartender. She pressed her hand over her glass. "You trying to get me drunk? I'm not sleeping with you, Tuck."

He gave a playful snort on her neck. "I'm not expecting that."

"Don't you have someone special?"

"Do you, Carrie?"

"No time." She had given up men sometime between Senior Week in college and her first ninety-hour workweek on Dave's staff. No time—and impossible standards. Where could she find someone with Dave's character, her brother's intelligence, and Tuck's good looks?

"We're almost thirty, over the hill." Tuck rubbed his eyes. "Do you ever think about settling down?"

"I'm not going to marry you, Tuck."

He laughed, glanced at the drink in front of her. "Don't you want that?"

"The drink? Sure do. The hangover? No way. Help yourself."

"Life is one big hangover, Carrie." Tuck drained her glass. "Your candidate would say I've got an empty spot in my heart. Longing for apple pie and Jesus. Right?"

"We sell the apple pie and we live by Jesus. What's wrong with that?"

"You gotta let me quote you on that."

"No. We're off the record, remember?"

"Tomorrow, then. Say it again tomorrow." The tomorrow came out as *tu-mur-ru.*

"Tucker, you're worn out. Let's get you back to the hotel." She grabbed the back of his stool, swiveled it so he was facing her. She found his billfold in his blazer, threw a fifty-dollar bill onto the bar, added a twenty from her wallet as a tip.

He leaned against her. "I'm not sleeping with you, Carrie."

She tightened her arm around his waist and walked him outside. The icy night air did nothing to promote Tuck's steadiness. The three blocks to the Radisson might as well be three miles. She should have called a cab. Not like there'd be one on the street. This city was dead after eight.

Carrie avoided Main Street, took one road over. No reason to parade an inebriated reporter in front of the MoveIn people. And the last thing she needed was Victoria Peters getting word that Tuck had a drinking problem. She'd had her own candidate for this story, some wet-behind-the-ears kid she'd known from MIT.

Carrie had vouched for Tucker Keyes to Will. She won, Victoria pouted.

Now the heir to a great newspaper stumbled past trash cans and into Dumpsters.

"We're almost there. A few more steps." Carrie tightened her arm around his waist, but he was too tall to get leverage. "Tuck, please. Just stand up."

"Can't," he said, going down to one knee. "Gonna be sick."

She wrapped her arms around his waist as he curled forward and vomited. When he finished, he hung there like a puppet. How sadly pathetic. She gagged at the stench.

"Need some help?"

Carrie startled, almost let Tuck fall face-first onto the pavement. "Are you stalking me?"

Jared O'Dea grabbed Tuck's arm. "Did you want me to?"

"What're you doing here?"

"Filling up water jugs from behind the coffee shop." Jared smiled. The dim light accentuated his cheekbones.

"Don't you have people to do that for you?" Carrie said.

He wrapped an arm around Tuck's waist. "Don't you have people to do this for you?"

She tugged Tuck's other arm, as if he were a rag doll that they fought over. "He isn't part of the campaign. Just . . ."

"An ol' fren," Tuck said, eyes fluttering.

"What he said. An old friend."

Jared laughed. "We're off the clock, Carrie. I'm not going to exploit . . . whatever this is. Let's get him back to his room. Before he freezes to death."

"What about your water?"

"It's not going anywhere." Jared smiled. "And neither am I."

Tuesday after midnight

Tucker Keyes got sick one last time before passing out. At least they had gotten him back to the hotel and up to his suite before the last explosion.

"I am so sorry," Carrie said as she tried to wipe the mess off Jared's shirt. "He got you everywhere."

"Your pal does good work."

Carrie took deep breaths through her mouth. "Run down to your . . . tent or whatever you call it. Get a change of clothes and I'll wash these up here."

"We're protestors. It's not like we have walk-in closets."

"Then take those off and I'll do a quick wash and dry for you. You can have a shower while you wait. Or is that against your creed?"

"Running the washer for one set of clothes?" He shook a finger at her comically. "Not eco-friendly."

"Neither is recycled bourbon down the front of your shirt." Carrie tossed him the dry-cleaning bag from the closet. Jared went into the bathroom and handed it out a minute later.

She took change from Tuck's pocket and went down four flights to the laundry. How bizarre—the operative, the heir, and the protestor—all in one room. Like a late-night comedy. Or a horror film.

Jared was in the shower when Carrie returned. He sang something vaguely operatic. Of course the guy with the red hair and easy chatter would be an Irish tenor.

As she washed her hands, she eyed his personal belongings. A billfold. A cell phone. A generic water bottle. A small key, probably to a padlock. She stuck her head into the bathroom. "How's it feel in there?"

"Good for the bones on a cold night."

"Take your time. My compliments."

"Right. Leech off the drunk one-percenter."

"Oh, shut up and enjoy the shower." She closed the door and waited. The water continued to run. She grabbed her cell phone from her bag, went back to the vanity.

The billfold was thin, a few ones, a twenty. No scraps of paper with phone numbers or email addresses. The driver's license listed Michael J. O'Dea as a Washington state driver. He was thirty-four years old. She snapped a quick picture of his license. Jason Polke could run it for her.

No credit cards, no union cards, not even a library card. Just a license and some money. The absence of anything beyond a simple ID was more incriminating in her mind than a phone number for the opposition party or a powerful union would be.

"Hey, you want something to eat?" she called out.

"I can't take favors from you." Still in the shower.

"Room service," she said. "Compliments of Mr. One Percent."

"At this time of night?"

"I know the overnight prep cook. He's a big Dawson guy, takes care of us."

"Great. Order me anything with red meat."

"You don't need vegan?"

"Hardly. On the street, we live on peanut butter and jelly."

Will said the MoveIn encampment felt like a trap ready to spring. And as engaging as Jared O'Dea was, Carrie agreed. Given the right spark, they could ignite. And what if . . . what if they were involved in this Jericho thing? The feds took these incidents seriously. Rumors were the FBI had enlisted the help of the hacking group Anonymous to design a scenario that would replicate Joshua's rogue, early-warning messages.

The shower stopped. "Did you call down yet?" he said.

"No, I'm still looking at the menu." She crept away from the vanity, found the room-service menu. "How does chicken and grilled vegetables sound?"

"Not red enough. Can I get a burger?"

Carrie laughed. "Want fries with that?"

"And a milk shake. Now that I've been co-opted by the Dawsons, might as well sell the rest of my soul." He came out of the bathroom in a thick terry robe. His hair hung in damp curls on his shoulders.

"You can dry your hair," Carrie said. "The laundry's still got forty-five minutes."

Jared plopped on the chair across from the sofa. "Nah, I'll let it frizz."

"Trim the beard? I can dig you up a disposable razor or some scissors."

He rubbed his stubble. "Destroy my image? No thanks."

"How about a beer? Or is that bad for the image too?"

"Hmm. Now you're tempting the dirty-dog capitalist in my soul. Yeah, sure. I'll have one if you'll join me."

Carrie keyed open the honor bar, took out two Coronas. How many sins would she pile on this pregnancy before she said good-bye to it?

"Is your room this nice?" he asked.

"I wish. I'm stuck in a standard room. Which I have to share with another gal from the staff."

"Why? Dawson is worth a billion bucks."

"Which he spends wisely. As he will insist this nation do."

Jared stretched his leg across the coffee table, nudged her knee. "Truce, remember? I've been good. So you need to be."

Carrie had a sudden urge *not* to be good. Where was this coming from? Apart from that treacherous slipup in the golden sunshine and warm leaves, she wasn't one for quick sex. Had to be hormones. A flood of progesterone or whatever it was that drove someone in her state of mishap.

Stop. Jared was completely irrelevant to their mission. Boost Dave in the polls, set him up as either a dark horse for this cycle or a stronger candidate in four years. Will had the vision. And darn it all, her brother had self-restraint. If he had taught her anything, it was *don't let anything slip.*

Jared nudged her again. "So, how does one become a political staffer?"

"I was born to it. My mother has held various administrative cabinet posts. At the moment, she is ambassador to Germany. My older brother—"

"William Connors. He married the daughter of the famous Bobby Joe Fallon."

"Ah, you Googled me. Lowly operative that I am."

"You tend to be irresistible, Carrie."

"Glad I'm rising in your estimation."

Jared raised his bottle. "Underestimating you would be a grave mistake."

She leaned across the table, clinked her bottle against his. "Ditto. So why a protestor?"

"You didn't Google me?"

"Sorry, I did not." What a liar—of course she had. "What drives you to live in a tent in the gloom of November?"

"We've got college students with staggering debt, chronically unemployed folks, and homeowners with underwater mortgages or losing their houses. We see bailouts and tax breaks and big money flowing into politicians and coming back out to Wall Street and we say—hey, look at us! Because we're looking at you and we're appalled at what we see."

"I get that," Carrie said. "But you're avoiding the question."

"I was in finance at a major company, on the VP track. I saw how screwed up this whole system is and how it's the average Joes and Janes who are getting squeezed. If you know economics, you know consumer debt was used for the past fifteen years to mollify the middle class. Now our debt—and the debt used to fatten up the special interest groups—is going to kill us."

"You're singing a Dawson song."

"No. He hums the melody but he's still Mr. One Percent. You realize that, don't you? This whole Common Sense thing is a veil over the real message."

"What is the real message?" Carrie said.

"If you can't keep up, too bad for you because we're going to leave you in the dust."

"My goodness, I thought I was cynical."

Jared came around the table and sat next to her on the sofa. His skin was so fair that she could see the pulse in his neck. "You're as lost as the rest of us, Carrie. You just don't know it."

She pressed her hand to his mouth because she couldn't think of any way else to keep from kissing him. "Don't," she whispered. "Don't go there."

He nuzzled her palm. "I'm already there, Carrie. Already there."

ten

Tuesday morning

CARRIE STARED AT THE CEILING. A FEW MORE DAYS.

Dave had his secrets, Will had his, and even Melanie must have secrets that could never see the light of day. This would be Carrie's. Of all the things she had done, this pregnancy would shame her the most.

Be tough. Be resolved. Be willing to do what needs doing. These lessons she learned at her brother's knee.

She rolled over in bed, felt the room roll with her. Victoria blissfully slept in the other bed. This sharing of rooms was nearly intolerable.

Carrie had her own trust fund. She should have rented herself a suite like the one Tuck had snagged. Will had nixed that notion. Not while MoveIn was camping out in the park across the street. *We live simply so no one can claim we're out of touch,* he'd said.

The one good thing about shared rooms was being able to keep an eye on Victoria Peters. The speed at which she had risen in the Dawson hierarchy was mystifying. Carrie hadn't put in all these years for Dave just so some dewy-eyed girl could hop right over her in the org chart. Victoria came to bed late, often up with Will because she was the liaison with the Senate office and that staff needed oversight.

Carrie sat up and immediately the room spun. Who knew a baby could wage war on its carrier? Maybe he was battling for survival. No—don't go there. It was embryonic tissue, barely differentiated into a clump of cells.

Blast that Tucker Keyes for keeping her out so late—and Jared O'Dea for keeping her up even later. She got up and tiptoed to the bathroom. Sinking to her knees, she turned on the shower, her trick for hiding her vomiting.

When she had exhausted her stomach contents, she pressed her head to the side of the tub. The porcelain was blessedly cool. She needed a minute to let the nausea settle. Not much to look at down here on the floor. The trash—was that a prescription bottle under *Time* magazine? More than one.

She grabbed a tissue and took the pill bottles out of the trash. Vicodin, ibuprofen, Gabapentin—all prescribed to Victoria. Interesting. Maybe she had an old injury and some nerve pain. It would have to be pretty bad. A couple of teammates from Carrie's hockey team had taken a combination like that, but the Vicodin was given only for a few weeks.

Victoria had refills available on all three. If she had chronic pain, either she hid it or the pills worked well.

The knock on the door make her jump. "Caroline," Victoria said. "I need to get in."

She put the pill bottles and the magazine back in the trash and willed herself to stand up. She opened the door.

"What is up with you? Are you pregnant?" Victoria said, wiping sleep out of her eyes.

"Leave me alone." Room spinning, Carrie sat on the side of the tub. "I'm fine."

Victoria dampened a cloth, dabbed Carrie's face. "You think I don't hear you every morning? Is there something I can do to help?"

"Let me be. Please. Just let me be." Carrie pressed her face to her knees and gagged.

Victoria left, came back a minute later with a Coke. "Sometimes the carbonation helps nausea," she said. "And the sugar might get your blood pressure up."

Carrie took a couple sips. "I've got gastric reflux. The stress, the travel, the endless pizza, the infinite coffee." She liked her lie. It fit, it wasn't dire. And it should be good enough to buy herself a few more days without scrutiny. She would Google gastric reflux, see what over-the-counter remedies she should purchase to extend the lie.

While she was searching, Carrie would see what condition required Vicodin and Gabapentin. One never knew when a tidbit might come in handy.

Tuesday morning

Tuck's head felt like an overripe pumpkin about to implode on its own rot.

Sometime last night, someone brought him back to the hotel. Pulled off his pants. Covered him with a blanket. Sponged off his vomit. How bloody embarrassing.

Carrie. How much of the drunken fool had she seen? He needed to clean up. Be productive. Remember what lay ahead and the important role he could play.

His throat felt like a desert wasteland. How ironic that excessive drinking caused dehydration. He hiked himself up on his elbows, tried to stop the room from its unpleasant spin. The wet bar might as well be a hundred miles away.

He slowly slung his feet over the side of the bed. On the night table was a bottle of water, with a note from Carrie.

> No hair of the dog for you—it's going to be a busy day. Mea culpas scheduled all over N.H. Bus leaves at 8 a.m. The senator and Mrs. Dawson will squeeze you in between first and second stop.
>
> Hugs, Carrie

Bless you. He uncapped the bottle. The best he could do was an earthly blessing. If God existed, Tucker Reynolds Keyes could not—or would not—lay claim on the Almighty's resources.

Those nights at school when the conversation devolved to the "Does God exist?" question—Tuck was always out in the cold. He had grown up in Washington, DC, where power was God.

He had crossed the room to the honor bar without realizing it. No hair of the dog, Carrie said. If they were canines, she would be a junkyard dog in the best of every sense. Tough. Protective. Scrappy.

J.L. would be a bloodhound. Dawson would be a lab, friendly and kind. As for Tucker Reynolds Keyes, could a leopard change its spots? Wait. No. The analogy rested on dogs, not cats.

Suddenly he had a glass in his hand, as if the hotel could serve him without Tuck having to muster one thought. The room tilted and he fell, crashing face-first into the credenza. He had a sudden urge to urinate but he couldn't get up, couldn't save himself from all his worldly blessings.

"God," he whispered.

God would not whisper back. He was too busy forgiving the likes of David Dawson to smile down on a twenty-eight-year-old drunk who just peed himself.

Tuesday morning

"Dave, I don't understand." Melanie blinked back tears. "How did this happen?"

They huddled over the oak table in the situation room. The door to Will's room was ajar. Carrie was in there, making phone calls and playing chaperone. Dave was never alone behind a closed door with any woman but his family.

Dave shook his head. "I don't even know what to say, except that we're so busy managing public perception that we forget to guard against our own fleshly nature."

"We? What does that mean—*we*?"

"Sorry, royal we. This is all on me. I believed my own press that I was upstanding and righteous and justified and I forgot that I could be as big a jerk as any other man."

"Miranda must have been devastated." Melanie couldn't picture him having a single drink, let alone getting drunk. "This is why you wanted me to join the campaign. You knew you'd need someone to boost you with values voters."

"Yes, we knew this would be another 'war on families' sledgehammer for the opposition to pound me with."

"It's not like you to use people, Dave."

"That was not my intention. We've been asking you once a week for almost a year. I'd say it was a God-thing that you showed up last week—if I actually deserved this kind of blessing." He leaned forward, elbows on his knees. "Lanie, it's not just about the lifeline you bring to the campaign. On a personal level, we've prayed for you to be reunited with Will and Sophie. And to be able to expand the circle of friends we can just be ourselves with would be a major blessing."

Melanie shook her head. "You never should have let this come to an arrest."

"You sound like Bobby Joe." Dave leaned back, crossed his legs. "Are you advocating that we pay blackmail?"

"Absolutely not. You should have worked the episode with this Bowers girl into one of your speeches. A note of confession and repentance and then gone on. Paige Bowers couldn't extort you if you preempted her ammo."

"My story is one of redemption, Lanie. And as off course as this country may be, the voters still believe in redemption. Can you forgive me, Lanie?"

"Of course." Melanie squeezed his hand. "I do need you to answer one question. Was Will at that function with you in '07?" She knew the answer. Any gathering of high profile would include her husband, especially if lobbyists were present.

"Yes."

"Why didn't you ask him for a ride home?"

"I have no good answer to that," Dave said. "All I remember is how smoky the room was and how I wanted to get out of there."

"Was Will involved with these people at *any* point?"

Dave stood, brushed imaginary crumbs off his pants. Melanie's father had done the same thing every time he stood up, even in the privacy of his office. Cleaning up before taking the podium or greeting someone was an instinctive measure born of too many dry dinner rolls on the stump.

If only it were so easy to brush off a scandal.

"If you have concerns about how Will has conducted himself, you'll have to ask him."

"'No comment' is a comment."

"He's doing therapy. He has asked Miranda and me to pray for him during this time."

"Therapy because he has a prostitute problem of his own?"

"Because your marriage is at the point that you'd even be

asking me these kinds of questions. I'm sorry for you, Lanie. I want only the best for you." He turned to leave.

"Dave. Wait." Melanie stood up, resisted brushing off her own imaginary crumbs. "What about Hannah? How is she taking this?"

"We told her last year as part of the consideration of making a run. She was—in her words—*grossed out*, but understood we had to be honest about what a presidential campaign could bring."

"Does Sophie know?"

"I assume so. The girls are close."

Things were simpler from the sidelines. *Strength and wisdom and oh, how I need courage, Father.*

"Dave," she said. "I'm in."

They stood with hands on each other's shoulders, forehead to forehead, Dave praying for wisdom and humility and patience. At some point, Carrie wandered in and bowed her head with them.

Melanie said "amen" to his prayer and kept hers close and silent, though it echoed within her. *Help me, Father. I am not up for any of it.*

Tuesday afternoon

Six hours after his disastrous morning, Tuck was in Washington, DC. Relatively sober, he was ready to claim his place in journalistic history.

"Don't bring that Bowers woman into the newsroom," John Larter Keyes had advised. "I've got the political desk after me. The lot of 'em think you're a lightweight. Suddenly they all want onto the Dawson bus."

"Tough snickers." Tuck balanced his phone and a bag of groceries as he keyed in the code for his condo. "Caroline Connors will only work with me."

His grandfather cleared his throat. "Don't sleep with her."

"Who?"

"Either one. The Connors woman or the prostitute."

"Won't be a problem, sir." Tuck had never paid for sex and wasn't about to. Carrie, on the other hand—he didn't want to sleep with her, he wanted to make love to her. Real love, the kind that comes with sweet words and staying power.

A few minutes after he got settled, the doorbell rang. Tuck opened the door to Paige Bowers.

He envisioned hookers as skanked-out meth addicts with sagging breasts and yellow teeth. This woman was more Helen of Troy than streetwalker.

The police report said she was thirty-nine. The only signs of age were faint lines around her mouth and her forehead. Her lips were opulent. Her long brown hair was spiced with auburn. Her eyes were so light blue they made him think of moonlight. No wonder Dave Dawson got into a car with her.

"Please, have a seat," Tuck said. "Can I get you something to drink?"

"Water is fine." She gave his living room an appreciative glance and then sat on the sofa. She wore yoga pants, the waistband folded down to reveal a firm abdomen, a tight T-shirt, and a sheen of workout sweat.

"I read your movie reviews," Paige said. "You're good. If you hate a film, I hate it. How did you luck into my story?"

"Connections."

"Hmm. I thought so. The Dawsons were quick to sit down with you."

"Damage control. Thank you for meeting me here."

"We're all doing damage control." Paige positioned a pillow behind her back, then curled her legs under her. "I'm not guilty, you know."

Tuck scratched his nose. She must think him a bloody prep-school fool in his button-down peach shirt, designer jeans, and loafers with no socks. He placed his phone on the table between them. "Do you mind if I record?"

Paige pulled her phone from her bag, the latest model iPhone. "We'll both record. That way there will be no misspeaking."

"You say you're not guilty. They have you on the wire, asking for money."

"No. You only hear me make the introductions. Shane took over after that. I had no idea what he was going to do, and I had no part in asking for money. The recording will exonerate me. I threatened nothing, I did nothing wrong. That's what I want you to print."

"Sure," Tuck said, annoyed.

"Do not use the word *allege*. I state unequivocally that I did not ask for any hush money. And I also would like first-look before you submit."

First-look? Either she'd been coached or she was an old hand at damage control. "That wasn't part of our agreement," Tuck said.

Paige dug into her bag, took out the envelope of cash Tuck had passed to her lawyer last night. "I can walk now if you have qualms about my collaboration."

"Tell you what—why don't we talk and then you stay here while I write the article?"

She gave him a Mona Lisa smile. "What do I do while you're writing?"

"I have a very nice home theater. You can have a private viewing of the holiday movies that won't be out for a couple of weeks."

"Fine. But do not hit Send until I see it. And if it takes you longer than"—she checked her phone—"three hours, I'll have to charge you for my time."

"I will not let you use me as a propaganda machine."

"So it's only all right if the Dawsons use you? You do understand that the only difference between a professional escort and a legislator is that the escort gives value for the money she takes."

Tuck laughed. "They're not using me. They might think they are, but trust me—I'm my own man."

This ability to lie to women was the devil's gift, or perhaps genetic destiny. Grandfather claimed to have bedded Marilyn Monroe right under John Kennedy's nose. A decade later the old man had gone on to Faye Dunaway and Diane Keaton. Name the Oscar nominee and John Larter Keyes had slept with them. *Allegedly.*

"I assume you want to get into the Dawson stuff right away. Or did you want to get to know each other first? Considering you're paying twenty thousand dollars, I should be . . . accommodating."

She stared at him in open invitation. Paige Bowers would give him a magnificent moment and then it would be over. And the emptiness would resume.

"Tell me everything," Tuck said. "Every blessed thing you know about Dave Dawson and his people."

Paige nudged him with her foot. "Dawson I'll give you. Anything more will cost you."

"Do you have anything worth telling?"

"I'll report," she said with a smile. "You decide."

eleven

Wednesday afternoon

EVEN AFTER A DAY IN PRAYER AND REFLECTION, Melanie still couldn't grasp how Dave could be so stupid. How on earth Will *let* him be so stupid. She had made her decision—she would stay with the campaign and fight. Fight for her husband. Fight for Dave and Miranda.

Fight for what she believed in. This country had been built on solid values, on solid families. Both were under assault. If they fell, the nation would fall.

Since they weren't going home to Nashville, Melanie would make a home for them in New Hampshire. This morning she had rented a condo residence in the Radisson and spent the afternoon decorating.

Will came into the condo, eyebrows raised. "Victoria said you left a message about meeting you up here. What is this?"

"The closest to home I could make it."

Three bedrooms meant Will could have a quiet office space and Sophie could have a sanctuary from the campaign. The galley kitchen was fully stocked with dishes and utensils. Melanie's last foray was to the grocery store. It soothed her to plan meals for the three of them. Or more—this condo could be a refuge for the Dawsons, Carrie, Eli. Anyone who needed a break.

The Radisson residency suite was purposely bland to soothe long-term corporate visitors. Melanie had purchased colorful pillows for the bedrooms and the sitting area, vibrant blues and greens to warm the dull décor. She had bought a lovely oak table that could be used for dining or for study.

Will let out a long whistle. "The campaign can't afford this."

"*We* can afford it."

"We already have a suite."

"That mess two floors down? Phones ringing all day and night, people always barging in? If we're going to be together as a family, we need family space."

Melanie slipped her arm through his. He needed a haircut. His curls brushed his collar, more silver than she remembered. "Momma used to do this. You remember, don't you? She said it kept Bobby Joe grounded when he was on the road. She traveled with linens, a bread knife, and a slow cooker. Even if we were passing through for a night, we'd have our own pillows and blankets, and a bowl of stew before bed."

Will's shoulders loosened as he undid his tie. "So, this means you're staying, Lanie?"

"It's a three-month lease. So I guess I am. I have another surprise for you." She steered him into the third bedroom, to the chair she had paid an extra hundred bucks to get immediately delivered.

"A recliner?" Will said. "I don't understand."

"Sit. Your back is a mess. I can see it in your face and the way you stand. You can take quick breaks in here, put your feet up, work your phone and tablet. The girls need a place to do their schoolwork where they aren't distracted. And you need a place to rest. We can even have Thanksgiving here tomorrow."

"We're scheduled for a couple of shelters," Will said.

"Then schedule us in for later." Melanie struggled to keep the annoyance out of her voice.

Will walked to the slider. The condo was on the eighth floor. The balcony was on the street side of the hotel. From up here, the MoveIn camp in Veteran's Park was a patchwork of bright blue, army green, and faded khaki. Ironic how Melanie had rented a condo and they were huddled under plastic and canvas.

Their gesture spoke of street activism and sacrifice. Her gesture—*please, Father, help him understand*—said that she'd make home where Will was. It was the best she could do for now. She prayed Beth could help her do better.

Melanie tentatively curled her little finger around his. "If I am going to take on speaking engagements, I want Sophie with me or with a responsible adult."

Will let go of her hand. "You can't walk two feet around here without bumping into a responsible adult."

"Your staff and volunteers are not family, Will."

"The world is not an evil place." His mouth tightened. "For Pete's sake, give her some room to breathe. We've raised her well."

"*We've* raised her well?"

"Here we go," he said. "You went five minutes without casting the first recrimination. Five stinkin' minutes! Should I sit down for the rest? You've probably got ten years to unload on me." Will dropped into the recliner, levered up the footrest so hard that the chair banged. "Go ahead. Tell me what a crappy husband and father I am."

Melanie sat on the arm of the recliner, took his hand. "I'm just . . . overwhelmed. I know you are too."

"Your chipping away at me doesn't help, Lanie. Not at all."

"I'm sorry," she said. "I am so sorry."

"No, it's me. Late afternoon is cranky time." Will kicked off his shoes, stretched his neck. "I appreciate what you did here. What's that good smell?"

"Homemade beef stew. Momma's recipe from the old days."

She brushed back his hair. Maybe she could pick up good scissors, trim it tomorrow. Or she would ask Carrie to schedule in a trip to the barber.

Carrie no longer kept his schedule. Melanie would have to go through Victoria.

"This feels good," Will said. "Getting the feet up for a few minutes. Your mother was a smart woman."

Melanie sat on the arm of the chair, kissed his head. "She and Bobby Joe would be so proud of you."

"I call him, you know. A couple times a week. He usually thinks I'm one of his cronies from thirty years ago. That's okay. It's nice to hear his voice."

She pressed her lips to his ear. "Just promise me Sophie will be safe. The Jericho group and that creep Joshua, right in our faces. And I know Dave gets death threats."

"The feds are on the hackers. And you know every candidate gets threats. We have security. A staff that's close. Everyone watches out for Sophie and Hannah. And the Whittaker kid too."

"I know. I just . . . it's a mother question, that's all."

Will closed his eyes, leaned into her arm. "I'm sorry I gave you a hard time. This is good, you and me here."

Melanie kissed his cheek and left him to nap.

Wednesday evening

Extended family could be a curse or a blessing.

In the case of Dillon Whittaker, extended family was a blessing, albeit an odd one. Melanie could see the resemblance between her daughter Destiny and the half brother they discovered a couple of years back. He was tall like his half sister, skinny where she was willowy. Both were creative, both quick to ask questions.

Melanie and Will had dropped Destiny off at college in Illinois when she was eighteen. Three weeks later she turned up in Los Angeles as an unpaid personal assistant to an Oscar-winning makeup artist. They had refused to support their daughter's folly so she paid the rent and bought food with the money she made designing tattoos.

Dillon had left home at the same age. His liver disease had kept him isolated and lonely for too long. This postgrad year at Prescott Academy seemed like a good compromise, though Melanie knew his parents had to be as apprehensive as she had been when Sophie came to New Hampshire.

"You're not going home for Thanksgiving, Dillon?" Melanie asked.

"Nah, too much hassle with the travel. My parents are coming up here this weekend. Lucky them with their private jet. Besides, I want to film the MoveIn people." Dillon was on his second bowl and had consumed three pieces of corn bread.

"He films and I interview," Sophie said. "We make a good documentary team."

"It'll be fun," Hannah said. "Mike said he'd go with us so we have an adult."

Melanie glanced at Will, expecting him to say no. He raised his eyebrows at her, then went back to picking at his salad. The campaign's chief strategist was going to take an afternoon off just so three teens could mingle with the riffraff? Clearly Hannah heard only what she wanted to hear.

"That's an unattractive idea," Melanie said, "getting into that MoveIn crowd."

"They're people too," Sophie said.

"Who think their earnestness makes them immune to criticism."

"You can come with us and see," Hannah said. "They're friendly."

Why didn't Will say anything? "How do you know they're friendly?" Melanie asked.

"They shared their brownies with us a couple days ago," Sophie said. "They didn't bake properly on the camp stove so they gave us cups and spoons to eat them like pudding."

"You ate something they gave you? Or should I say—you got close enough so they could offer you food? You do know that some people bake marijuana into brownies."

"Please," Sophie said. "We're not stupid."

"The brownies were just that. Nice and gooey," Hannah said. "They're always cooking something yummy over there."

"It's okay if you guys are polite," Will said, finally entering the discussion. "Ingesting anything they give you is not intelligent. At a couple of those Occupy camps four years ago, lots of drugs were going around. Including"—he stared directly at Sophie—"roofies. You know about those date-rape drugs, don't you?"

"Oh, Dad," Sophie said. "Why is it always sex with you old people?"

Melanie dropped her spoon. "Sophia Rachel Connors!"

"I'm sorry. Excuse me, I didn't mean to be so rude," Sophie said. "It's just . . . all you guys talk about is how dangerous the world is."

"We do that for a reason," Melanie said.

"It's okay, Soph. I get the same warnings." Dillon patted her arm, then glanced at Melanie. "Before I leave campus I have to report my whereabouts to my godmother. She lives a few miles from Prescott. If I'm not at school, she needs to know where I am. If I don't report in on time, she gets itchy. And if I ever was, like, not where I was supposed to be? Trust me, I'd hear about it from the Texas branch of the family. And probably Destiny too."

"There's a reason we get frantic," Melanie said.

"Concerned," Will said, an edge to his voice. "Being frantic doesn't help anyone."

Dillon glanced around the table. "I'll admit the MoveIn folks are like jack-in-the-boxes with those signs and slogans. But don't we have to expect . . . or at least hope . . . that Jesus is working among the weird people of this world? That He's not just confining Himself to those of us who say grace before their meals and eat with linen napkins? Not that I mind good dining, Mrs. Connors."

"Of course," Will said. "We just expect you to be careful."

"Common sense," Melanie said.

"Then you come with us," Sophie said. "If Jesus was here today—"

"He is here," Dillon said.

"Noted," Sophie said. "Let's say He was walking the streets of Manchester. Wouldn't He go to the people living on the street before He came to this nice Radisson condo?"

"They're not on the streets because of circumstance," Melanie said. "They chose to adopt the face of poverty while playing their own politics. Jesus always expects honesty."

"So does that mean Jesus would ignore them?" Hannah said. "He, like, ate with tax collectors."

"And Pharisees," Dillon said, "though He usually spoiled their appetites."

"Come with us," Sophie said. "I'll interview, Dillon will film. You can get a firsthand look at their issues, Mom. It'll be cool. Please."

"Your mother's got events, starting Friday." Will glanced at his phone. "I'll have Carrie take you."

Melanie resisted the urge to rub the goose bumps out of her arm. "The sun sets early this time of year. Make sure you're out of there by then." She turned to Will. "And you make sure Carrie is with them every second."

Will got up, spooned himself more stew from the Crock-Pot. He kissed the top of Melanie's head. "Great meal," he said and then dropped his voice. "Lighten up. They're not four-year-olds."

The doorbell rang. Sophie ran to answer it. "Hey! Tori's here."

Victoria Peters wore a pink V-neck sweater, short skirt, and knee-high leather boots. She looked straight at Will and with no pleasantries said, "I need you. Something that can't be left unattended."

He laid his napkin on the table and stood. "Sorry, guys." He followed Victoria out.

Will didn't even ask what the crisis was. Victoria snapped her fingers and he left. Just like that.

"Dil, you like her," Sophie said. "Admit it. You've got the frog eyes anytime she's around."

"What guy doesn't like her?" Dillon said, then blushed. "Except Mr. C. I mean, he likes her because she does her job and all . . ."

"It's okay, Dillon. I get it." Melanie touched the back of his hand. "What happened to Carrie? She used to be her brother's keeper. Professionally, that is."

"Nothing." Sophie's eyes shifted side to side.

Hiding something. Sophie was an inexperienced liar.

"Carrie got promoted," Dillon said. "That's what you told me, Soph. She's got 'senior' in her title now. So Mr. C. promoted Tori to do her stuff. She's, like, good at everything and all that. And she's . . . you know."

Hannah poked his arm. "She's hot. Say it, silly."

The girls laughed as Dillon flushed. "The point is—she could rule the world," he said. "We're a downgrade for her. No offense, Mrs. Connors."

Melanie fidgeted with her fork. Was Caroline's promotion really that? Or had Will shuffled her aside?

New Hampshire was not home. Their serene brick house with its gardens and porches was home. Nashville, the country music capital of the world, was home. Hope Chapel, where the Connors and the Dawsons had worshipped for many years, was home.

Melanie's attempt to turn this condo into a home away from home was pathetic. She should have known Will would flee as soon as he had an excuse.

Friday morning

Dave's campaign was in disaster-recovery mode, and still Will insisted they take time out for a therapy session. That had to be a good sign. A healthy gesture.

Beth opened the session with prayer. Melanie tried to follow but the drumbeat in her head was too insistent.

Change my heart. Or is it change my body? Dear God, how can this happen? Change . . . change . . . oh Lord, change . . .

"Don't think of me as a shrink," Beth Sierra said. "Think of me as a coach."

Melanie folded her arms across her chest and crossed her legs at the ankles. Her body language shouted, "I don't want to be here." What choice did she have? It was this or nothing.

"I'm a little cold," she said. "Do you mind if I use that throw?"

"Of course."

Will handed the throw to Melanie. She draped it over her shoulders, allowing her arms to relax in her lap. They'd both steered away from sitting together on the sofa.

Beth didn't miss a beat, just curled up on the sofa with a pad and pen. "I'm going to ask some questions to try to get to know you a little more as a couple."

Will sat with shoulders straight, hair neatly combed. That wouldn't last past this hour. The smallest hint of stress would make him tug at his curls or brush them back from his face.

"Tell me what first drew the two of you together," Beth said.

Will began, telling about his volunteer work with Bobby Joe, losing track through college, and then getting to know each other again on the campaign trail.

Beth smiled. "Good start. You've given me the *how*. Now give me the *what*—what drew you together?"

"Will was electric," Melanie said. "My dad was the Speaker of the House for years. It was no big deal to have presidential candidates—including two who became presidents—in our home. These men and their wives all had charisma of some sort. Good people, for the most part." She took a breath, felt her heart flutter, and couldn't find her voice.

"Will's electricity was different?" Beth said.

"Will believed. He believed with a passion and certainty that I wasn't used to."

Beth glanced at Will, then turned back to Melanie. "What did he believe?"

"Will," she said. "Can you . . . ?"

"I believed then what I believe now," he said. "That God calls each of us to know Him, serve Him. That Jesus died so that sinners like us could have a relationship with Him. That marriage is intended to reflect Christ's passion and commitment to His bride, the church."

"And was faith always a strong certainty for you, Will?" Beth asked.

"No. At one time, faith was . . . what you did on Sunday and what kept you from being a jerk on other days. That changed when I was about fourteen and my mother took me hunting."

Melanie laughed. "I love your mother. She can throw a black-tie dinner party or skin a squirrel and still look fantastic."

"She loves you back." Will smiled at her, turned his smile to Beth. "My father owned a company that manufactured pharmaceutical filtration devices. Things you don't think of, like the filters that keep bacteria out of your drugs. Dad was always at work or lobbying in DC, so my mother took on educating me to be a proper son of Tennessee. That includes hunting. It was autumn and the trees were a brilliant red and yellow. Like a sunrise wrapped over me. The air cut through my skin and made me vibrate. Not with cold but with . . . I guess, just being alive.

"I was alone in the deer blind. Mom was about twenty yards away. I picked at the bark of the tree as I waited. And it hit me in a flash, how the morning and the trees and the air and, yep, my mother—they were all wonderfully made. I had this rush," Will said, hands lifted up in instinctive praise. "This rush of knowing, of understanding what Jesus loved. Whom He loved. And what a gift it all was, and what a challenge His gift was to me. Fourteen-year-old, goofy-haired, squeaky-voiced me.

"For about a year, I thought maybe I should be a missionary. You know, save the world for Jesus? Then I took a look at my own hometown, saw how people struggled and how nothing seemed to work the way it was supposed to. I saw it in my father's business, all the regulators. Yes, these were good, safe rules. But no one above us in government seemed to understand what it took to provide jobs.

"Election time came around, and one of Bobby Joe's people opened a call center in our town. I went inside and saw fire in the candidate's eyes. I asked my parents for permission to volunteer there after school, and Mom said it was good that I thought about the wider world and Dad said don't let them steal your dreams.

And it only took me a few weeks to see how that could happen. And then Bobby Joe came in for a fund-raiser and he brought his daughter." He nodded at Melanie.

"And the electricity?" Beth said. "If we could get back to you, Melanie."

"I was so used to compromise," Melanie said. "Raised on shifting expectations and staying one step ahead of potential voters. I didn't know what it meant to pursue something so entirely. Plus Will was not terrible looking."

"Thanks, pal," Will said with a laugh.

"Will decided he would grab onto this slippery eel we call public service and he would wrestle it into submission. There was something so beautifully fixed in him. He electrified me, made me want to be as alive as he was."

"And is that electricity gone?" Beth said softly.

"No." Melanie reached across the table for Will's hand. He squeezed hers, then let go. "He's still that guy, even after all these years in Washington. We just grew up, that's all. Learned it's risky to be so . . . idealistic."

The word *risky* hung in the air for a full five seconds. She expected Beth to snatch it, maybe pound Melanie with it. Beth let it just dangle out there while Will gave a smug smile.

Beth stood. "More tea for anyone?"

"I don't know," Melanie said. "Are we finished?"

"What do you think?" Beth cut more lemon slices, set them out on the tray.

"That's a shrink question," Melanie said. "You said you wouldn't do that."

"I said I was here to coach. So we've got another player to get on the field."

"Your turn, Will. What drew you to me?" Melanie asked.

"Before I knew your last name was Fallon—when you were just Lanie on the phones—there was something so open and casual and confident about you. Like a star drawing me effortlessly into its orbit."

Melanie broke her cookie in half, dunked it in her tea. When was the last time she *felt* either open or casual? "And we're here because I'm no longer . . . open?"

"Think about it, Lanie." Will's voice was ragged. Fighting tears, she realized. "We had a world together. Then it was like you closed the door and left me out in the cold. It was you and the girls. When Destiny left, things got even stuffier in your world. Like all you needed was Sophie and anything beyond that—including me—was an intrusion."

"You want to know how it felt to me, Will? I'll tell you. I stood in that proverbial door and said, 'Come home, please come home,' and you stayed away."

"No, that's not true. I came home and you'd find another door to lock me out with. So I did what I could to be a good father and did the work God set before me. And every once in a while, I'd knock and your body might be there, but Melanie Fallon Connors—that woman who was open and casual, that woman who chose me—didn't want me anymore."

Will stood, went to the French doors. The skies were gray. Clouds pressing in already. Melanie knew he had a town hall in Derry to get to. She was scheduled to sit with Mike McGregor and work on talking points.

There was a huge world outside this room. All the doors in the world couldn't keep them safe. "He's right," Melanie said. "And I'm right. So what do we do?"

Will sat on the arm of her chair and took her hand. "Yeah, what do we do?"

"We get to work," Beth said. "That's what we do. First thing—see how you're holding hands? I want you to do that for five minutes, twice a day."

"I don't know if we'll be scheduled together twice a day," Will said. He kept his hand over Melanie's but the grasp had lessened. He was getting ready to let go.

"Make it happen," Beth said. "Remember that you two are in your own campaign. And I want you both to begin journaling individually, starting with your deepest fears. Write out every fear you recall having up to this point in your life, going as far back into your childhood as you can remember. And be as detailed as you can about your current fears about your marriage relationship."

Will pressed his lips together, the muscle in his jaw flinching.

"Any questions?" Beth said.

Melanie swallowed her last sip of tea. "What if one of my biggest fears is doing this very exercise?"

"Write that down in your journal too," Beth replied without hesitating. "Now I'm going to pray you out the door and on your way, and I will see you—and your journal entries—in a couple of days."

twelve

Friday morning

Carrie scrolled to the Lord's Heritage website as she waited for the elevator.

Melanie's website had a short film on fetal development. Carrie clicked off after week eight. She didn't need to see the heart developing and the fins that miraculously became hands and feet, and the little face.

If Dave made it to the presidency, Will would be the White House Chief of Staff. When he burned out after three years—like they all did—she would climb right into her brother's chair.

There was no room for children in her career path. Mother had raised her to be a career woman, and Will had helped make that happen. What would it be like to kick back for a few years and raise a child? She had money in a trust so she wouldn't have to worry about income. Childcare was another matter. No way would Carrie stick her baby with a nanny.

If it hadn't been for Will and the Dawsons, Washington would have been a lonely place growing up. If she had a baby, she would raise that baby.

Will would volunteer to help, but could she ask him to curtail his work to help raise a baby born out of wedlock? Melanie would support her if Carrie moved to Nashville. That was impossible. Carrie had DC in her blood and couldn't imagine living anywhere else.

What about love? If she stepped out of the rat race, would she find something—someone—unexpected?

She had dated goofy-looking guys. Successful guys. Funny and wry and Mother-approved. Scratch the surface and they were just like her—ambitious, driven, and, yes—self-centered.

Tucker Keyes would marry her in an instant. His grandfather would rejoice because he respected the bloodlines on her mother's side. What if Tuck never grew up? She couldn't bear the thought of her child losing a father in an overdose or immature stunt.

Carrie should pray for him. Pray away the drinking and whatever drugs he cruised with. Pray for his soul and his sobriety.

It was easy to "amen" Will or the Dawsons. Alone, her prayers caught like a bone in her throat.

God, forgive me because I can't get out of my own way. And take a look at Tucker Reynolds Keyes, Father. He really needs You.

—

Friday afternoon

Melanie volunteered to drive back to the hotel so Will could check his messages. She hadn't even pulled out of Beth's driveway before he was on the phone with Victoria. He spoke in rapid-fire code that she couldn't follow. Was it because she was thirty years behind the trends?

Or did Will and his assistant have a special shorthand?

She would not give in to such thoughts. Especially after the kind words and fond memories they had just shared with Beth.

"No, I'm fine," he said before finally ending the call. His thumbs flew over the screen, scanning texts faster than the eye could process. The brain worked in amazing ways. Gleaning the meaningful from the chaff.

"Does Victoria know we're doing therapy?" Melanie asked.

"No. Why would you even ask that?"

"Dave knows."

"Of course he knows," Will said. "I can't be absent from the campaign for two hours at a time unless he understands why."

"I'm not sure I understand why. Why are we doing this now, Will?"

He ran both hands through his hair, leaving tracks in the gel he must have applied after his shower.

"I didn't know how intense this would be," Will said. "When I worked with your dad, he took all this on his shoulders. I just breezed through, ignorant of the load he carried."

Melanie tapped the steering wheel. "I asked about us. Not the campaign."

"*Us* is the point. I need there to be an *us*. Or I need to stop worrying about it."

"Dave's run is probably going to be over in February. We couldn't wait until then?"

Will chewed his thumb. "Maybe we should wait until our next session to discuss your reservations about therapy. And Dave's candidacy."

"My concern is that adding two hours of therapy to your schedule will add to your general stress level. Why not wait until Dave has to drop out?"

"Dave is going to be president."

"He's going to have a tough time surviving Paige Bowers. You know the media is laughing at him. That's more damaging than a head-on attack. You know that."

"The media will have redder meat to chew on shortly," Will said.

"What? Don't get into dirty tricks. It's not worth selling your soul for a few votes."

"Are you lecturing me, Melanie?"

"Are you staring at me, William?"

Will laughed. "I can't help it. If you only knew how much . . . I can't help it."

Strength and courage, Melanie told herself. "Is Victoria as good as Carrie?"

"No one is better than my sister. However, Victoria is easier to get along with. Why all the questions?"

"I'm just freaked by Beth poking into our lives."

"She hasn't poked into anything. She's asking us to do the poking."

"What's going to be at the top of your list when you do your journal?"

Will laughed. "You know darn well, Lanie."

"You are afraid of being wrong. You always have been."

"When I mess up, it's not just me. We're doing good things, Lanie. We want good things for this country and there are enemies arrayed against us. We can't afford any more screwups. You know that."

"Yes." She rubbed his shoulder. "I do know that."

"And you? What's numero uno for you?"

"I fear . . ." Melanie took a deep breath. She'd never said these words aloud. "Alone," she said. "I fear being alone."

"You don't have to be alone." Will clutched her hand. "Please tell me you know that."

Melanie pulled the car into a parking lot. She leaned over the center console and touched her finger to his lips. "Bear with me just a little longer. Please?"

Saturday morning

It was so wrong to let the presence of Victoria Peters make her uneasy. Campaign work was tedious, a string of tight quarters with long days and nights. With Caroline doing more senior staff work, it was normal for Will to keep his assistant close. The question was—how close?

Was the marriage counseling an excuse for Will to use if he filed for divorce? *I did everything I could but I just couldn't make it work.*

Or was Melanie so emotionally fragile right now that she imagined a relationship that wasn't there? The thought of Will and Victoria together was like psychological pornography. Once the picture formed in Melanie's mind, it seemed impossible to paint over.

She had to know so she arranged a trip to Jeanne Donegan's farm. The cover story was that Melanie wanted to search for unusual shots to create a YouTube video. Dillon's parents had refused to allow him to keep his expensive film-editing equipment at Prescott Academy. They shipped the equipment to his godmother's home in Groveland for safekeeping.

Jeanne Donegan and her husband lived on an expansive farm in the Merrimack River Valley where they kept free-range cows for organic milk, cheese, and yogurt.

Sophie, Hannah, and Dillon made the trek to the Donegans' farm with Melanie. She knew that, to Dillon's chagrin, their affection for him was more sisterly than anything else. He was in rare form, showing the girls every bit of his equipment. Finally, Sophie persuaded Melanie to let them take the car and go to a movie.

Before digging into the raw film, Melanie accepted a mug of hot cocoa, made with real chocolate and whole milk. She forced herself to make small talk with Jeanne as a thank-you for letting them invade the Donegan home.

"Dillon storyboards at school," Jeanne Donegan said. "He comes here once a week and edits. He really does have a fine eye."

"That's what his sister tells me."

Jeanne was a lovely lady with thick blond-streaked hair and expressive blue eyes. As Julia Whittaker's best friend, she had been there for the pregnancy and Destiny's birth. Melanie felt a twinge of envy that this woman knew her daughter before she did.

"What was Destiny like?" Melanie asked. "Before she was born."

"That child entered this world with a loud wail and fists clenched. And now look—a married woman, successful in her craft, committed in her faith. You and your husband are wonderful parents."

"Thanks." Melanie tightened her grip on the mug.

"Julia asked me to confirm . . ." Jeanne paused. ". . . that Dillon's work on the campaign is really work and not fooling around."

"They have nothing to worry about. Dillon is generally quite mature." Melanie smiled. "Except when it comes to girls. He gets tongue-tied and foot-tangled."

"It was a step of faith, letting him come to Prescott Academy. It is hard to let go and let your kid learn their own lessons. With three daughters, I prayed day and night. Still do."

"Amen." Melanie accepted a refill on the hot cocoa. It was nice to sit and chat with someone who didn't think she was a helicopter mom or a cold, uncaring wife. Small blessings. *Thank You, Jesus.*

Saturday afternoon

Dillon had prowled around the campaign for almost three full months, gathering candid film, unscripted interviews, shooting crowded rooms and the open sky for brilliant effect. He recorded each session with a stationary camera and a handheld.

Lots of film to scan. Melanie was grateful he had taught her how to fast-forward. She found nothing to clarify her husband's affinity for Victoria in the handheld shots. Will kept to the background. Victoria was a steadier presence, the "go-fer" during events and a coordinator at the call center.

The stationary film was more revealing. The September film showed workers and volunteers very aware of the camera's eye. Melanie smiled as Dillon appeared in his own film, sometimes lying on the floor or climbing on a chair to catch the image he chased.

Melanie smiled as Eli DuPont walked through a shot, flossing his teeth. Volunteers got caught straightening their underwear, picking their noses, or doing other harmless activities best done out of the public eye.

She grimaced when she saw herself. She'd smile brilliantly when anyone engaged her, but her gaze moved side to side.

Whenever Will crossed the path of the camera, he was always a man on a mission. Victoria was usually at his side or close behind. A couple of times, he studied her when she wasn't looking. He wasn't alone. Every guy—college age to senior citizen—gazed at her in admiration. They would turn away, often red-faced, if Victoria caught their stares.

A modest woman would have blushed. A bold woman would have wiggled her hips to accentuate the attraction. Victoria Peters just gave the camera a knowing smile. What was that about?

Dave Dawson seemed immune to Victoria's attributes. He lived by the credo "Someone is always watching." Even if CNN or his wife didn't see, he believed God Almighty did. How Dave slipped into Paige Bowers's car for an instant was beyond Melanie.

Human frailty was fraught with far more peril than being caught flossing your teeth at your desk or pulling out a wedgie.

Mike McGregor also didn't show much interest in Victoria. Strange, because they seemed like a perfect match. Single. Attractive. And apparently quite amusing because Hannah and Sophie giggled every time he approached.

Without sound, Melanie couldn't tell what charmed the girls so thoroughly. Fairly often, he deliberately changed his path to hug them and make them laugh.

She reversed to October, studied the video, and watched Mike McGregor at work. Touching Sophie's hand. Hugging Hannah. Tickling a couple of the college volunteers. Dispensing candy. Tossing foam balls or play-wrestling. Kissing Sophie's forehead—and lingering over her hair when only the camera was there as witness.

Mike McGregor might as well be a faith healer as often as he laid hands on the girls.

Yet there was nothing Melanie could tag as wholly inappropriate. It was the quantity more than the quality that spooked her. The quantity—and the adoring way her daughter looked back at him.

Saturday night

Will and Melanie had the situation room to themselves. A rare hush had fallen on Dave's New Hampshire headquarters. Dave, Miranda, and key staffers had trekked to Portsmouth for a meet-and-greet at the Naval Shipyard. Even Victoria had dislodged herself from Will to make the trip.

Melanie had insisted Sophie and Hannah stay in Manchester. They were upstairs in the condo, watching a movie. No doubt whining that she was too restrictive.

Melanie handed Will the stills she had printed from Dillon's film. "I think Mike McGregor is hitting on Sophie. Maybe even Hannah."

"You've got to be kidding," Will said. "To even think of such a thing is sick."

"I'm sick?" Melanie said. "Look at this man, his hands always on our daughter."

"If you define 'hands on' as touching a shoulder or giving a hug, then most of us are guilty. Including you. Turn the spotlight on yourself, Lanie. Your perspective is warped." Will softened his voice. "Don't you see that? You fear what's *not* there."

"Please, Will. Just tell him to stay away from Sophie."

"If I saw something, I would act immediately . . . but I don't, Lanie. And you cannot go showing these around." Will jammed the photos into the shredder, turned it on.

"Stop! What are you doing?" Melanie said. The whir of the shredder felt like tiny paper cuts, ripping apart the only evidence she had.

"Don't you understand?" Will said. "You can't make accusations that only exist in your twisted imagination. You could ruin Mike McGregor by even suggesting this kind of thing."

"I'm twisted? Is that how you see me, Will? Twisted?"

"No." Will touched her cheek. "You're . . . scared."

"I know, I know." Melanie pressed his hand to her heart. "I can't tell you how hard it is to *know* . . . that I'm freaking out but still freak out anyway."

Will brushed her hair from her face. "At least once a month, Carrie gives the lecture about improper conduct to all our volunteers—and staff. Miranda and I have carefully discussed this kind of thing with Sophie and Hannah."

"You can't discuss it enough," Melanie whispered. The moment the words escaped her, she recognized the weakness of such a statement. Perhaps *she* had become a clanging cymbal that Sophie couldn't hear.

"Tell you what," Will said. "I need to make a couple of phone calls. And then we'll go upstairs. Maybe pop some popcorn and watch a movie with the girls."

Melanie clung to Will. A homework moment, courtesy of Beth Sierra. She hated this teeter-totter of emotions.

"Can we just . . . talk to the girls?"

"You cannot mention Mike. We can't get into slander."

It's not slander if it's the truth. But what if Will was right and she was obsessing? These days hugging was a common form of communication for teens. "I won't."

"Okay, we'll go talk to the girls. Remind them about proper conduct," Will said. "I can catch up with Texas and Colorado later."

They took the stairs up to the condo. Though Melanie's legs ached, Will lagged behind her. He was out of shape and not eating right. Grueling didn't even begin to describe the tax this put on the body. Maybe Bobby Joe would still be well today if he hadn't poured himself so completely into every campaign and every cause.

They found Sophie and Hannah in the living room, munching grilled cheese sandwiches and giggling over pictures on Sophie's phone.

"Hey, guys. What's so funny?" Will asked.

"Nothing," Sophie said. She swiped away whatever they found so amusing. "What's up?"

"You two are real troopers," Will said. "Everyone appreciates the work you've done."

"Wow," Sophie said. "Sounds like we're going to get fired, Hannah."

Melanie smiled. "From what everyone says, you two should be getting raises."

"Fifty percent," Will said. "At least."

"Fifty percent of nothing is still nothing," Hannah said. "How about business cards instead. And maybe Channing Tatum as my security guy."

Sophie waved her quiet. "What's up?"

"We just wanted to remind you about how . . . intimate . . . campaigns get."

Sophie groaned. "Yeah, yeah. You know that's sick, Mom. Even thinking that could happen is creepy. Tell her, Hannah."

"It's . . . unsettling," Hannah said. "As if."

"As if we didn't have a single brain between us," Sophie said.

"Just use your brain," Melanie said. "That's all we're saying. Think. And tell me or someone you trust if anyone approaches you in an uncomfortable fashion."

"Sure. Fine." Sophie glared at Melanie for an uncomfortable few seconds before turning to Hannah. "Let's go finish our homework." They retreated to Sophie's bedroom.

"They don't believe us," Melanie said.

Will threw up his hands. "Fine. Just take her home. That's what you want, isn't it?"

"I am not going anywhere," Melanie said.

"Keep telling yourself that. Maybe someday you'll believe it. I'm going downstairs."

"Nice, Will. Run away. Like you always do."

"Me? Your life has been one big road race in the opposite direction."

"You're the one who outgrew Nashville. Not me."

"This is getting us nowhere. I've got work to do." Will left without a good-bye.

"Mom?" Sophie peeked out of her bedroom. "Are you okay?"

"Fine, honey. Go finish up your homework."

She was *not* okay. Her past clung to her like shrink-wrap. Why couldn't Will at least consider talking to Mike? This was not her imagination. She knew what she had been like at Sophie's age. She aggressively pursued what she wanted.

Beth would say that Melanie had been prey. Beth would be wrong.

Melanie had seen what she wanted and gone for it.

November 1979

Presidential Primary Season

thirteen

MELANIE WONDERED HOW OLD HE WAS. WHAT DID it matter? They say love is eternal. A few minutes or years shouldn't matter in the face of forever.

"You were great tonight," he said.

Normally she'd just say thank you and defer the compliment. This was not the time for modesty. "Thanks."

"You had the personal narrative thing going and—*bam!*—slid right into the message seamlessly. Like a pro, baby. Like a pro."

She glanced sideways so she could see his face in the lights of the oncoming traffic. One of the girls at headquarters said he looked like Harrison Ford. Or maybe like Sean Connery. All Melanie knew was that Carl Linder burned with a passion that was real and not manufactured for the news cycle.

He went on and on, and she let him—wearing his praise like a cashmere wrap. He was a well-known strategist. She was a teenaged volunteer. Sure, she was Bobby Joe's kid, but she was more mature than many of her father's staff members.

"The way you kept the energy up in the room," Carl said. "Students can be the best because they're so hungry to make their own views count. But they can be nasty if they're not engaged. It's not just talking about the campaign or the Olympics—it was you. You had them—"

He grabbed her hand, tapped her palm. "Right here."

"That's good," she said. She didn't dare move, not while his hand still rested on hers.

Carl turned his attention to his driving. Back roads, poorly lit, a touch icy. Somehow the other young staffers ended up in the van for the trip back. Everyone knew that he liked to drive alone, have the time to debrief and strategize. Not tonight, though. He asked Melanie if she wanted a ride back with him to headquarters.

So they could talk, he said. She was a great conversationalist, he had said more than once. And she was so grateful he never added "for a kid."

Her parents were in Iowa for a few nights. They didn't see her as a teenager. They saw her as the political asset that she was. Everyone said she was incredibly helpful. People Carl respected and had worked with for a long time sang her praises. They always talked about how she motivated young people and inspired the jaded. How she could debate circles around people on street corners and in three-piece suits. How she worked tirelessly and devotedly.

And how she always looked darn good while she did it. That's what *he* said.

He took his hand away and flexed his wrist so sharply that his watch clanked against his cufflink.

"Tired?" she asked.

"Who's got time to be tired?" He stretched his fingers. "Just sore from shaking too many hands. Which is always a good thing."

"Hands. Hands . . ." She jolted upright. "Oh no."

"*Oh no* what?"

"I forgot to grab the antiseptic wipes at the . . . where were we tonight?"

"It tends to blur, doesn't it?" He snapped his fingers. "Littleton. Store that for posterity. Your first official appearance for the campaign was at the Littleton Grange Hall."

"I don't even know what a grange is." The road curved left and she leaned with it, close enough to smell his musky shampoo.

"Let's just say it's another proud American tradition that has become endangered to the point of near extinction."

What a fool, her age exposed by not knowing what a stupid grange was. "Does it matter?" she whispered as she leaned back. The rental was a Lincoln Continental. Soft leather, heated seats, good for dreaming. The backseat was big enough to stretch out on.

Their bodies touching. Their breath mingling.

Focus, she told herself. "Does it even matter if the grange becomes extinct?"

"Doesn't it?" He drummed his fingers on the Diet Coke in the drink holder. It was a hollow sound with the fizz gone.

She grabbed his hand and massaged her thumbs into his palm. "Not really."

He folded his long fingers over both her hands, capturing her. "And why not?"

"Because when good things like granges or World War II veterans or, I don't know, black-and-white television—" She brought her hands, still wrapped in his, to her chin. "When good things from the past fade away, that makes an opportunity for something even better to take its place."

He pulled his hand away and she thought, *He's counting the years and I've come up short.*

When he pulled the car to the side of the road and gently cupped her cheek, she stopped thinking. Stopped counting everything—except her lucky stars that Carl had chosen her.

First Week of December

Presidential Primary Season

fourteen

Sunday night

TUCK SLIPPED ON A TURTLENECK, MUSING ABOUT which bar he'd hit this evening. The interview with Paige was golden and he needed to relax, process what she'd told him.

Process how Carrie would react when she learned the news about her brother. Carrie had held Tuck at arm's length since that drunk night she'd had to muscle him back from Martha's Exchange. He'd be temperate tonight. He had vowed to change his life, do things better. Sure, the Dawson campaign was small potatoes, but those people were *alive*. Tuck envied that sense of purpose and destiny.

His iPad pinged. *Ignore it*. Probably his grandfather, wanting to deliver a forty-minute treatise on Dan Rather. A now-familiar scarlet flashed on the screen. Another Joshua hack?

Tuck checked his phone, flipped on the television. Everything ran red.

He dialed Carrie on the landline, caught her in her room. "I'm asleep," she said.

"Joshua is back. I'm coming down."

Tuck took the stairs down, half afraid that somehow this Jericho group could trap him in the elevator. Stupid thought. He followed the tirade on his iPhone.

The puppet was dressed in a suit and tie. Ghastly with its skull head and jerky motions. "I am Joshua and I can be anywhere. I can be anyone. I can re-create myself bit by bit, millisecond by millisecond."

Carrie opened the door to him, tablet in hand.

"What do you think?" Tuck asked.

"Egotistic, narcissistic, garbage-spewing, back-patting fool."

"I am Legion," the Joshua skull said.

"Wow," Carrie said. "Add delusions of grandiosity to my description."

He'd have to be legion. One hacker couldn't move through the communication systems like this cat did. Lots of fingers pointed at the international hacker group called Anonymous. Easy to accuse, impossible to prove. The apparent control of satellite communications was terrifying, though J.L. said the feds had warned media not to even speculate about that.

People were not stupid, no matter how much his grandfather believed in the "sucker born every minute" theory of P. T. Barnum.

Carrie slipped her arm around Tuck, snuggled against him. She explained the biblical significance of Jericho, how Joshua and the Israelites marched around the city for seven days and then shouted. "The walls came down," she said.

"Chilling," Tuck said. The cartoon on-screen might be a joke, but what this group could potentially do was no laughing matter. With enough intelligence and skill, they could bring down banking, communication networks, or even mess with infrastructure like traffic systems or power plants.

"The name Joshua is a nice fit," the marionette said, "even though the analogy grinds to a halt somewhere between 'as for me and my house' and the rubble from which that house was built. No matter. Analogies are meant for quick processing.

"Our heroism is now characterized as terrorism. You sheep

and goats are so far removed from freedom, you can't recognize us as the vanguard we must be."

The Joshua creature laughed, its jawbones making an unholy clatter. It raised its bony hand, pointing at the camera in Jacob Marley fashion. "Get ready, you Bible thumpers, Starbucks sippers, Pilates strivers, Weight Watchers, Dexter lovers, McMansion dwellers, SUV drivers, Valium chewers, Ward Cleavers.

"Get ready—because I am coming for you."

The screen blanked and resumed Tuck's desktop icons. Carrie collapsed against him, the sweat on her face dampening his cheek.

"It's okay," he said.

"Last time it was lights out at the arena. What could it be this time?"

"No one can grab disparate communications vehicles—satellites, cable, servers—and not leave a Sasquatch-sized footprint. The feds will track down these guys by tomorrow."

Carrie relaxed and Tuck decided it was a good thing he was experienced at lying to women because he could hide the dread lurking deep inside his bones. If this Jericho thing advanced beyond cheesy dialogue into directed action, chaos could result.

A nation in chaos was a nation at war with itself.

Monday morning

For the first time in days, it wasn't the baby—fetus—making Carrie sick. Victoria had awakened her fifteen minutes ago, telling her that Joshua had made good on his threat. The Jericho group had struck and it was ugly. She'd pulled on sweats and followed her roommate to the situation room where Will was being briefed via phone.

The only folks missing were the Dawsons, Melanie, and Eli DuPont. Thankfully, Sophie and Hannah had gone with them, heading for a seacoast Chamber of Commerce breakfast.

Will finally hung up and addressed them. "It's confirmed," he said, and everyone groaned. Joshua's theatrics had gone from prank to threat to disaster.

The Jericho group had broken into the national database of health records and selectively released Dave Dawson's medical records and those of anyone associated with the campaign.

"How bad is it?" Victoria asked.

"It depends on who is hiding what," Carrie said. Thank heavens she hadn't gone to an ob-gyn to confirm her pregnancy. Other than puking her guts out every morning, she was healthy as a horse.

Mike McGregor hustled into the room, a cell phone in each hand. "It's a massive security breach. It's all the campaigns, even some locals. The NSA, FBI—all the alphabets—are going crazy."

"What about the president?" Carrie said. "They get his stuff?"

"Lame duck. No one cares," Mike said.

"Where are the records posted?" Will asked.

"Everywhere," Victoria said, fingers flying on her keypad. "They downloaded onto WikiLeaks first. Haines got his taken down within an hour but they've all been reposted on underground sites. Google any one of our names—and this goes even for the volunteers—and the first hit is on our health records. Which means they not only broke into Health and Human Services, they also got Google, Bing, the rest of the search engines, and manipulated them like a puppet master."

Mike swore. "When they passed the healthcare bill, they promised our data would be secure."

Carrie and Will laughed. Cynicism was in their DNA.

"Doing a selective extraction requires a tremendous skill level," Victoria said. "Not just in getting by all the firewalls but in knowing *whose* names to target."

"Staff are public record," Carrie said. "How did they know who our volunteers are?"

"Bresler's people said the same thing," Mike said.

"The hackers have people inside," Will said. "That's the only answer."

The thought of someone treacherous working side by side with her or Will or Dave was absolutely chilling. Carrie scanned the room, took in the faces she had known since she was a teenager in Dave's office. No one was a saint—how could they be in this business? But to betray the entire organization? The feds would be peering down their throats by the afternoon.

"Okay, enough detective work," Will said. "Mike, let's be the first to speak publicly. Have Dave go live as soon as he can get to a camera."

"He's got a couple crews this morning," Carrie said. *Thank you, Paige Bowers.*

"Position it as 'incredible invasion of privacy' and 'how Dave saw this coming because it was dangerous letting the federal government be a repository of our personal data.'" Will rubbed his temples. "That kind of thing."

"We need to dig out the video of Dave's filibuster in the Senate. He did at least twenty minutes on the healthcare database," Carrie said. "And didn't he write an editorial for the *Wall Street Journal*?"

"Don't go too hard," Mike said, "or they'll think we did this."

"Victoria, call everyone on the list to let them know what happened and that it's not just us who got hit." Will turned to Carrie. "I need a minute with you."

She grabbed her tablet and phone and followed him into the hall. "We need to know what can hurt us," Will said. "Go through our records."

"Talk about invasion of privacy," Carrie said, though she had thought the same thing.

"The press is going to do it anyway. Fortunately, the vultures will go for Haines and Sanders first so we should have some time for damage control on our side."

"And if I find something?"

"Tell me. I'll figure out how to handle it."

"What if it's something you don't want to know?" Carrie said.

He frowned. "Do you know something I might *not* want to know?"

"Nope. Just reminding you of the consequences of peeking behind the curtain."

"Do it as fast as you can, Caroline. I don't want to be blindsided." Will glanced up and down the hall, then went back into the situation room.

Carrie debated going to her room. Victoria might come in and want to know why she wasn't working alongside the rest of them. Blast that Joshua! Her procedure was scheduled for this afternoon. She'd have to postpone. It was early. She had time.

She took the elevator to the ground floor and wandered into the hotel's breakfast room. It was empty and dark, tables washed and trash carted away. She sat near a window. It was a gray day—weren't they all this time of year? Snow would brighten up the brown grass and barren trees.

Two more months until the New Hampshire primary. How strange to think that they'd put in a full year, to watch it all dissolve on one cold night in February.

Carrie popped a Coke and began reading. It took her about twenty seconds to find something in Dave's record. She texted Will.

Dave takes painkillers and an antidepressant.

Fibromyalgia

Will texted back.

He's going to mention it in his presser. No prob.

Miranda had a mammogram in October and a biopsy on Halloween. Benign, *thank You, God.* They hadn't said a word, just waited in silence. That was the Dawson way—smile, bless you, and soldier on.

Eli DuPont had a gastric bypass four years ago. If it had yielded results, Carrie didn't see it. She cringed at his weight and blood pressure at his last physical. The guy would pop a literal gasket someday if he didn't take his health more seriously.

Victoria's history was unremarkable. Strange. Her prescriptions weren't listed. Carrie had seen the bottles in the trash. None of them appeared in Victoria's medical record, nor was there any record of injury or chronic pain. No time to worry about that now.

Will had a sinus infection in April. It was alarming how far back these records went. He'd had his tonsils out when he was twenty-seven. Carrie had totally forgotten about that surgery. At six years old, she was so excited because he shared his ice cream with her.

Sophie and Hannah were still under a pediatrician's care. Their records yielded nothing other than immunizations. Interesting how Hannah had gotten the HPV shot and Sophie had not. Did Melanie think Sophie would go nuts if she was immunized? Hey, fellas, I'm protected against vaginal warts! Whoee, let's get it on!

A rap on the window made her jump.

Jared pressed his face against the glass. He'd mentioned that someone in the kitchen gave him the leftover rolls and muffins every morning.

"Go away," she said. "I'm working."

He shook his head, pointed to his ear. She typed, I'm working and turned her tablet so he could see it. He smiled, put his index finger to his lips and then to the window. *Corny*, Carrie thought, even as she placed her finger on the glass against his.

Carrie shooed him away, got back to work. When she had finished with staff and volunteers, she'd look up his records. *Dear God, please don't let him be involved in this.*

Melanie was next. Her record was unremarkable until eight years ago. Her sister-in-law had a miscarriage. Three days later she had her tubes tied. Did Will know this? For two years after, she was on antianxiety drugs.

There was no shame in any of this—unless Melanie had never told Will. He would have told Carrie if another baby was on the way. She scrolled through procedure pages, found the one that her sister-in-law had signed.

Patient is estranged from husband; notification of spouse is waived.

Carrie couldn't imagine any wife keeping a miscarriage and sterilization secret from her husband. That would explain the Xanax prescription. Carrie texted Will.

Come to the breakfast nook.

Can't it wait?

No. Now.

Maybe Carrie shouldn't tell him. She could urge him to call Melanie, let her come clean. Or maybe roll the dice. Their opponents or media allies wouldn't even read her record unless they remembered she was Bobby Joe's daughter. And Will had enemies because he was so good at his job.

Her brother stomped in, arms flexed as if ready for a fight. "This better be good."

"Did you know Melanie was pregnant eight years ago?"

"What? What are you talking about?"

Carrie turned the screen so he could read it. "You really didn't know?"

He rubbed his face. The red marks on his forehead answered her question.

"Was it your baby?" Carrie asked.

"Stop. How can you even ask such a thing?"

"It's the question that people will ask if they find this."

"And I'll say that they are scum. I'll swear that I knew all along and they had no right to intrude into my and my wife's private grief. Dave's already gone live with his outrage and the others are popping up. Haines and Sanders have enough clout so that anyone who brings up this kind of personal information will be shunned."

"What about Lanie?" Carrie said, though she really wanted to say, *What about me, Billy? I'm pregnant and I'm scared*. How Melanie must have felt, going through this without him.

"That's irrelevant."

"Irrelevant? And you wonder why you have trouble in your marriage."

"What else can I do, Caroline? She never told me about being pregnant and never told me that she'd gotten her tubes tied. So what do I do now—throw it in her face? What good will that do?"

"I'm sorry," Carrie said. "I wish things were better for you. And her too."

Her brother clenched and unclenched his fist. Swallowing

anger, worry, all of it. She watched as he took it all in, put it deep inside in some emotional vault, and focused on the next step. When Will was like this, she usually prayed for him.

God wouldn't hear her now.

"Billy," she whispered. "What do we do?"

"Let it go." Will kissed the top of her head. "It's not your problem. Just keep looking." He mustered a smile for her and then left the room.

Keep looking. Did she even want to know what other secrets were hidden here? Secrets intended to be kept between patients and doctors? And God—*God, forgive me—please, God, forgive me because I'm trying to keep a secret from You.*

fifteen

Tuesday morning

The attorney general of the United States held a press conference, threatening anyone who published health information with massive fines and maximum jail time. The FBI and NSA investigated the hacking full-time. Health and Human Services scrambled to reassure citizens that their records were safely encrypted.

Homeland Security raised the threat level. Carrie laughed about that with Tuck. Trying to flush out terror-hackers was like trying to knit a sweater out of cooked spaghetti.

Jason Polke told Will that they thought the same hackers pulled the stunt at the ice rink. The Chinese, maybe even Al-Qaeda, could be behind it. State and federal governments were working around the clock to clean up their security.

All the candidates were so outraged, no one dared use any of the information. Mutual assured destruction, Will called it. Stockpiling, Carrie knew. Sitting on data, waiting to sling arrows at each other from the forest.

Was it possible MoveIn had anything to do with this? When she searched for Michael J. O'Dea, birth date of March 6, 1982, nothing popped. It seemed the Movers were exempt from the hacking or the feds were getting the data locked down. Or perhaps his license was a fake. She would love to poke at him about this.

What are you really, Jared—sociopathic or smitten?

Destiny called her at midday, gave her the excuse needed to track down Jared at the encampment. Destiny Connors Aviles was Carrie's niece. Though genetically they weren't related, they had always connected. Both were ambitious. Wry. Sharp-witted. Even though Destiny was a bit of a freak with her art and Carrie was buttoned-down Beltway, they remained good friends. After discussion of the Joshua creep and his Jericho threats, Destiny got to the reason she had called.

"My bro is up there, poking around."

"I know," Carrie said. "I'm always tripping over those big feet of his. You guys are from a race of hobbits."

"He needs a solid, if you can make the time. He wants to interview MoveIn. His parents say he can't unless he is accompanied by an adult. Can you go over with him sometime and let him poke around? I know you're busy saving the world and all, but it would make the Whittakers happy."

"Sure," Carrie said, grateful for the excuse to wander into Jared's world. "I'll keep an eye out for him."

"And while you're watching stuff, Carrie . . ." Destiny took a deep breath. "Just between us, can you keep an eye on that dark-haired woman? The one who has glued herself to my father?"

"Don't ask me to go there," Carrie said. "I know nothing and I plan to keep it that way."

"He's *your* brother, Carrie. I'm asking you as family."

Jared claimed his encampment was family. They were public-relations arrows aimed at the heart of next year's elections. They were in training-camp mode right now. What would happen once the primary elections began and the Movers began serious protesting? They'd take headlines away from what really mattered.

National pressure had kept the media from coming out with medical secrets. What would stop MoveIn from making signs or speeches with the information they gleaned from the medical records?

After ending the call with Destiny, Carrie bundled in jeans, hiking boots, and a down jacket for the trek across the street. It was a balmy forty degrees but she could smell snow in the air. The only good thing about New Hampshire was the skiing. Will said she could take a couple days off at Christmas. Mother would want her in Belgium.

The notion of skiing, of flying free in a pristine white world, made Carrie sigh. Two days without this intrigue or slog. Maybe Tuck would come with her. He was a black-diamond skier. Everything came so easy for him. Sports. School. Women.

Privilege and money opened the whole world to people like him and Carrie. Tuck was tangled in a hole of what she assumed was self-loathing. She was knotted by a microscopic clump of cells threatening to make its own world deep inside her.

The nausea was as bad as ever, and she'd had some fainting spells. Low blood pressure, according to the machine at the local pharmacy. She had rescheduled the procedure for the day after tomorrow.

And then she could start praying again. She would explain to her heavenly Father that this pregnancy was impossible. She had been careless. She had sinned. She was strong but not strong enough for this. Surely God would understand.

For now, focus on the task at hand. Sophie writing a documentary and Dillon filming it. Though some of their cuts were unwittingly funny and amateurish, they hit their strides in other sections.

Carrie crossed the street to Veteran's Park. The encampment would have been shut down if the governor of New Hampshire hadn't stepped in. He was the hero of MoveIn in Manchester, Nashua, and Concord. It would be on his head if this went bad. Sanctimonious fool.

Carrie ducked under the police tape that bounded the encampment and picked her way through the tents.

Porta Potties were lined up at the edge of the sidewalk. A gift from Manchester's mayor. If these people had to search out places to do their business, they would have been gone a month ago.

An older woman sat on a bench, knitting mittens. She wore a baseball cap over a bald skull. Cancer victim? The poor thing was all jutting bone and blistered skin. Her hazel eyes were clear and burned with life.

"I'm looking for Jared," Carrie said. "The redhead?"

The woman pointed at a military-type tent in the middle of the park. "That way. And thanks for visiting. You look cold, dear. Would you like a set of mittens?"

"No, thank you," Carrie said. It made her uncomfortable to look at the disease-ravaged woman. Surely the cold must be agonizing for her. Was she here as a last defiant act before death claimed her?

A college student in a UMASS sweatshirt and Patriots cap cooked hot dogs on a small grill. Her friends passed around paper plates like they were china. Plywood on sawhorses formed makeshift tables. The "diners" sat on large plastic buckets.

At rush hour, they'd pound those buckets in a drum circle. What was the point? What did banging on hollow plastic get anyone? She supposed it was their equivalent of Dave's door-to-door campaign.

Dave had a message. MoveIn had a presence. Which was more powerful in the end? Neither one, she knew. It was all about the money.

A man with a Santa Claus beard huddled in the meager

sunshine and wrote in a journal. Two hearing-impaired men held a heated conversation in sign language. A toddler in a snowsuit played in the empty fountain while another child skateboarded around her. Two women watched them. Were they MoveIn or just passing through the park?

And if they were part of the encampment, shouldn't Family Services know about these children? Carrie had seen three or four young kids in the past month. A woman in the Nashua MoveIn—at Sanders's headquarters—was interviewed on *60 Minutes* because she had left her four children and husband in North Carolina to "move in" for the duration. She claimed it was far more important to show solidarity with the movement than to drive her kids to soccer.

Carrie's mother had had the same calling, though hers led to hallowed halls and hushed conference rooms. It was Will or the nanny who made sure she got to hockey practice and dance lessons. Melanie made her birthday cakes and Destiny went with her to Six Flags to help her celebrate.

Carrie paused before entering the tent. She needed to compose herself. People like Jared were experts at reading faces and body language. Like those fake mediums on television read their marks, charismatic leaders did the same.

The wind gusted, making the tarps and tents flutter with the familiar *whap whap*. A Mover in the New York City occupation had recorded a rap to the beat of snapping plastic.

Jared came out of the tent to meet her. Someone must have seen her poking around and called to warn him. His hair was pulled back tight, showing his muscular jaw and a birthmark in front of his left ear. He wore a camouflage sweatshirt, ragged jeans, and a big grin.

"Hey," he said. "What brings you here?"

Disarming. The kind of instant ease that made people comfortable. Made them like you. The same charisma propelled people like Dave Dawson into the public eye while cynical operatives like Carrie and Will stayed out of sight and did the dirty work.

Carrie resisted the urge to wipe her hands on her jacket. Her skin was cold but everything inside her boiled. Would she still be so drawn to Jared after the procedure when this insane storm of hormones was put to rest?

"I need a favor," she said. "We've got a teen who has been filming us for a school project. He'd like to come by here, learn more about you. Run some film."

"What if he likes us better than you?"

"Trust me," Carrie said. "That will not be allowed."

"Come on in." Jared linked his arm through hers. "Let me check my schedule."

Inside, the tent looked like the Dawson situation room, with folding tables and chairs and nests of extension cords and surge protectors. They had WiFi, a gift from City Hall. She could hear the generator grinding away, providing power to the cause.

"So what do you think?" he said. "It's not the Radisson but it is the twenty-first century."

"It must get cold over here at night."

"There are ways to stay warm." Jared tipped his head and smiled sheepishly. "I owe you a return on your hospitality if you want to check it out. You gave me a shower, we'll give you a campfire."

"Jared," Carrie said. "What are we doing in here? I mean, really."

"Consorting." Jared leaned close, his breath warm on her cheeks.

She leaned closer, a moth to his flame. When he kissed her, she thought, *Oh, this is a bad idea.* And then she kissed him back.

Tuesday afternoon

Melanie and Will sat on Beth's sofa. She had held her breath for days, wondering if anyone would dig deep into her medical records. How far back would they go? Maybe they were like legal documents, destroyed after seven years.

She had spent yesterday afternoon in a mild panic, waiting for Will to storm into the condo and ask, *How could you let our son die?* She had been three months pregnant when she lost the baby. Will never knew because she had still been trying to work up the energy to tell him. He would insist that she needed to move to Washington. She would insist he come back home for good.

The truth was, she would have had to raise the baby by herself—just as she had with Sophie. The miscarriage had been a mixed bag of emotions.

"Melanie," Beth said, "you seem unsettled." Their therapist wore muted colors today, a silk gray top and heather-gray slacks. The ballet slippers were back, with crimson stockings.

She laughed. "What gave me away? The tic above my eyebrow or the tremor in my hand?"

"You're safe here," Beth said. "I want to make sure you understand that."

"I just feel like . . . you've heard about me for all these months and I wasn't here to speak for myself. I feel out of step."

"And whose fault is that?" Will said. "I had to practically bludgeon you into coming."

"Is that true?" Beth asked. "Do you feel forced into this, Melanie?"

"Yes. No. I don't know. I just want us to find a place where we both feel . . . safe."

"Safe is your word," Will said. "Not mine."

"What is your word?" Melanie asked.

"Welcome. I want to feel welcome in my own marriage."

"I want you to feel welcome." Melanie tossed the pillow aside so she could scoot next to him. She laced her fingers through his.

They had followed Beth's prescription and remembered to make physical contact twice a day. She liked being this close, feeling the strength of his hand, the warmth of his skin. Smelling the coffee on his breath, his lemon shampoo.

This close, she thought, folding one ankle over the other, *but no closer. Father, please . . . what can I do?*

"You have both committed to refreshing your relationship," Beth said. "That is the biggest hurdle and you're already over it. Let's dive in."

Will got up, went to the minifridge, popped a Red Bull. He sat back down, found the coaster for his drink. How at home he seems here. And what a delay tactic. So she wasn't the only one struggling in this.

"Let's look at some basics," Beth said. "Over the past year, how often have you calmly discussed your sexual and relational expectations of one another?"

"We don't talk about sex," Melanie said. "Do we, Will?"

He shrugged. "There hasn't been anything to talk about."

"Ouch," Melanie said.

"I'm sorry. But if we're not honest, simply talking about unmet expectations won't work. I tried that a long time ago."

This won't work anyway. It didn't take a shrink to know that something inside her had turned to stone.

"What about relational expectations?" Beth said.

"I want him home more," Melanie said. "Sophie needs a father."

"See what I mean?" Will's tone was sharp. "It doesn't take long to get to Sophie. I'm the bad guy because I'm not home, and I'm the bad guy because I brought Sophie to New Hampshire so we could enjoy this once-in-a-lifetime experience. Together."

"There hasn't been fruitful communication in the past year," Beth said. "Is that what I'm hearing?"

"Loud and clear," Will said.

"In general, then," Beth said. "How often have you discussed relationship matters over the course of your marriage?"

"Will, have we ever?" Melanie said.

"We did when Dave decided to run for the Senate," Will said. "I took you to dinner and talked about what a win would mean. When we were in the House, Dave and I came home weekends because we had district meetings. But the Senate is a different animal. Lanie, I asked you to please move to DC with me." He turned to Beth. "There're some lovely towns in Maryland and Virginia. We could have made a nice home for Sophie. I would have been home every night. Maybe not for dinner all the time. But I would have slept in my own bed every night."

"And you preferred to stay in Nashville, Melanie?" Beth said.

"She said the Beltway wasn't safe," Will said.

"One sec, Will. Let her answer." Beth nodded at Melanie. "Is that the reason? You feel Washington isn't safe?"

"I suppose," Melanie said.

"She grew up there," Will said. "Her momma made a nice home for her and Bobby Joe. I still don't understand the disconnect."

"I grew up among power," Melanie said, "and that whatever-it-takes attitude to hold on to that power. Living there, you never turn it off. We have family in Nashville, a church fellowship, community activities. And no one is sweet-talking you to your face while sharpening a knife for your back."

"How did we get from our sex life to backstabbing?" Will said.

"This is relational," Melanie said. "You chose Dave over me and Sophie."

"That kind of loyalty used to be patriotic. John Adams was away from his family for years as an envoy to France."

"You're not John Adams," Melanie said. "And I'm certainly not Abigail."

"The point is that *this* is my job. And yes, it's my calling. You have a calling, Lanie. One that you could do anywhere in the world. But I need to be in DC. And I have begged you to be there with me. Over and over."

Melanie wrapped her arms around her chest. She'd endured twenty years of this circular logic. His world revolved around congressional politics; hers revolved around Sophie and whatever books God put on her heart to write, whatever causes she was inspired to champion. She always thought Lord's Heritage was the link between his world and hers. Information, call to action, call to devotion.

And yet, she and Will had never managed to find the link between his heart and hers. Respect, admiration, commitment—they paled without passion to drive them.

"It's like we're not even married anymore," she said in a low voice.

"You're out of practice. But you're married," Beth said. "Otherwise you wouldn't be sitting on my sofa right now."

Will slipped his arm around Melanie's shoulder. "I'm here, you're here. This is our safe place for now."

"Let me ask about that word *safe*," Beth said. "Will used it, attributed that need to you, Melanie. Why is that important to you?"

"A home should be safe. And ours is."

"Safe from what?" Beth asked.

"Turn on the television, walk down the street, go outside. There's danger everywhere. Look at this Jericho thing. We don't even know who these people are but they've already turned us inside out."

"I know what the news says. I know what this world is. The question is *you*, Melanie. What do you need to be safe from?"

"Is it me?" Will said softly.

"No." Melanie clutched his hand. "Of course not."

Beth let that sit for a moment and then said, "Let's shift into another gear. What's the best thing about your relationship?"

"Easy. My wife understands my work," Will said. "She understands what we're trying to do and why we're doing it. That's not a small thing. She is my sounding board, my reality check."

"Your sanity check," Melanie said.

"My refuge," Will said. "Maybe not physically but professionally. Spiritually."

"If that's so," Melanie said, "why didn't you tell me about Dave and his accident? I'm sure you've heard about that, Beth."

"Good question," Beth said. "Will, you said she was a sounding board."

"Dave drank too much and lost his cool. He told Miranda that night it happened, told me the next day. If I confessed all Dave's or Carrie's or anyone else's sins to Lanie, we'd both go crazy."

"You should have told me the instant Dave decided to involve the police," Melanie said. "I had a right to know before I had Miranda begging me to stay and work on the campaign."

Will shifted in his seat. "We've asked you once a week for the past two years, since the inception of the campaign. Perhaps it's God's timing, your finally showing up on the week the story would break."

"That's a crock," Melanie said. "Tell him, Beth."

"You tell him," Beth said. "So far you're doing a great job."

"You let me walk into it without full knowledge of what I was getting into." Melanie stared at Will, biting back the impulse to ask what good Victoria Peters was to him as an assistant if he couldn't spare three minutes to tell her about Dave and this link with a prostitute.

"Lanie, I have a hundred things going on. You know that. And Dave wanted to be the one to tell you."

"Melanie," Beth said. "Let's get back to the original question."

"I forgot the question."

"What is the best thing about our relationship?" Will asked.

"Did you hear yourself when you answered?" Melanie said. "You framed your reply in context of yourself. She listens to *me*, she understands *me*, blah blah."

"Wow, nice to see you show some emotion," Will said.

Melanie got up, walked to the French doors. They were original to the house. She could tell because of the settling of the glass in the frames and how the cold snaked under the door. Beth could have replaced them with expensive replicas and kept the character of the room—and the cold out.

Perhaps Beth Sierra was willing to endure a little cold to preserve what had lasted two hundred years. Or perhaps she couldn't find the energy to move forward with reconstruction.

"We are healthy enough," Melanie said, "strong enough to lead independent lives and to cherish the work each other does. And Will calls me every night. Not text or email. He makes sure I hear his voice and he hears mine. And we talk about his day or his week. That's not him being self-centered. He knows I want to know. He knows I want his legislative efforts to succeed because I see families failing and it breaks my heart.

"And he listens to me. We speak in shorthand and understand each other immediately."

"What about physical contact?" Beth said. "Do you use shorthand there?"

Will got up and stood behind Melanie, one hand on her shoulder. "I touch her, she stiffens."

"She's not stiffening now," Beth said.

Melanie breathed softly. She didn't dare move now because anything she did—pull away, lean closer—would be a symptom she'd have to explain.

"She feels safe. Nothing more," Will said. "And that makes me sad."

"Melanie," Beth said. "How does that make *you* feel?"

"How do you think it makes me feel? Guilty. So guilty."

"Why?" Will said.

She turned to face him. "Because I'm not who you want me to be."

He wrapped his arms around her, held her tightly. "Even when you're a thousand miles away, you are still bone of my bone, flesh of my flesh. Hold on to that, Lanie. Hold on."

Melanie heard the door open and Beth's receding footsteps.

"We drove her out of the room," Will whispered.

"Maybe she expects us to rip off each other's clothes or something."

"Wouldn't that be fun," Will said.

Melanie nestled against his chest. "Positively scandalous."

"I love you. No matter what erupts around us, I need you to know that."

"I know, Will. And that's what makes this so hard. I love you too."

He kissed the top of her head. "You're here, I'm here. It's a start."

sixteen

Wednesday afternoon

"Bummer that Sophie isn't here," Dillon said.

"Yeah. Bummer," Carrie said, though she was annoyed at having to be her niece's stand-in. Because Sophie was told not to enter the encampment, Carrie volunteered to read the questions Sophie had prepared. Dillon said he'd film Sophie later and then edit the film so it would look like Sophie had been the one asking questions.

Carrie and Jared stared at each other across one of the plywood tables. He wore his hair down, the curls wild around his face. For effect, Carrie knew. Even on the street, perception was everything.

"So do you want to hear my condition for doing this interview?" he said.

"Shush." Carrie nodded at Dillon. "We've got children in the room."

"I heard that," Dillon said. "I'm not a child. And this is not a room."

"Every question you ask me," Jared said, "you also have to answer."

"What is the point of that?" Carrie said.

"I want to know you like you know me."

"Dillon is just going to have to cut it out."

"Good practice for the kid. Assuming you agree?"

"Yeah, I suppose. As long as you understand that I have to be careful." Caution had been drilled into Carrie from childhood. Watch what you say, what you wear, what you drink or eat. Your opponents, the press, and now civilians with cell phones prowled about, searching for a slipup.

Primaries were more about endurance than anything else. Make it to February without busting a gut or shaming your party and you might have a chance. Sneeze the wrong way before then and the whole campaign could tumble down.

That Sanders video was proof of that. Will was saving it until after Christmas. Show the governor what they had, let him leave quietly—if he threw his support behind Dave.

"Sound check," Dillon said. "There will be ambient noise from the street and from people moving around."

"A good metaphor for why our voices aren't heard," Jared said.

Carrie rolled her eyes. Why did she continue this flirtation? To think that she and Jared O'Dea could have anything beyond some untimely physical attraction was bizarre. And look what that untimely October attraction had produced.

Dillon made a few other adjustments and then counted them down. A sudden shyness overtook Carrie as she stared into the light over the lens. All her life, she had worked in the background and out of the camera's eye.

"Action," Dillon said. Carrie tried not to laugh.

"Why MoveIn?" she asked, reading Sophie's notes. "Why not resurrect Occupy Wall Street?"

Jared stared at the camera. Dillon motioned for him to look at Carrie.

"Occupy was the face of discontent," Jared said. "A Noah's

ark—if you will—of grievances. The term *occupy* implies warfare, the inhabiting and controlling of hostile territory. *MoveIn* says that we're here and we're staying. That we are willing and eager to join in the hard work and the sacrifice, and we expect the American people and their representatives to do the same. We keep our message undiluted."

"And what is that message?"

"That's question number two," Jared said. "First you need to answer the same question. Why Dave Dawson? Why not Jack Haines or Hal Sanders?"

"I've known Senator Dawson since I was a little girl. We're family. 'Common Sense for America' is not just a slogan. It's how we operate in the senator's office and it's how we operate in our field offices."

"Here come the talking points," Jared said. "I want to know you, Carrie. Not what you've been programmed to say."

Carrie ignored him. "Don't spend what you don't have. Free our resources and our businesses from burdensome regulations. Respect the environment; don't worship it. Reward hard work. Transform the entitlement system into something that encourages personal responsibility, hard work, and a wonderful future."

"Just words," Jared said. "Change the punctuation and the accent and you still have the same-old, same-old. At MoveIn, we hope for something better. That's why we work hard, to make the *same-old* new again."

"And your message?"

"That the greatest resources in this nation are the working people, and they deserve to share in the bounty that their labor produces."

"So you're a union movement?" Carrie said.

"We're an equality movement."

"You can give Dillon the speech later. Next question: What is a typical day like?"

"We want our camps to be a microcosm of what this country should be. Mornings we spend on ensuring our environment is clean. Picking up litter, taking out the trash, keeping our common area spotless. Before lunch we meet, listen to each other's ideas and concerns, and take a vote if we can't come to consensus. We plan the day's activities based on current news. The sign-holding starts right after lunch and goes on until Senator Dawson is back in the hotel."

"Wait a minute," Carrie said. "How do you know he's in the hotel?"

"Your turn to answer the question," Jared said. "What's a typical day like for you?"

Goose bumps crept up Carrie's neck. Was the security so lax that Jared or his people got into the Radisson's parking garage? It required a keycard to unlock the gates. Even the pedestrian gate needed an access card.

How hard would it be to hack a hotel and get access? Could Jared have anything to do with this Jericho thing?

"Tell me how you know the senator is back in the hotel," Carrie said. "Or this interview is over."

"So it's over." He got up to leave. "I'm only doing this as a favor to you."

"Wait." Carrie ran after him, took his arm. "Mute us," she told Dillon over her shoulder.

Dillon fiddled with his equipment, gave her a nod.

Jared's bicep tightened. Fight or flight. She walked him out of camera view, ducking behind a World War II monument in case Dillon had adjusted the stationary camera to catch their conversation.

"I don't mean to be a nuisance," she said. "I just need to know how you know."

"You, Carrie. The balcony appearance."

"I stopped turning on the light out there."

He laughed. "Some spy you'd make. The drapes veil the light and you're backlit as you stand out there. You look lonely. Like you've been deserted in the midst of a crowd."

"All that from me just taking a break in the night air?" She'd beg Will for a room change. If he continued to be obstinate, she'd move out of the hotel.

And yet she could barely admit to herself that she liked being six stories up, able to look down on MoveIn—and Jared—anytime she wanted.

He laced his fingers through hers. "There are nights that I'm tempted to scale the wall."

"Your Romeo act doesn't cut it," Carrie said. "I'm still furious."

"Will this cut it?" Jared leaned in.

Stop him, she told herself. *Stop* this *before Dillon wanders over and catches it.* She wanted to pull away. After one more moment, one more taste of his kiss—

"Caroline Connors! What are you doing?"

Carrie startled, turned to see her sister-in-law glaring at her. "What are you doing here?"

"I walked over with Sophie," Melanie said. "She's waiting back at the table with Dillon."

Jared extended his hand. "I'm Jared O'Dea. And you are . . ."

"Melanie Connors." She shook his hand.

"Ah. The Lord's Heritage guru." Jared smiled. "I check it every day."

"Hmm. I hope you find it useful."

Jared's face remained composed, his eyes with an impish glimmer.

"We need to get back," Carrie said. "Dillon only has so much time until the light changes."

"Thank you for doing this, Mr. O'Dea," Melanie said. "It'll be a good experience for my daughter."

Jared gave a quick smile, then walked back to the table. Sophie sat there, dressed in one of her mother's suits. Hair pulled into a knot, small hoops in her ears.

Melanie took Carrie's arm, held her back so Jared could get out of earshot. "Does anyone in the campaign know?"

"Know what?"

"That you're having an affair with some guy from MoveIn."

"You see affairs around every corner, sister," Carrie said. "You might want to get some help with that. Oh, that's right, you are."

"That's not your business."

"And this is not yours," Carrie said.

"We'll see about that. And by the way," Melanie said, "you're going to Iowa tonight."

"What? I was scheduled to run New Hampshire while Will is gone. You have no right to ask for that change." She couldn't keep delaying. Every day made the pregnancy more real, the tissue more differentiated into . . . *dear God* . . . a baby.

"Will promised to make any accommodation I requested. I want Victoria to assist my appearances this week. So you need to take her place."

Carrie's mind ran at triple speed. She had to reschedule the appointment. Pack for Iowa. Worry about Victoria making another move on her territory.

"Why her?" Carrie said. "I killed myself getting you scheduled on short notice."

"Because"—Melanie stepped close to Carrie—"I see affairs around every corner."

"Oh." She wanted to scream at her sister-in-law about the chaos her newfound jealousy would provide. That would accomplish nothing. "I am sorry about what I said."

"Don't be sorry, Caroline. Be family. For Will's sake and mine—please, be family."

Thursday morning

The networks and news outlets made a grave mistake in not cultivating sources in the Dawson campaign. Now they were being punished for it, Tuck knew. For a little while longer, Eli DuPont fed him cake and made the others scramble for crumbs from Tuck's table.

With no viable leads in the Jericho story, national media had followed Dawson to Iowa on this "mea culpa" trip. Imagine if his health records had revealed an STD? What a feeding frenzy that would have caused. Nothing there, unfortunately. Or maybe fortunately—Tuck liked doing this and would have been sad to see his new career cut short.

The talking heads conspired to drum the "War on Families" theme by sending female reporters to pester Dawson. He took it all with his usual equanimity as he shook hands at a food pantry, ate donuts at a coffee shop, spoke to the Iowa Garden Association. The only men in the press corps were the ones holding the cameras.

And Tucker Reynolds Keyes.

Not all about the Pulitzer, J.L. said. But even Grandfather had to admit Tuck's writing was snappy and captivating. Tuck reframed the Dawson-Bowers story as a soap opera in his mind and the Jericho threat as a blockbuster movie. That made the words come easily.

Dave and Miranda Dawson had been very open for the past few days, reliving every emotion and challenge. Their accounts always ended with the Christian version of happily ever after. The senator used his faith like Wite-Out to cover anything unsightly in his character. Repent, forgive, move on.

Not so fast. The story had a wart on it the size of a pumpkin.

Out of courtesy, he'd arranged to meet Carrie here in his hotel room and let her know what his time with Paige Bowers had sprung.

It would be nice to have a drink now. Just a shot to calm the nerves. He paced his hotel room, checking the time, watching CNN on mute, glancing at the empty minifridge. This was a working-class hotel—continental breakfast, indoor pool, and BYOB.

Tuck dug through his bag, uncapped the Maker's Mark, sniffed it, put his lips to the bottle. Liquor was an excellent tranquilizer. Tasted good and dulled the unanswerable questions. No, he would not. He had chosen a course, and he would see it through.

Carrie finally showed up at his door, her face drawn and eyes shadowed.

"Are you all right?" he said.

"Fine," she said. "I just need to use your bathroom." She came out a minute later, smelling of toothpaste.

"Sit down." Tuck pulled out a chair at the table.

"I've only got five minutes," Carrie said. "They've packed every moment with appearances."

"You're sick."

"It's that blasted Iowa Garden Club. I'm allergic to their centerpieces."

"Hmm." *Don't smile. This is going to be tough for her.* "You know I'd do anything for you, Carrie."

She patted his hand. "Don't put me in a position to make promises I can't keep."

How patronizing. Interesting how sobriety promoted clearer observation. "I interviewed Paige Bowers," he said.

"What? When? Where?"

"The day the story came out," Tuck said. "In DC."

"Why would you do that? She's not supposed to be commenting on this 'ongoing investigation.' "

Tuck shrugged. "I didn't know I had to ask your permission."

"Yeah. Sure." Carrie stood, paced the same steps he had trod moments ago. "It was just a ride home. If she said something different, she's lying."

"She confirmed that it was just a ride home. I think the voters like knowing he's human." He leaned the chair back and stretched out his legs. The prospect of watching Carrie implode gave him a sick thrill. Always in control, Caroline Connors would let you get only so close before she dropped the veil. After all these years in politics, she might not even know who she really was. Did she know who her brother was?

"Tucker, just get to it. Okay?"

Tuck tabbed on his iPad and brought up the raw video from his interview with Paige. Carrie took the tablet from him and watched. He took one of Carrie's earbuds so he could listen in and judge her reaction as the story unfolded.

". . . just an accident," Paige Bowers said. "The senator paid for the damage to my car, even though the accident was my fault. Mrs. Dawson prayed for me and then I hustled them out because I didn't have time for what they were selling."

Tuck heard himself question her about who sponsored her "appearance," hoping she'd bite. He fished for a juicy scandal, a catchy headline—sluts, senators, and the *whatever* corporation or labor union that greased their skids.

After a minute of his prodding, Paige went on with her story. "After the thing with the senator, one of his staffers called me. This guy—Billy—wanted a time for himself. So we got into a routine. He'd book a hotel room, I'd meet him, and he'd get what he came for. Afterward he would thank me and leave good money. I was disappointed that it didn't last long."

Tuck heard himself ask, "Billy who?"

Paige Bowers smiled. Talk about the cat with a bowlful of canaries. "Senator Dawson's right-hand guy. William Connors."

Carrie pressed her hand to her mouth. Her fingers whitened on the iPad.

"We had a good thing going for a few weeks. And then one day," Paige explained, "he said he appreciated what I did for him but he had to move on. I assumed prostate trouble because that's what happens with some of these men as they age. I took good care of Billy when he was with me. He really—"

Carrie snatched the iPad away and slammed it onto the bed. "You're not using this. Will is not running for office, he doesn't vote on bills, he doesn't make policy."

"Spare me," Tuck said. "I've done the background. A brilliant bill—excuse the pun—comes out of that office, it's Will Connors who wrote it, not Dave Dawson. You, of all people, should know your brother is Machiavelli to Dawson's Abe Lincoln."

"That's a horrendously mixed metaphor." Carrie sat on the arm of his chair. "We're friends, Tucker. This is ugly. But it's not news."

"I'm a Keyes. I can make this news."

Her eyes widened. "Why would you do that?"

"It's my job, Carrie."

She took a deep breath, clenched her fists. For a moment Tuck thought she would punch him. Her hands relaxed, her gaze quieted. She stood on tiptoes and whispered, her lips brushing his ear, "Give me a day. I'll get you something better and we can make a trade."

Fascinating, how she manufactured composure out of thin air. "I've already written the story. J.L. is pestering me for an early look. He wants to run it above the fold."

"I've got something better, Tuck. I promise. Huge. The question is—do we go with you or with CNN or NBC, now that they're here?"

"I paid a ton of money for all the rights to Paige Bowers's years in Washington. I knew I could glean more stories from her and I was right."

"So I'll buy those rights from you. If you knew the size of the story, you would see whatever she sold you isn't worth anything compared to what I've got," she said. "If I pass it to someone else, your meager story about my brother will just evaporate in the mushroom cloud of what I've got."

"Stop talking about it and show me."

"Give me a day so I can clear it for you. Then shall we regroup?"

"Sure. Okay, tomorrow by lunch or else we're going to press on Sunday with the Billy story."

"Thanks, pal." She kissed him, not a chaste kiss and not a "let's get it on" kiss. A middle-of-the-road, "here's a taste so deliver and then we'll see" kiss.

Not enough, not nearly enough. Never enough with Carrie Connors.

seventeen

Thursday midday

MELANIE PACED BETH'S OFFICE. HER HANDS FELT like ice and yet sweat pooled under her hair. The world outside was a grim blur, brown and withered oak leaves on the trees and the sky smudged gray and overcast.

"Did you ask Will this question?"

"What goes on in his session is confidential," Beth said. "You know that, Melanie. I can only share the information he's cleared me to share."

"So if he was having an affair, you wouldn't tell me?"

"Why are you going there?"

Melanie plopped into the rocking chair. "Maybe he doesn't come home because he doesn't *need* to."

"How about we leave Will alone for now and go back to the question I asked." Beth gave her a bland smile. "If you haven't experienced sexual satisfaction in your marriage, have you had that need met by other people?"

"No. Absolutely not."

"What about other activities?"

"Here's my life, Beth. I homeschool Sophie in the morning and then she goes to her high school for chemistry and cheerleading.

We do gymnastics on noncheering days. You think I invest in her too much. And if you say, 'Do you?' I swear I'll kick my way through one of these walls."

"What else keeps you busy?"

"Lord's Heritage, of course. I have volunteer researchers and columnists but it's like lassoing a wild beast. We track local legislation and other developments, make sure parents are aware of the ramifications for their children. For example, one small city in the Northeast decided that parents of high school students had no right to see their grades."

"Really? That's bizarre."

"That's the world we live in. Lord's Heritage connected concerned parents with some national resources and helped get the ruling reversed."

"So you're a lobbying group?"

"We're advocates for strong families. We're under assault on every front. Taken as a whole, this culture is overwhelming. Taken one small step at a time—like this grade privacy issue—and we can make a difference. Sometimes we advocate outright, but mostly we connect concerned folks with people who can help."

"Do you have any physical activities you enjoy? Pilates. Skateboarding. Skydiving."

Melanie bit her thumbnail. "I watch DVDs of black-and-white movies. You think I'm withdrawn, don't you? Hiding out from the world."

"What's changed, that you're getting back into politics, and at the highest level?"

Melanie stood. "You know what changed. Will gave me an ultimatum. I like you, Beth. And Will trusts you. Think of this from my point of view—I arrive in New Hampshire to check on my daughter, and my husband informs me that I need to go into counseling with someone I've never met. And he expects me to talk about my sex life or he's going to start divorce proceedings. A normal person might find that a wee bit annoying."

Beth opened her mouth to reply but Melanie held up her index finger. "And furthermore, I think I'm normal and it's this society that's hopping with hormones and expects the rest of us to leap up and down and say, 'Oh, do me, do me!' When did the pursuit of sexual pleasure overtake the pursuit of godliness?"

"It hasn't," Beth said. "It just gets far better press. But the two aren't juxtapositions. Christians can be holy and horny at the same time. It's how God made us—both spiritual and sexual beings. The beauty is when the two meet in marriage."

"It's never that easy," Melanie said. "I know that from my ministry and you know that from your practice."

"Agreed," Beth said. "Grab your coat. Let's go for a walk."

"Why? It's cold out there."

"Let's see how it feels to get into that fresh air, warm up our muscles a bit. How does that sound? Riverwalk is just a block over. You'll enjoy it."

They grabbed coats, scarves, and gloves and headed through Beth's back gate. Melanie appreciated the change of scenery. The air had a bite to it, and the water was dark and secretive. She pulled her jacket tightly around her, held on to the collar with both hands.

"I'd like to ask you," Beth said, "to do something that may make you uncomfortable."

"What could possibly be worse than journaling all of my fears?"

"I want you to complete a sexual history form."

"A *what*!" Melanie said.

"This is a way to guide you through recalling every sexually charged encounter you've had—with anyone, ever. You'll indicate how old you were, how old your partner was, what role this person played in your life at the time, and other tidbits of information that would be helpful for us to examine."

"It sounds . . . sordid."

"If we have a road map of all your experiences, we can draw lines, connect dots, and get a bigger picture of the lens through which you view your own sexuality."

"I don't see what the ugly past has to do with today."

"This exercise is not intended as a value judgment, Melanie. And not intended to shame you. It's merely gathering data to be analyzed. A scientific study of social behavior."

"Why in the world would I need to drudge up all of those details? Wouldn't that be like dredging this river for bodies that have been missing for thirty years?"

"To the person who lost their loved one that long ago, finding a body in that river would answer so many questions, bring much-needed closure. Don't you want answers? Solve the mystery of what's happened in your life and marriage?"

"Not if the answers are going to hurt worse than the mystery itself."

"You are an intelligent woman. Consider where you are today—do you understand that it's going to hurt a lot worse *not* to look at your life and change what needs changing than it will to keep ignoring your sexual and emotional history?"

Father, how can I do this? How can I trust this woman to look at what I've done and not despise me?

"It just seems so hard, so unnecessary."

"Remember, you are not just a forty-eight-year-old woman," Beth said. "You are also the eight-year-old that you once were, and the thirteen-year-old, and the thirty-year-old. Everything you've experienced is still a part of you. Sweeping it all under the rug and calling it 'the past' doesn't make it go away. It just creates a bigger pile under the rug for you to trip over."

"Why did we have to come out here to discuss this?" Melanie asked. "Were you afraid I'd start throwing things in your office or create a scene?"

Beth laughed. "I wanted to show you my favorite place to sit and think. It's ahead, about a hundred feet."

Melanie walked in silence. The Merrimack River, once the lifeblood of this city, had provided the power to drive the mills. Now it was just something to walk along or kayak on. Cold and forsaken. A place to hide secrets.

"Let's sit for a minute," Beth said.

The bench was granite, a simple seat with no back. A plaque on the side of the heavy stone identified that it had been given in the name of someone long dead. Someone whose secrets would never be dredged up.

Melanie could keep walking. Leave Beth to sit and ponder while she walked into the city center, found a cab, went to the airport, and flew back to Tennessee where the rivers didn't freeze and where no one put a claim on her secrets.

Beth extended her hand. "Please, Melanie. Sit."

Dear Father, give me the strength to fight for my marriage.

Her knees wobbled and Melanie had to sit or she would fall. Beth slipped her arm through Melanie's. She felt warm. The brusque air and wide river didn't sap her of energy. Will had met the therapist at church, had a good connection. If anything, Melanie would have to trust his judgment that Beth was safe. There was that word again.

"What are we doing here?" Melanie asked.

"You're not the only woman with ghosts in her past. Ghosts that own more of her soul than she realizes."

Melanie asked, "You too?"

"When Paul and I had a bad patch in our marriage, I spent many hours working through my own sexual history. My husband died far too young, but we had a good last few years because

I had done the work and he had done the work, and we'd both done the forgiving and the rebuilding."

"Why can't the past stay buried?"

"We don't have to be defined by what we've done, but it does help to understand the nature of what we've done . . . and more importantly, why. If we don't discover the answers to those questions, we are in danger of repeating history."

"Trust me. I am not going to repeat my history."

"Don't you owe it to yourself to understand why you're feeling so cold toward Will?"

"You asked me to journal my fears. Well . . . my second biggest fear is that I'll never understand why I freeze whenever my husband touches me."

"If that's number two, what's number one?"

"That I *will* understand."

Thursday afternoon

Billy. Carrie's pet name for her brother. Her trustworthy Christian brother—exposed by a high-priced hooker. She vomited again, pregnancy sickness and utter shock sending her stomach into overdrive.

And he gave that prostitute the name Carrie had given him.

When she was a little girl, she couldn't call him Will. That was what her mother called him, and she always sounded angry, spitting out the name like it was a bad taste in her mouth. Her brother believed that Mother had broken up his parents' marriage.

So Carrie called him Billy. No one else was allowed to. The name was her special bond with her brother.

When she grew up, Carrie called him Will because that's what Melanie called him, and Dave and Miranda, and everyone on staff.

She swished toothpaste around in her mouth, spit it out. She had missed the car to the luncheon. Will texted, furious because she was supposed to be in the advance party. She texted back, told him to get back to the hotel immediately.

Y?

More to the Bowers story

There had been a long pause and she wondered if someone had grabbed him to talk. Finally he texted back:

U can't come here?

no. private. come NOW

B there ASAP

Fifteen minutes later he stormed into her hotel room. "This better be important. Dave's got crowds . . . It's pretty bloody amazing out there. You can just feel the momentum shift."

"Tucker Keyes has Paige Bowers on tape," Carrie said. "She gives excruciating detail about a regular customer named Billy. It took her a couple of alleged 'dates' to figure out who he was. He was a steady customer for a while so she kept her mouth shut. She's talking now."

Will tapped his fingers on top of the television as if he were trying to anchor himself in place. "I don't know what to say. I'm sorry, Caroline. What is Keyes going to do?"

"*The Journal* has it above the fold for Sunday. Part of a bigger story about 'high times with hookers' in DC. I said it wasn't news but he knows, Will. Tucker knows it'll resurrect the Dave story, give his own career more juice."

He sat on the bed, head in hands. Carrie touched his shoulder. "You know and I know this is Melanie's fault. The ice princess."

"Don't talk about her like that."

"Would you rather I blame you? Fine. It was you who dragged Dave into that party, wasn't it? Maybe you're the one who arranged for the hookers in the first place."

"It was the typical lobbyist gathering, which meant it was my job to be there. Dave came along because he needed to get out of the office. It was a long time ago. Why would media care? Especially with this Jericho thing."

"You've got enemies, Will. Men, women—heck, whole organizations—who want to take you down. Dave has smiled through fifteen years in Congress while you wielded the axe. You know people aren't afraid of him. It's you they step around with trepidation."

"And now we have to be afraid of Tucker Keyes? What happened to the leash, Caroline? Your puppy bites."

"Don't take that tone with me. I'm not the one rolling around with—" She clenched her teeth to stop the accusation. She had rolled around too. Rolled around in fragrant leaves with the man whose last name she couldn't remember until she went through the donor report. She was in no position to accuse her brother of anything.

His shoulders hunched. "You know how things were with me and Melanie. Before I . . . contracted with Paige . . . I was losing my mind. Paige Bowers was like a pressure valve."

"If this comes out, it'll put an end to that reconciliation you pretend to have going."

"Why are you biting my head off?" Will asked.

"Because your wife bumped me here to Iowa so she could personally babysit Victoria Peters. Because you wear *that* girl like a set of drapes. How many bimbo eruptions should we expect?"

He threw up his hands. "Do you have anything for me other than sarcasm?"

Carrie sat next to him, drained. "Just tell me, Will. Tell me how to help you."

"You can't get Keyes to hold my part of the story?"

"Short of sleeping with him—no. And I'm not dropping trou to save your sorry backside."

"You think I want that? I may push you hard, Caroline, but we're family."

"We've got the Sanders video. Wave that in front of Tuck and he'll drop the little fish for the whale."

"No." Will shook his head. "You know we're timing it for the first week in January. Dave wants to sit down with Sanders privately and help him see reason. He's convinced Sanders will do what's right for the party and withdraw. Maybe we could get the governor to do an exit interview with Tucker Keyes and—"

"No, no. Sanders is not going to sit with anyone once you force him out of the race. And Tuck won't bite on a fluff article anyway." Carrie dug her fingers into his shoulder. "Was it worth it? Sleeping with that woman?"

He flushed. "It was Paige Bowers or have an affair. I wasn't about to do that to Melanie or to some other woman who would be looking for love while I was just looking for . . . what I needed."

"Why didn't you just divorce her? Living in limbo is its own hell."

"Scripture says—"

"Hold on there, bro. Scripture pretty much went out the window when you dropped your money on a prostitute."

"You think I don't know that? You think it doesn't eat at me to know what I did?"

"I know it does." Just like what Carrie needed to do ate at her. "Do you still want this marriage?"

"I love Lanie."

"I love Lanie too. But I recognize what she is."

"What's that, Caroline?" He closed his eyes. "What is she?"

"She's damaged. And you've never dealt with whatever it is that makes her so . . . sensitive."

"I ran away from it. But no more."

"So let's clean this thing up and let you move on. I trade the Sanders video for what Tuck has and you live to fight another day."

"We don't want to destroy Sanders," Will said. "We just want him out of the race."

"You did what you did, and Hal Sanders did what he did." She took his hand. "Whose side do you think I'm going to come down on?"

"Dave said no."

"Don't forget what's at stake here. Dave is on the scale with you. Dave and you on one side and that foul-mouthed bigot Sanders on the other. Do you want to add Lanie and Sophie on your side? Can you bear all that weight, Atlas?"

"Sanders has a family too."

"Frame it bigger, then. Who is better for the country? Hal Sanders—who never saw a federal grant he could pass up? The man who subsidized abortion clinics with state funds?"

Hypocrite, she told herself even as that phrase passed her lips.

She stood, clamped her hands on his shoulders. "You and

I could be in the corporate world making real money. Running Dad's company or maybe an investment fund. Instead, you chose public service, and I followed you. We are doing this for our country. Right?"

"That—and for Dave," Will said.

"You made Dave the man he is."

"God made Dave the man he is."

"You won't pull the trigger, will you?" She shoved him. "You gutless wimp."

"The purpose of acquiring that video was to force Sanders to withdraw. We promised Dave that's what we would do."

"*You* promised Dave. I didn't."

"You work for me, Caroline. And I'm saying no. We'll find something else to feed Keyes."

"Tucker Keyes is like a coyote with a squirrel. He's dying to rip it open, get at those guts, howl at the sky. If you want Dave to stay viable—if you want your marriage to stay viable—I have to do this. Now."

"You heard me, Caroline. I gave Dave my word. No."

Her brother had been caught in a lonely limbo. How much was his fault and how much was Melanie's—only God knew. And God would forgive whatever mess their marriage was in and Carrie would too.

Throwing his pearls before swine by letting a prostitute call him Billy? That was nearly unforgivable in her book. *Nearly*, but not completely.

"You want to know why you've got such a messed-up marriage, William Connors? Because you didn't find the energy to fight for your family. But I will."

She stomped out of the room.

—

Friday morning

If Victoria Peters was trying to drive a wedge between Will and Melanie, she hid it well. She had been as sweet as summer corn for the past two days. Then again, this was high-level politics where obfuscation was an art form.

Melanie poured a glass of water and set it on the shelf under the podium. She was scheduled to speak in fifteen minutes. Miranda would join her in about an hour for a meet-and-greet of the combined Concord and Portsmouth Women's Clubs. She would do a Q&A afterward. Eli DuPont had provided talking points that Melanie didn't need.

She felt a peace about speaking in support of Dave.

If only she could find the same peace about therapy. How often had she recommended therapy to women who had contacted her for help? And here she was, being a wuss about it. She was far more comfortable speaking to two hundred women—some of whom would be hostile—than she was chatting with Beth Sierra.

"Is there anything else I can get you?" Victoria asked.

"No, thank you," Melanie said.

"Do you need the ladies' room? There's a private john off that short hall."

"I'm good," Melanie said, feeling awkward. Which was worse—if this girl did have designs on her husband? Or if she didn't and Melanie imagined the worst about her?

Beth Sierra seemed to be an excellent therapist, but she couldn't know what it was like to be in a campaign. Those long evenings, working into the night, barriers coming down. A touch of the hand to comfort or a hug to encourage. Those touches and hugs becoming more frequent. Lingering.

And you become so hungry for what started as incidental contact—what you are desperate now to have—that you make time and space to be alone and to draw together, closer and more fevered.

Dear Lord—please, Lord—I just need to know the truth. About Will and this girl. And about me.

". . . get into speaking?" Victoria said.

"I'm sorry. What did you say?"

"I was asking how you got into speaking."

"I wrote a book."

Victoria smiled. "*When the Mountain Doesn't Move.* I've read it more than once."

"When the second book came out—*When the Sea Won't Quiet*—I started getting requests to speak. A local church asked me to meet with their women's fellowship group and speak on unanswered prayer. I absolutely agonized over my talk."

"You were a kid when you started in politics. You spent a ton of time talking to people."

"That was usually one-on-one or to kids my age. The first time I spoke to a large group—people who had read my book and expected some sort of wisdom—the nerves took over. I had to jam my elbows into my ribs to stop my shoulders from shaking. When I got in front of those women and realized they were like me—concerned for their families, their communities, their faith—it was like having a conversation. Once I started, I couldn't stop.

"And it wasn't about what I had to say to them. It was about what we had to say to each other. As with the website, I make it clear that I am not an expert. I'm a . . . connector. Enough about me, Victoria. How did you get this job?"

"No family ties or anything." Victoria fluttered her fingers in an excuse-me wave. "Sorry, I didn't mean . . . I wasn't referring to you, of course. I meant Carrie." The girl paused, as if gauging Melanie's reaction.

Straight face. Bobby Joe had taught Melanie that from the

age of six. Give nothing away. He had taught Will the same thing, and Will had passed it on to Carrie. No wonder they didn't communicate.

"Carrie had the internship and all that," Victoria said. "Practically from the time she could walk. My dad is a philosophy professor. I didn't know anyone. Well, I do now. Obviously."

Melanie smiled, somewhat surprised that a young woman who looked so put together would have trouble telling the story of what clearly was important to her.

"Did you do poli-sci in school?"

"I majored in communications. MIT, of all places."

"MIT?" Melanie laughed. "My dear, you do not look like the stereotype."

"You should see me with my glasses instead of these contacts and with my hair not straightened. I am the prototypical nerd. I didn't have much of a choice, not there."

"Why did you go to MIT to major in a nonscience?"

Victoria smiled. "Because those guys and gals need someone to be their public face. All of our technology starts with them. So I needed to know what they knew—at least to be able to explain it."

Melanie had a quick chill. "Do you have any . . . insight on this Jericho thing?"

Victoria shook her head. "It's organized, it's brilliant, and it's scary."

She went on with technical details that lost Melanie within seconds. "Whoa," she said, laughing. "Why didn't you go into high tech with Apple or Microsoft? Why politics?"

"I didn't plan on politics until I realized that government will function in the future like Apple or Facebook."

"Really? That's a scary thought."

"I suppose," Victoria said. "Which is why we need good people with common sense and integrity. I believe I can make a difference with Senator Dawson. I applied for an internship with Eli DuPont's office when I was in grad school. I came on full-time after graduation."

"And you moved to Will's staff for the campaign?"

"No, before that. I discovered that I liked the policy side more than the press side. I'm a geek *and* a wonk."

"And the campaign? Someone told me you were the Senate office liaison."

"I basically do whatever Will asks me to do. I'd love a little more independence like Carrie has. Just paying the dues for now."

"And your five-year plan?"

Victoria flushed.

"I'm sorry. I didn't mean to . . . make this feel like a job interview."

"It's just that I'd like to have a child by the time I'm thirty. That kind of thinking doesn't bode well for a long career in the Capitol. My plan is go to law or business school while I'm home with them. Then get back into this."

Will was forty-nine years old. In DC years, that was plenty young enough to take on a younger wife, start a second family. No one raised an eyebrow when that happened. Except maybe wife number one.

Melanie glanced at her hands, hadn't realized she'd been sliding her wedding ring on and off. Talk about obvious body language. "How many would you like?"

"Degrees?"

"Kids."

This girl couldn't possibly be as empty-headed as she sounded. You don't get through Georgetown or by Eli DuPont with a half-full intellect. Especially with a degree from MIT. Either Melanie made her nervous or the girl was playing her.

"As many as my husband and I can handle."

"You're married? I'm sorry, I didn't realize."

"No, no." Victoria waved her hands. "No husband. Not even a hint of one on the horizon. Maybe when the senator is in the White House, I'll meet someone."

"You're confident Dave is going to win?"

"Your husband makes sure that we all believe that. And it isn't a hard sell. The senator is inspiring. As are you."

"That's kind of you to say." Melanie tugged at her sweater, a ripe flush rising up her neck. That's all she needed now—menopause.

"My mom has been a member of Lord's Heritage for years. In fact . . ." Victoria dug around in her bag, came up with Melanie's latest book, *When the Day Is Like Night*. Can you sign this for her after the event? She'll be so wild."

"Sure. Let's do it now. What's her name?"

"Polly."

Melanie used a Sharpie to write: Bless you, Polly, for sharing your treasure of a daughter with us. In His name, Melanie Connors.

She drew a double line under her last name. How obvious. Infantile. Even as she flung a prayer for forgiveness, she thought, *So blooming what?* She might have fallen for the wide-eyed, naïve act ten years ago. But not today.

She could only pray Will knew better than to fall for it too.

eighteen

Friday midday

MELANIE WAS FULLY WARMED UP, INTENSE, interesting, funny. She had done this for long enough to know it wasn't her talk that was chilling the stares of the women in the audience. She continued to speak, praying for a small sign that someone was listening with open ears.

". . . and do you know that oral STDs have skyrocketed among middle school kids? And yet, we're assured it's okay because it's natural and who are we to attach any judgment to a natural act?

"Meanwhile, it's our daughters who kneel at the altar of sex when they should be standing up for themselves. Women of every age are bombarded with messages. You're not pretty enough. You're not skinny enough. You're not young enough. Or"—Melanie paused—"sexy enough."

That got some laughs, some groans.

"You have no value except as consumers. Your worth and yours and yours . . ." She pointed to a redhead in the front row, then an Asian gal farther back, and the dark-skinned woman who stood in the last row. "Your worth is determined by the number of men you can dominate or seduce, and the number of women you can outrank or outshine."

"Is that what Paige Bowers did to the senator?" a woman with long gray hair yelled out. "Dominate and seduce?"

Some boos. Too many laughs.

Lord, please. Please . . . give me words. Give me wisdom.

"Here's my talking point on that: Dave Dawson got drunk, took a ride home with a prostitute, was dreadfully sorry, and asked his wife and Paige Bowers to forgive him. That is all.

"Now here's what my heart says: Anyone can make a mistake. I certainly have. I have known Dave and Miranda Dawson my whole life and I believe—I *know*—that they have told the complete truth. That is why I can stand here today to talk about things that concern us as women and David Dawson as a candidate."

Melanie scanned the crowd, breathing a little too quickly. She stepped back from the microphone to slow down her heartbeat and to let her own silent groan rise to the throne of grace. "Any other questions on Dave Dawson's sex life?"

She waited, prayed there would be none. And there weren't. *Thank You, Jesus, and help me reach these ladies.*

"Both parties think the voters want to be coddled and soothed. They think we can't take a challenge," Melanie said. "Are they right?"

This brought a chorus of nos. "You know what they say about women? That we historically vote for progressive candidates because we want to ensure a safety net for our families. You all know my daddy—Bobby Joe Fallon?"

That drew applause from the gray hairs in the audience.

"He got it wrong too, and he was a smart guy. 'Soft hearts, open hands, and mush for brains,' he used to say. 'All it takes is a handsome face and a pocketbook of promises and you've got them.'

"Ladies, the power is in your hands to determine the course of your lives and the lives of your families. Show them. Show these people in Washington, DC, who think you need your hand held. Show them that you know better. Show them you won't run scared.

"Don't let people in government tell you who you are and who you are called to be—especially when they're trying to fit you to their political purposes and not the purpose God lays out for you.

"I get that you're tired. We all are. We're tired of factions, tired of hot-button issues, tired of talking heads, tired of dirty tricks."

"Tired of no one listening to us," someone yelled out.

Melanie stopped. She felt a deep current running through the group, absorbing it through her skin rather than her mind.

Adrenaline saying, Run! Hide!

"Are you afraid?" She slowly scanned the gathering. No one moved. No one even blinked. Deer in the headlights. Just like she had been these past too many years.

"I'm afraid too." Melanie's voice dropped to a mere whisper. She leaned into the microphone and said it again. "I am afraid too."

"What are you afraid of?" This from a young woman in a bright yellow bandana.

"Oh, goodness. It's a whole laundry list. I'm afraid for my daughter . . ." She glanced at Victoria, who was thumbing through her phone. Texting Will perhaps, to tell him his wife had gone off script. "She's sixteen and I'm afraid that because I homeschooled her, she's too sweet and gullible. I fear for her because this is a world that devours *sweet* and *gullible*."

A couple of middle-aged women nodded. Melanie looked at the UNH girl. "What's your name?"

"Katie."

"What do you fear?"

"Not having a job when I graduate. And all those staggering loans I took."

The girl sitting next to her nodded and said, "Not having a job and having to live with my parents. No offense, ma'am."

Melanie smiled. "No offense taken. My eldest daughter left home at eighteen. She thought she was utterly fearless. She knew everything and her dad and I knew *nothing*. Every night I prayed that she'd learn the truth without . . ." *Say it. Be truthful.* "Getting pregnant. Or raped. Or, dear God, murdered. I lived in fear every day and every night."

"What happened?"

"She got a clue."

That drew laughter. A blonde with cornrows stood, defiantly thrusting out her chest. "I fear getting pregnant. Because no birth control is one hundred percent. I fear not being allowed to choose for myself what happens with my body. You—you and Dave Dawson—want to stop abortions. Take away my right."

"We want to stop the *need* for abortion," Melanie said. This drew a mixed response. Melanie held up her hands. "We want to make our sisters and daughters and friends strong enough to just say no.

"Why don't we?" This from a woman with long, gray hair and a Red Sox sweatshirt.

"I know why I didn't," Melanie said. "I was afraid I couldn't keep a guy if I said no."

"You saying you weren't a virgin when you got married?" someone yelled.

She tightened her hands on the podium. "I was afraid to be a virgin. How sick is that?"

"I'm with you. Afraid to say no," Katie from UNH said. "I pretend the sex is my idea, that I'm in control. But without it—I am alone because now guys see it as their right. And I have to pretend I'm happy about all this hooking up. But . . ." She glanced around, almost cowering. "I'm ashamed."

"I am afraid that there's no such thing as forgiveness," a white-haired woman said. "Or repentance."

The crowd opened up, speaking fears faster than Melanie could think until she was no longer sure where theirs ended and hers began.

"I am afraid of not being valued."

"I'm afraid to do my best at school . . . work . . . even church . . . because smart women are intimidating to men."

"I worry that the only way to keep a man is to give him everything he wants even though he might not deserve it. And no matter what it might cost us."

"I fear I have to turn myself inside out to please people. To feel loved."

"I'm afraid there's no such thing as love."

"Or respect. Patience. Courtesy."

"No way to pay my car payment. My heating bill. My student loans. My rent. Patience and respect and all that crap won't keep my family warm this winter."

"I'm afraid my child will get molested. Or kidnapped. Or get cancer."

A woman with big eyes and a thick ponytail stood on her chair. "I am afraid that all men—like your pal Dawson—talk a good game but when the lights go out, they prefer the whore to the wife."

The gal with the blond cornrows followed suit, climbing onto her chair. "And I am afraid of women who stand by their men. They give our husbands and boyfriends carte blanche to do whatever they want."

A woman at the side entrance said, "I'm afraid if I don't stand by my man, then I'll be standing alone. And I am afraid of being alone."

Melanie leaned into the microphone, whispered it again. "I am too. I am afraid of being alone. And I'm afraid that it's sinful to have such a fear. To worry that God isn't enough when I am alone."

"And I'm afraid that there is no God," the woman in the Red Sox sweatshirt shouted. "Then we're all alone and what we are—who we are—is just dust."

Melanie leaned on her elbows and grasped the front of the podium. The room spun and it didn't matter how locked her knees were or how straight her back was, she was going down.

"Sometimes," Melanie whispered, her lips brushing the microphone, "sometimes I fear that too. That God exists but when He looks at me, He only sees dust. And I know that isn't true but sometimes the fear is so overwhelming, it's a veil over the truth."

She felt an arm through hers—Victoria's—and heard her voice, or maybe it was the Holy Spirit speaking.

Hold on. I've got you.

Friday afternoon

Pure Americana. The land of sleigh bells, Christmas cards, and Jimmy Stewart movies. The kind he'd never known.

The Christmas Faire, hosted by the unified churches of Des Moines, was a portrait of the heartland. With the smell of cinnamon rolls and pine boughs, the ring of Santa's *ho ho ho*, and children's laughter, the organizers hadn't needed to add the *e* to the word *fair* to rouse nostalgia.

Dave Dawson had worked the crowd, then done a quick press conference on the front lawn. Tuck was the only media person still at the fair. The vultures of FOX News, CNN, and NBC had booked it to the Chipotle's down the street as soon as Dave Dawson's Q&A finished.

The senator had sailed through the rocky waters and, by force of his good nature, seemed to be putting the Bowers thing behind him. The latest polls showed he had actually picked up four percentage points in Iowa and New Hampshire. The evangelicals had hiccupped, according to the polls, but had stayed with Dawson and kept his base solid. Dawson was the cheerful repentant who radiated optimism and stability. New voters embraced his newly confessed humanity as if to say, "We know this about all you politicians, but you're the only one honest enough to admit it."

The follow-up to Tuck's interview had only served to bolster this narrative. And now *The Journal*—under Tuck's byline—was ready to tarnish the campaign again by shining the light on Will Connors. It was one thing to have a one-nighter with a hooker; quite another to go back a second and third time.

The revelation imperiled Tuck's nascent career. If his investigation took Dawson down, he'd have to hook on with another candidate or go back to writing movie reviews. He'd lose the only advantage he had—Carrie Connors.

What did it matter? That was the question, the reason he had left his shiny condo and sleek lifestyle behind. What did anything matter?

Tuck strolled up and down the craft tables, feeling like he'd been cast into a Norman Rockwellian Twilight Zone. He faked admiration for the old-fashioned wares. Quilts. Wooden toys. Handmade jewelry. Potholders and kitchen towels. Knit mittens and snow hats. Watercolor landscapes and charcoal portraits. Crocheted throws and needlepoint pillows. And what Sub-Zero, granite-topped kitchen could exist without a toaster cover?

On and on, America regaled the holidays with the work of her hands. Most of the crafters were silver-haired. Did anyone younger than sixty know how to crochet these days? Why bother when you can buy a throw at Kohl's for less than the raw materials must cost at a local yarn store? Americans poured out their wallets on cheap merchandise made in China or Pakistan or India while complaining all the jobs had gone overseas.

Empty gloom. His blood sugar must be low. He wandered

into the lunch line. The chalkboard listed corn chowder, with chicken salad or tuna stuffed into hot dog rolls, perfected by hot cocoa and a slice of mile-high apple pie.

Had the sleek and polished Paige Bowers ever made an apple pie from scratch? She had the skill set for the Beltway, would likely starve in middle America. The DC crowd would consider the crafts and the chowder and the Christmas tunes that played incessantly as something to be massaged, seduced, polled, locked down. All the while secretly despising and scorning this fair and these people.

Tuck excused his way out of line. He had to get out of here. He felt like a wart on this landscape of goodwill to men. He pushed through a door marked Exit. It took him a dizzy moment to recognize where he had stumbled into. Pews, pulpit, choir loft. Hymnals, Bibles, welcome packets.

A simple wooden cross.

What was the last church he'd visited? Probably one of the lofty cathedrals in Europe. Rather than Romanesque architecture, flying buttresses, and plaster cornices, this sanctuary was decorated with an artificial Christmas tree and children's homemade ornaments.

He sat in the front pew, looked up at the cross. Whassup, man?

Nothing. And so you have it—nil, zero, nada. Man as God was the best that Tuck could imagine, and he'd already gotten an F on that test. No saving grace.

Except for the one in his pocket. He took out his Maker's Mark. All that staying dry had gotten him was an endless echo that couldn't be silenced.

"Bottoms up," he said, lifting the flask to the cross. Was this blasphemy—or prophecy?

Friday afternoon

"Tucker. Wake up."

Tuck blinked. "Carrie?" The afternoon sun made her hair shine like a halo.

"You've been drinking," she said.

"Postprandial delight."

"Whatever. We need to talk." She sat next to him. "Not here. This is the last place I want to show you what I've got."

"I'm sick of hotels. I like it here."

"Fine. If you want to do it with that cross staring us in the face, so be it." Carrie held up an iPod, offered him her earbuds. "Watch this."

She wouldn't let go of the iPod. He understood why. Iowa might be the heartland of America and a cousin of the Bible Belt, but Tuck and Carrie were children of the Beltway. They could shaft each other without a moment's notice.

Governor Hal Sanders came on-screen, plastic cup in one hand and fat cigar in the other. Someone must have forgotten to confiscate everyone's electronic devices as guests entered the party. That was easy enough to get around—just bring in two cell phones so you could give up the one and use the other to record. For high-stakes meetings with donors or lobbyists, Tuck had heard of people playing suicide bomber, sneaking their phones into the room in their underwear or shoes.

Sanders's booming bass came through, loud and merry. Part of his electoral success was due to that voice—solid gravitas with a twinkle of Ronald Regan. Three or four good ol' boys from upper-state New York surrounded Sanders. They were telling jokes, bad ones that amused the intoxicated group.

Tuck glanced at Carrie, eyebrows raised.

"Just wait," she said, snuggling next to him. He pressed his face to her hair, breathed in a scent that he imagined was almond and cream. If she ever did succumb to his charms, would he still love her in the morning? Or was he doomed to a lifetime of empty encounters until he fell victim to his prostate and a shredded liver?

"Here it comes," she said. "Pay attention."

Sanders blew smoke rings at the ceiling. The governor was the big dog in this race, the one guy who pundits thought could knock out the vice president. That was clear from the too-eager looks in the faces of the men who surrounded him. Lampreys, completely attached to their shark.

"Three guys go into a bar," Sanders said, smirking. "One was a . . ." The joke continued with offensive nomenclature for African-Americans, Latinos, and Asians.

"Really?" Tuck said, mouth open. "This guy is really saying this?"

"From his mouth to our ears," Carrie said.

With the racist content that followed, Sanders was a dead duck. Tuck knew it in an instant, and Carrie knew he knew it. She gave him a smug, *See, told ya so* smile.

It was sad that no one in Sanders's trusted circle flinched at the language he spewed. How pathetic that the person with the moral compass—and a live iPod—was the minority in this gathering. And the jokes kept coming, with no one safe from the offensive humor.

"Will the person who recorded it come forward?" Tuck asked.

"To you, yes. To the public, absolutely not." Carrie poked his arm. "Do we have a deal? You get the iPod and the name, details of when and where and anything else you might need. And I get your rights to Paige Bowers. Every single part of her story. I will reimburse you for whatever you paid her."

"Dawson knows you're doing this?"

Carrie blinked. He'd hit a nerve.

"Oh," Tuck said. "You're doing this *ex parte*."

"Plausible deniability. You will preserve that. None of this goes in writing but the bottom line has to be the truth—Dave does not know I am giving this to you. This story has to be broken as if coming from the guy who recorded this."

Tuck touched her hair. She wasn't the bubbly kind of blonde. More honey than sugar. "Then how do we seal the bargain?"

Carrie locked her blue eyes on him. No summer skies here. Always a storm brewing. He closed his eyes as she kissed him long and deep. He wanted to put his hands on her, lock his body to hers, sate this yearning he'd had since the first day he met her.

He was afraid of her and she knew it. So he took what she gave and no more.

Second Week of December

Presidential Primary Season

nineteen

Tuesday morning

"So how's the homework going?" Beth asked.

"Scary," Will said. "No man likes to be reminded of his fallibility."

"You're doing it," Beth said. "That shows courage. Melanie?"

Melanie sat across from Will. It was rare, she realized, to face each other. That was probably why Beth had asked them to sit here instead of on the sofa.

"Mine is not so much scary as it is long-winded. It embarrasses me to have such a long list. Are we turning in these fears to you?"

"No. It's your tool. Use it whenever something gives you pause."

"Or makes the hairs on the back of my neck stick up?" Melanie said.

"Do you want to talk about that?" Beth asked.

Will shook his head so imperceptibly that only Melanie could have possibly caught it.

"No," Melanie said. "I'm just feeling a bit worn down. Too many events."

"It takes courage," Will said, "to keep going out, day after day. Knowing that forces are stacked against you, wanting to take your guy down. Melanie has handled everything the campaign has thrown at her." He reached for her hand. "If you listed what you've overcome rather than what you fear, I think it would be a much longer list."

"Will's right," Beth said. "Give yourselves a star on that one. So let's get to the fun part. And I'm going to ask you to speak to your partner as if I'm not here."

Melanie held her breath. This couldn't be good.

"What was sex like the first few months of your marriage?" Beth said. "Did you enjoy it? Was it satisfying? Did you anticipate being with each other?"

"It was fun," Will said. "We did the celibate thing—remember how hard that was? The honeymoon in Aruba was one big celebration. We'd soak up sun during the day and then at night, we'd lie with the window open and the island wind blowing over us and we would just take our time with each other. That carried over into marriage for a while. I'd think of Melanie—"

"You're speaking to her," Beth prompted. "Not me."

Will turned back to Melanie. "At work, I'd think of you and thank God you were in my life. My partner. My friend. My lover. We did have a satisfying life together at first, right?"

Melanie folded her hands. She had the urge to hide them in her lap. She would not give in to the body language that said, "No, not anymore."

"We did," she said. "I enjoyed it and, Will, every moment was genuine. No faking. No need to because I couldn't get enough of you."

"How about before you were married?" Beth said. "Did you come into the relationship feeling guilt or shame about any sort of sexual involvement with one another?"

"Of course," Will said. "I thought about you a lot, Lanie. Worried about the foreplay-type stuff we were doing. The odd thing was that, unlike other couples, we weren't using sex to smooth over the other parts of our relationship. We respected our differences, celebrated what we shared. Physical intimacy was a bonus. Maybe you see that differently?"

"I felt guilty about everything," Melanie said. "I wanted to be close to you, Will. Whenever we saw each other, I thought about how strong your arms were, how safe I felt—oh my, there's that word again."

"Did you have some reason to want safety?" Beth asked.

If Melanie even mentioned Sophie in this session, Will would walk out. "I used the wrong word," Melanie said. "I should have said that I felt like I was . . . home. And then we'd kiss and we'd slip across lines that aren't spelled out in Scripture. I mean, was I pure because every cell in my body was dedicated only to Will? Or was I so wrong to have these urges before we were married?"

"You project that on Sophie," Will said.

"That's ridiculous."

"Really? Come on, Lanie. Be truthful."

Melanie knocked her fists together. She had avoided the subject and her husband used it as a club against her. "Blame me for wanting to keep our daughter sa—"

"You act like she's a hormonal time bomb. You cast all your anxiety onto her. Can't you see that?"

"What I see," Melanie said, "is that you're not the psychologist here. Tell him, Beth."

"He needs to be able to express himself freely," Beth said, then turned to Will. "Here's a more current question: When did things begin to slow down sexually? Do you remember the circumstances?"

"Will, you go first." Melanie gave in to the urge to fold her hands in her lap. "Please."

Will took a deep breath. "We married my senior year in college because ironically she said *she* couldn't wait. The premarital longing and the vigor of our newlywed lovemaking was not faked. And then, after a year or so . . . she withdrew. It was as if someone had turned off all her nerve endings.

"We wanted to have a child but we didn't seem to be able to have enough sex to conceive. Destiny fell into our laps. Someone who knew her grandmother and knew we would be wonderful parents brought us together. So our baby came, and then my wife just . . . went away.

"'Am I unattractive to you?' I would ask.

"'No, not a bit,' she would say. And her eyes seemed to confirm that, the way she looked at me like she couldn't wait to get to me. When I touched her, she hardened, as if she were having a fight-or-flight reaction.

"When Dave was in the House, I came home almost every weekend. I had a studio apartment in Maryland for during the week. I had promised Lanie we could buy a nice house in a good neighborhood—Maryland, Virginia—and join a solid church. She'd agree, but when the time came for her to come to DC and look at real estate, she'd have some excuse or another.

"When Sophie was born, I knew there was no dislodging her.

"I stayed home for six months, ran Dave's Tennessee office, did some consulting work for Bobby Joe. I prayed that my wife would give me one sign of encouragement. Something to make me leave DC and cling to her.

"One kiss, one *real* kiss, was all it would have taken. But you couldn't even give me that, Lanie."

The pause that followed was so uncomfortable, Melanie wanted to cover her head with her arms and pretend she wasn't in the room. Beth let the silence stretch for a good minute before speaking. "Thank you, Will. We can follow up on all this at our next session. Melanie, I'd like to hear your point of view on this."

Melanie remembered the intimacy of being so physically close that the spiritual wrapped around them and the almighty Father whispered, *Yes—know each other and help each other know Me.*

"Early in our marriage, we were playful and warm," Melanie said. "Torrid is probably the better modifier. Sex was *truly* lovemaking. We slowed down a bit as time passed. That was normal—who could keep up the pace of newlywed sex? On our first anniversary, I surprised Will at his office. He was working in financial services and I was still working part-time in my father's Tennessee office. We were talking about children, not sure if it was too early.

"I was so excited about our anniversary that I did something ridiculously cliché. I went to Will's office in a raincoat and nothing else but high-heeled sandals. I had planned it for weeks, gotten a fresh manicure and pedicure that morning, used my most expensive perfume, groomed as expertly as I knew how.

"Even the ride to his office was exciting. At a stoplight, I flirted with the guy in the next lane because . . . I could. It was as if nectar oozed out of my pores.

"I announced myself to the receptionist and waited, tapping my toes and stroking my hair. Will came out, tie loosened, sleeves rolled up, the hair on his arms still golden from summer sunshine. He wore his hair longer then and it was all I could do not to run my fingers through his curls as people walked through the lobby on their way to lunch.

"He escorted me into his office—after first taking me to his manager's desk to introduce us. My heart sang at the fun of it all. We went into Will's office. I locked the door and unbuttoned my coat.

"He just stared at me, teeth clenched. 'How could you?' I thought, *How could I?* He made me button my coat, told me I had embarrassed him at work.

"'What were you thinking?' he said. 'Driving over here like

that—what if you were in an accident or stopped for speeding? It's all so . . . inappropriate.'

"The heat drained from me so completely that my legs shook. *He is right*, I thought. Inappropriate was a mild term for what I had done. Misbegotten might be the best term.

"That night he came home with flowers and a bottle of wine. When he wanted to make love, I just couldn't get into the mood. He apologized and excused my gesture as naiveté.

"I realized I could not trust my judgment. That what I considered romantic and daring was just silly.

"I focused on making a good home. At the same time, Will got involved with Dave's first campaign. Most nights my husband was too tired to do anything but fall into bed. He worked full-time, did law school part-time, and campaigned in every spare moment for Dave.

"So many nights away. So many nights that I was lonely. The intervals between lovemaking increased. When we did manage to be together, his need was so urgent that it scared me. Because our lovemaking was so infrequent, Will felt like a stranger.

"We adopted Destiny. Even *she* will admit she was a hellacious child. Colicky, hated to sleep, hated to be held, hated to be put down. We loved her with our whole hearts. Ten years later, Sophie was our miracle baby."

Will didn't even look sideways at her. Should she tell him that they had another pregnancy—one that she had kept secret? The thought of raising a third child without a full-time father had been daunting. And yet, she was still ashamed at the relief she felt when she miscarried.

God, forgive me and hold my baby tight.

"With two children and Will away from home so often, I didn't have energy for sex. Dave Dawson's entry into politics became an outlet for Will's energy. They traveled the district, knocking on doors. Sometimes we'd campaign as a family. Destiny would go with Will and I would put Sophie in the stroller and go with Miranda.

"We would laugh at our circumstances in those early years and say, 'Maybe when we're eighty.' It was as if neither of us cared if our sex life wasn't the one-flesh union God intended. We respected each other, shared each other's callings. As dreadful as politics is, federal service is Will's ministry. I've never questioned that.

"He asked me to move to DC when Dave went from the House to the Senate. I thought the stability of our family was far more important than his convenience. So the girls and I stayed in Nashville."

Melanie felt the sob coming, could do nothing to stop it. She tried, pressing her fist to her breastbone, holding her breath, trying to stop words. "I chose my security over Will. I know that makes me a bad wife and, yes, a cold woman.

"But that's the trap I'm in and I see no way out for Will. Or for me."

Tuesday early afternoon

Melanie kissed Will on the cheek and said, "Drive safely."

"Aren't you coming back?" They had come in two cars at her suggestion.

"I have some shopping to do. I want to get something more comfortable and yet sophisticated for tonight." Some dinner or whatever in Portsmouth—she had volunteered to go with the Dawsons, shake hands, radiate serenity.

She didn't have a drop of peace left, not after that grueling session with Will and Beth.

Will got into the car, turned it on. "Lanie, I never meant *inappropriate*."

"I know. It's not your fault that I poured so much into the word. Now get going . . ." Part of her wanted to walk away from the embarrassment of having to recount that moment. The other part wanted him back in the situation room where he could keep an eye on their daughter.

"Lanie, I am so grateful you're doing this. None of it is easy."

"Turn off the car, Will. Just for a minute. Please."

He did as she asked and got out of the car. She slid her arms around his waist—he was so thin now—and leaned her head on his shoulder. "I'm sorry," she said. "It's me, not you."

Will kissed the top of her head. "It's both of us, baby."

"Pray that I'll be brave."

He cupped her face with his hands and they stared at each other while he prayed for strength and courage and persistence. When Will thanked God for every bit of her, the tears came. They held the stare, let the sadness trickle down their cheeks. When he finally said "amen," she pressed her lips to his tears.

"Go," she said. "I've got to find a dress."

"I love you," he said. "No matter what the years have done to us and we have done to ourselves and each other—that hasn't changed, Lanie. Believe that."

"I do. Now go." Melanie patted the top of the car, waved as he drove away. He didn't know that she had a solo appointment with Beth this afternoon. Three hours so they could go through her sexual history. Three grim, hellish hours.

Strength. Courage. Persistence. Her heavenly Father heard Will's prayer. She would hold on to that. Cling to that.

Melanie knew where she had to go while she waited for her appointment time. She grabbed her scarf and hat from her car and headed for Riverwalk. Two hours to sit on the bench Beth had shared with her. And face the past.

Then tell Beth about what she did all those years ago.

twenty

Tuesday afternoon

UNREAL. THE FBI AND THE SECRET SERVICE WERE in Manchester to interview folks. For some reason, Carrie was first on their agenda. Will was nowhere to be found and she needed him desperately.

She sent yet another text. Had he lost his phone? His response time was usually close to instantaneous, even in the middle of the night. Maybe they had him closeted away somewhere too—and imposed the ultimate indignity of taking away his phone.

Jason Polke had walked her to the Sheraton, pep-talking her the whole way. Now he was stuck in the hall outside the suite where they had set up temporary headquarters. Carrie was escorted into the living area and left to stew. Three years ago she had been vetted by the feds so she could obtain a Secret Clearance classification to work on Dave's defense work.

She had passed with flying colors.

Obviously they were here about the Jericho threats. Everyone hoped those stupid videos were nothing more than boastful and narcissistic indulgences. Joshua and his ghost hackers had demonstrated an ability to take over communications networks. Taking those networks down for longer than five minutes could take down this nation. Anyone with half a brain knew that.

What if this was about something else? Maybe Governor Sanders got wind of the video she had given to Tuck. The head of the NSA was a colleague of his from New York. Would they try to suppress it for him? Those kinds of deals got made every day—until someone finally got into a wash-my-back-and-I'll-stab-yours mode.

Carrie had vetted the laws regarding unauthorized recording. Because Sanders rolled out his ugly humor at a quasi-public gathering, there was little he could do to stop it except get some black-suited goons to put a scare in her.

The feds probably looked at her as some lower-level functionary of the Dawson organization. Pretty girl, still in her twenties, let's scare the stuffing out of her. Joke's on them because she played Division I ice hockey and wasn't afraid of anything.

Carrie jumped to her feet and pounded on the door to the adjoining room. "Hey," she shouted, "I've got work to do."

No answer. She glanced around, trying to find the agency version of a nanny cam.

"I'm leaving," she said. "Have a nice day."

The door opened, startling her. A young man with a two-day beard and thick glasses peered out at her. He wore a Guy Fawkes T-shirt and ratty jeans. "Sorry," he said. "We'll be with you in a moment."

"Sixty seconds," Carrie said. "Or I'm out of here."

After ten minutes, she got up to leave. The Guy Fawkes kid came into the room carrying a laptop. Following him was a grim woman in a gray pantsuit and a tall man in a white shirt, crimson tie, and navy pants.

He extended his hand. "Ms. Connors, sorry to make you wait. We were chasing down some details. I'm Special Agent Rick Bowse with the FBI. These are my colleagues, Agent Laurie Terrio of the Secret Service and tech specialist Garrett Ridley. Please, have a seat."

"Why is the Secret Service here?" Carrie asked. "Is there a threat on Dave?"

"No, nothing out of the ordinary," Laurie Terrio said. "It's our responsibility to investigate any hacking that threatens national security. Most people aren't aware of that, I suppose, because these incidents remain classified. Please, sit and we'll get started."

Carrie sat at the sofa, cursed to herself as she sank into the cushions. Oldest trick in the book for making someone feel inferior—sit someone in a too-soft seat—and she just fell for it. "So what can I do for you folks?" she said with forced bravado.

Agent Bowse swung around the desk chair. It had already been raised to accommodate his height and thus put his eye level a good eight inches above hers. *Oh, you big man. Flash that badge at me and make me tremble.*

"I'd like to get a few facts on record," he said.

"Are you recording this?" Carrie looked up at the Guy Fawkes nerd. He cringed. She held up her phone. "So you won't mind if I do."

Bowse glanced at Agent Terrio. As the agent reached for the phone, Carrie said, "No."

"Yes." The woman had a surprisingly girlish voice.

Carrie stood up. "Unless you can produce a warrant, absolutely not."

Agent Bowse snapped his fingers. The nerd passed him a file full of pages. Bowse flipped through until he found the one with Carrie's name on it.

"It's a FISA warrant," Carrie said, her heart pounding.

"Oh, good. She knows the Foreign Surveillance Intelligence Act," Terrio said.

"I have nothing to do with foreign anything," Carrie said. "And certainly nothing to do with terror except what you're trying to make me feel right now. Good luck with that."

Terrio pounded her fist into her palm. "We're not here to play."

Bowse held up his hand to shush his partner. "Ms. Connors, if you would just set your phone over on the television, we'll give it back when we're done here. We need to record this session to protect you, not to incriminate you."

"In what?"

Terrio sat on the arm of the sofa, taking her own superior position. "The release of federally secured health records."

Carrie held up her hands. "Hey, I'm a small fish in a very big sea. You need to be speaking with William Connors—"

"Her half brother," the nerd said.

Bowse and Carrie shot him the same dirty look.

"My brother is Senator Dawson's chief of staff and senior advisor on the campaign. I know what the rest of the world knows, basically. Will or Jason Polke—whom you could at least offer a chair to while he's out in the hall—could fill you in better than I can on what kind of security we use for the campaign."

Bowse wheeled the desk chair so close that his shins almost touched her knees. "NSA ran some profiles through a threat algorithm. We did that for all the campaigns and we've got other people we need to speak with. However . . ." He leaned forward so his nose was a few inches from hers. He had a day's worth of whiskers that she hadn't noticed earlier because they were gray, though his hair was brown. His breath smelled medicinal—maybe the mouthwash the hotel provided?

She'd bet anything that they left her to stew so they could get in a quick lunch.

"However . . . what? They teach you those pregnant pauses at Quantico? Can we get on with this? I've got work to do."

Garrett Ridley bounced on his heels as if he had just won a prize. "You had the highest threat matrix," he said. "That's why you get to go first."

Carrie's stomach went from zero to ballistic in the space of one sentence. "What? What threat matrix?"

Terrio put her hand on Carrie's shoulder. "Are you okay, Ms. Connors?"

"I'm going to . . . please . . ." She tried to reach past Ridley to grab the wastebasket. He panicked and shoved her so she landed against Terrio.

Carrie got the woman first and then, leaning forward so she wouldn't faint, she splattered Bowse's shoes with vomit.

"Get her a towel," Bowse said as Carrie pressed her face to her knees to stop the room from spinning. The last thing she remembered was a silent prayer.

Thank You, God, for morning sickness.

Tuesday late afternoon

"I was fifteen." Melanie's voice was hoarse from crying on the bench. The weeping continued in the solo session with Beth. The pain that had been a trickle since she was fifteen was now a flood.

"And your parents?"

"They trusted me to conduct myself like a good Christian daughter and a savvy Fallon operative. I was mature and yet entirely unprepared to be attracted to a man more than twice my age. Carl did little things like write me silly notes or bring me cookies. Not from a supermarket, mind you. He'd go a mile out of his way to get me whoopee pies from my favorite bakery in Nashville.

"When Carl joined the campaign, he was new and exciting and charismatic and he told me I was beautiful. Not pretty. Not cute.

Beautiful. And I realized he didn't see me as the Fallon protégé. He saw me as an equal. So I began dressing differently. Instead of jeans and T-shirts, I wore tops a little too tight and skirts a little shorter so he had to notice my womanly body. Momma said something to me but I ignored her and she got busy and forgot she had told me to stop dressing like a slut."

"Is that the word she used?" Beth asked. "Slut?"

"No. She probably told me not to dress so blatantly or inappropriately. *Slut* is the word emblazoned in my history. Because that's what I became."

"When was the first time he touched you," Beth said, "in an unambiguously sexual way? Beyond what you just told me."

"He didn't touch me. I touched him. I had to get something out of the storeroom. Carl was in there going through boxes of files on the top shelves. Mind you, this was before computers were on every desk. Bobby Joe's files were the 1970s version of Google. I went in and saw Carl perched on the ladder. His knees were at eye level to me. The way his calf muscle strained against the fabric of his pants—I just had to touch it.

"He smiled, said 'hey,' and kept looking. And I kept my fingers on his leg and pressed my palm to his calf. He slid down two steps and stared at me and I kept my hand on him. Touching his thigh now. And it felt so strong and he gazed at me like spring honey melting in the sun. That made me bold, so I . . . well, then the door opened. I jumped back and he said 'hey' to whomever it was who entered."

"And after that?" Beth said.

"There were opportunities to be alone if you really wanted to be and your parents weren't vigilant. It's staggering how easy it was for me to make happen."

"You made the arrangements?"

"Are you deaf?" Melanie said, struggling to breathe. It felt like she had ripped her own ribs open. "*I* was the seducer. Not Carl. *Me.* Melanie Fallon, the girl who couldn't open her blouse fast enough and do everything else that comes after. I did it. I did it and found what I thought was heaven and then he left. Carl left the campaign without a note or a kiss good-bye. He just left and I knew it was my fault. That I wasn't good enough to keep him.

"I had to prove to myself that I could be good enough. I knew what to do. I'm not so emotionally stunted that I don't know why I kept throwing myself at men. Ironically, Will is the *only* guy I didn't try to seduce. That electricity—that intensity was so powerful and unique in a guy still in his teen years. I was afraid that I'd either get fried by it or short him out. He had no idea how much I wanted to climb under his shirt.

"When he went to college, I almost bought a plane ticket to Boston. But I was afraid he would say no and I'd be humiliated. And there were plenty of guys close to home. Young guys who worked the campaigns or interned in Bobby Joe's office. One-night stands in college or at certain events. I knew which venues had coatrooms that would lock, or conference rooms off of dark halls. Can you imagine that?"

Beth nodded. "I can. You are not unique in this, Melanie. I have clients tell me similar versions. Different places, different circumstances, but the same feeling of guilt. Did Will know your history when you reconnected?"

"I told him I had lost my virginity. I've never told him how prodigious my activities were. I think he knows, don't you? I ran hot and cold early in our marriage, but the *hot* was so beyond anything he could have imagined that I must have scared him. When he had an out to go to DC, he took it."

"Really?" Beth said. "You scared him? Might you have scared yourself?"

"Yeah, I suppose. So much of what I did was when my father

was in office and the pickin's were ripe for an eager girl like me. I was terrified of going back into that. Or of putting my daughters in range of anything like that. Beth, I know my perspective is off. Warped, even. Hannah Dawson has lived in DC with her parents since she was born. And she's sweet and lovely and plenty safe."

"Do you see Sophie as any less?"

"No. But she's my daughter. My flesh and blood. I see how eager she is—how *alive* this experience has made her—and I hold my breath while I pray she doesn't do what I did."

Beth shifted in her seat, leaning forward. "Melanie, if a fifteen-year-old girl contacted Lord's Heritage and said she was having sex with a forty-year-old man, what would you do?"

"I'd get her in touch with a family therapist. Someone like you, I guess. Would you consider being one of our resources?"

Beth laughed. "That is such an obvious deflection, it's not worthy of you. Back to the question—what would your first assessment of the situation be?"

"That the girl was being molested."

"And you, Melanie? If *you* were the girl, what would your assessment be?"

"I know legally it was molestation and that emotionally or psychologically, the diagnosis is sexual abuse. But I know the part I played in it. And I know the barrage of escapades I let loose for six or seven years following that first thing with Carl. It was Will who saved me.

"Except . . . he didn't change me. I was still the same voracious girl. Like a keg of sexual dynamite that could detonate at any minute. When we were making love and it was so good, I was terrified that Will would loosen what I was holding back—what I was desperate for him never to see—and he would despise me. Like I despised myself."

Melanie pawed the tears out of her eyes so she could look

at Beth. "Do you see now who you're dealing with? Pretty ugly stuff."

"Melanie." Beth passed her a chunk of tissues. "When I look at you, I don't see a wild child, and I don't see your immature sexual escapades. I see a vibrant woman who has built a concrete wall around all of her sexual energies. A wall that not even her husband can break through. How long will you punish yourself for your premarital mistakes? And how long will you punish Will?"

"I never meant to punish him. I wanted to protect him. Protect him from me and my wickedness."

"A woman bursting with sexual energy is a blessing to a man, not a burden. I understand how your sexual energies scared you early on, before you knew how to control or channel them appropriately. But sexual energies oozing out in the wrong direction at the wrong time does not mean a young woman is wicked. Merely a fallen creature."

"I sure fell, didn't I? Fell for a man old enough to be my father."

"And he invited you to do so," Beth said. "He saw a vulnerability in you that your parents were too busy or too distracted to see. He exploited that vulnerability and was skillful enough—as abusers usually are—to make you think it was all your idea. You need to take a long look at that and see the little ways he groomed you, inched you along."

"What does that matter? Especially when it didn't stop there. It kept going and go—"

"Lanie, things are seldom black and white and I seldom make pronouncements. But I'm going to make one now, and I beg you to listen."

Melanie blew her nose. "I'm listening."

"What you experienced with Carl was sexual abuse—on his part, not yours. You were a child, and he was an adult. Even if you stripped naked and begged him to touch you, it was his responsibility to stop it. He didn't do that. He cultivated you with kindness and compliments and just enough off-center attention that you thought the contact was all your idea. The fun for people like him is getting their victims to initiate each step.

"You were only fifteen. That makes him guilty in the eyes of the law and guilty in the eyes of God. Perhaps, if we spend some time looking at him instead of you, you'll recognize and accept his guilt, and reject the shame you've been feeling all these years."

"Shame is exactly what I feel." Tears came freely now. "So much shame."

"I don't have to remind you what Jesus has done for you. How He died to remove all guilt and shame from us. You may believe that you have been damaged permanently. I wholeheartedly believe He can bind up every heart that has been crushed—even one like yours that has been crushed because of sexual abuse. Melanie, please tell me you're willing to work on this with me and with Will."

"Does he know that I . . ."

"Go ahead." Beth's voice was gentle. "It's good if you say it."

"Does he suspect that I . . . was abused?"

"We haven't discussed that. If he had broached the subject, I would have asked him to hold it so he could ask you, either alone or in session."

"What about you?"

"I suspected you might have been." Beth smiled. "There were indicators pointing to it."

"My helicoptering over my daughter?"

"Some of that is just good parenting. Don't beat yourself up for making reasonable decisions. What you might want to think about is how often you use the word *safe* and examine what undercurrents are running through your mind when that word comes up for you. Are you keeping your journal?"

"Yes. I still pretty much hate it."

Beth laughed. "That means it's effective."

"Where do we go from here?"

"We'll make a plan in your next session."

"And Will? What do I say to him?"

"Tell him what you told me."

After some more small talk, Beth walked her through the kitchen and out the side entrance. Like most therapists, she had different entrances and exits. Will sat on the steps.

"What are you doing here?" Melanie said.

"Will," Beth said. "This isn't appropriate."

"No, it's okay," Melanie said. "Go inside. I'm happy to see him. Go."

Beth nodded, went back inside.

Will stood, took her hands. "I saw something in your eyes when you talked about getting a dress. Something wasn't right. I checked your itinerary, saw personal time marked off, so I figured you'd be coming back to see Beth. I got lunch, answered emails, and thought I'd wait."

"Why?" Melanie said.

"In case . . . in case you needed me."

"I do need you." She stepped into his arms and stood there. Perfectly still and perfectly at peace until her toes got so cold she couldn't feel them.

twenty-one

Tuesday afternoon

"You didn't have to come," Carrie told Dave Dawson. The agents stood in the background, Bowse and Terrio stone-faced while their geek Ridley poked at a tablet.

Dave grinned, brushed her hair from her face. "I was the closest doc so Jason called me. Your blood pressure is coming back up. How do you feel?"

"Furious." She swung her legs off the sofa, thought about standing but didn't want to risk another spell of light-headedness. "They said I had a high threat matrix. I have no idea what they're talking about. Hey, you!"

No one blinked.

"I'm talking to you, agents! Do I need a lawyer?" Carrie said. "Or are you going to black-site me?"

Dave laughed. "She's feeling better. That said, Ms. Connors is not going to speak to you without a lawyer."

Terrio sat in the desk chair, lowered it to fit her height. "Senator, you can sit in on the interview if you'd like."

Carrie grabbed his wrist. "You don't have to. You've got . . . I forgot what event you're supposed to be at."

"It doesn't matter," he said. "We'll do this together."

Terrio launched into a batch of questions. Carrie said yes to all the background information. The feds would know all this anyway. She poised herself at the edge of the sofa, sitting as straight as she could. Dave relaxed next to her, arms behind his head. That was one of his most endearing and inspiring qualities—the world could be ending, Will and Carrie could be trying to stop endless disasters, and still Dave would keep a cool head.

"We've established that I am who I am—for better or worse," Carrie said. "Can we de-establish the idea that I'm part of your threat matrix?"

Dave held up one hand. "Before we get into your concerns, Agent Terrio and Agent Bowse, perhaps you could explain what the threat is?"

Terrio glanced up at Bowse. He nodded and she began.

"I don't need to tell you the sophistication of the attack that got into the Health and Human Services servers and released those medical records. A release of all might have been preferable to the specific theft of records related to the various presidential campaigns."

"Showing off," Carrie said. "Just like the stunt in the arena."

"It was an in-your-face to all of us in government," Dave said. "Most of us would rather have had our IRS data released than the most intimate—and guarded—details of our lives."

"Our tech people squashed that quickly," Terrio said with a nod to Garrett Ridley. "And it's not that we had a vulnerability in our systems. We have strong protection. What we're seeing is legacy 'worms' that were planted in the past, maybe even during software development. We're talking five, six years ago."

"That would require a conspiracy," Dave said.

"Immense," Ridley said. "To anticipate all this and then to selectively release records. Brilliant."

Carrie caught his grin. Chasing down cyberterrorists was like playing cowboy for a tech guy like him. "What do they want?"

Bowse sat on the edge of the coffee table. "It's not necessarily what they *want*. Globally, hackers have gotten into banks and drained funds, disabled governmental websites, crashed personal computers. The salient question is, what can they *do*? We're very concerned that our infrastructure is at stake. Taking over communications networks—even for a few minutes—is worrisome."

"Worrisome?" Carrie said. "It's a disaster."

"If they can get into utility control systems," Dave said, "they could release too much water at the Hoover Dam or turn the lights out in Chicago. If they got into transportation controls, they could fiddle with stoplights in Los Angeles or train-switching software and cause a horrific loss of life." He looked at Ridley. "Surely we're protected."

"From outside threats," Ridley said. "Unfortunately, we scour our software and still miss little back doors that these hackers use to get in."

"I don't care what you say," Carrie said. "The key question has to be what do they *want*?"

"We've received demands," Bowse said. "Most—probably all—are homegrown hackers trying to cash in on the medical records debacle. We don't have anything yet that we are taking seriously."

"Chaos," Terrio said, her voice deepening. "Chaos for chaos's sake."

"We don't know that," her associate said.

"We track national threats. We know those groups. We know the continuing war that China wages on our corporate servers and the Russian kids—in the pay of Moscow—wage on our financial networks. The NSA is kicking out too many whispers of anarchy for it not to become a shout. There's a philosophic string in cyberspace that advocates dismantling this government in one fell swoop to see what rushes in to take its place."

"I don't understand," Carrie said.

"It's the darkest part of the human heart," Dave said. "Tearing down authority."

"I have nothing to do with this." She clutched Dave's hand. "You know me—this is against everything I believe."

"I know that," Dave said, and then turned to Agent Terrio. "Can we get to why you're . . . detaining . . . Ms. Connors? We've got work to do and we wouldn't want to think that the FBI and Secret Service are slowing down our campaign."

"Fine." Terrio rolled her chair closer. "Senator, we need you to leave now."

"No." Dave folded his arms across his chest. "I'm on the Senate Intelligence Committee. Ms. Connors and I have secret clearances. So let's hear what you've got."

"Ms. Connors?"

"Yes," she said. "I want him to stay. So tell me about this highest-threat spiderweb I got caught in."

Ridley paced the room, throwing off technical terms that no one else seemed to understand. Bowse let him go a full two minutes before putting up his hand.

"The fact that volunteers' records were released indicated someone was onsite—with all the campaigns."

"Even the vice president's organization?"

Bowse nodded grimly. "Yes. So we ran an algorithm that matched people with high-level technical experience with street activists."

No. They can't know about a simple kiss or two.

"Ms. Connors connects with two people who fit the technical side. Her college friend, now embedded in the campaign media, Tucker Reynolds Keyes."

"Don't mess with the Keyes family," Dave said. "Not unless you're sure."

"They're not sure of anything," Carrie said, "if they're

throwing Tuck's name around. He barely has enough ambition to tie his shoes in the morning. He wouldn't be involved in anything like this."

"His psychological profile shows him as disaffected," Terrio said. "That's prime breeding ground for anarchists."

"Who's the other technical person?" Dave asked.

"Ms. Connors's roommate at the hotel. Victoria Peters."

Carrie laughed. "You're kidding, right? She's *so* establishment."

"We're just investigating opportunity right now," Bowse said. "She's got the comp-sci degree from MIT. So why is she a low-level functionary?"

"That woman wants my job, for Pete's sake. And she wants my brother."

"Shush," Dave said.

"Hold on a minute," Carrie said. "Victoria has a communications degree. Not comp-sci."

"Is that what she told you?" Terrio said.

"Give me my phone."

Bowse handed it to her. Carrie scrolled to the campaign's HR file, brought up Victoria's résumé, and showed it to Bowse. It listed Communications as Victoria's major, with a minor in Marketing Technology.

"Interesting," the agent said. "We went directly to MIT and saw the transcripts."

"Good grief," Dave said, "do we have any privacy at all?"

"You voted to renew the Patriot Act, Senator," Terrio said. "So we have these kinds of resources when we need them. Surely you can see why our profiling software kicked out Ms. Peters as a possible nexus. Ms. Peters has got a ton of programming, network design, all that stuff."

"And now we know she lied on her résumé," Bowse said.

"You said something about street activist?" Dave said.

"Ms. Connors is"—Terrio cleared her throat—"seeing the leader of Manchester MoveIn. A Michael Jared O'Dea?"

"Carrie?"

"It's nothing," she said. "He did a favor for Sophie and Dillon. That's it."

Ridley handed Terrio his tablet. She turned it to them, showing a photograph of Carrie and Jared kissing.

Carrie pressed her face to her knees. The feds must have insiders working MoveIn. To think someone saw her and Jared kissing and turned it into a national security threat was insane.

"You're seeing shadows where there are none." Dave grasped Carrie's elbow and helped her stand. "If you have real evidence, we'd be happy to hear it. Until then, we're done."

Bowse blocked the door. "We're not leaving," he said.

"We are," Dave said. "Now, are you getting out of the way or do I need to call my security man and tell him we've been unlawfully detained?"

"Better yet, I'll call Tucker Keyes," Carrie said, "and get this onto the front page of *The Journal*."

The agent opened the door. Dave and Carrie went out into the hall.

"This is real," Bowse said. "Be careful, Senator."

Jason stepped between Bowse and Dave and stood his ground until Dave and Carrie reached the stairs.

"You okay to go down?" Dave asked.

"I'm fine," she said. "And you are so my hero."

Two flights down, she had to stop and let her blood pressure catch up to her.

"Carrie," Dave said. "Is Michael Jared O'Dea the father of your baby?"

Tuesday evening

"You're enjoying this," Tuck said.

His grandfather flashed an impish smile. "Immensely. For years Huggable Hal has been insulated from any criticism by his pals in the media. It's about time someone exposed him."

He handed the iPod back to Tuck, holding it by a corner as if it were a soiled handkerchief. "Let me see the affidavits."

Tuck shuffled through his bag, brought out the paperwork. *The Journal*'s legal team and the leaker's lawyer had met extensively, made sure every jot and tittle was nailed down.

J.L. pawed through the pages. "Are you sure, Tucker? You need to be positive that the Dawson people aren't using you."

"They are using me. And I'm using them."

His grandfather pointed a crooked finger at him. "The Dawson people may be clean-cut Bible people but they *are* politicians. Don't ever doubt that under the skin, they're all the same."

"It's a win-win."

"Maybe. The one variable in this is you. You and that woman you moon over. I trust you to keep the drugs and booze out of this—"

"I'm not using anything." Tuck felt a flicker of guilt. Okay, so he had a beer before bed. At least he wasn't bar-hopping and woman-shopping anymore.

"You've been after that Connors woman for years."

"Not really."

"Not really?" His grandfather laughed with the barrel-toned wheeze that had been memorialized at several White House Correspondents' Dinners and *Saturday Night Live* shows. "What assurance do I have that she isn't pulling something deeper with this stunt? Something that will embarrass *The Journal* or us. I won't be disgraced, Tucker. Not now."

Tuck sighed. "I had a tech expert examine the video. He confirmed it's not doctored. And I paid for a security sweep to ensure the leaker is who he says he is. I could have done it myself, but I didn't want to get any fingerprints in the system."

J.L. dropped his chin so he could peer through the top of his trifocals. "Whatever are you talking about? Did you hire a private investigator?"

"Of a sort. I had a cybersnoop scan their email and texts for anything that would undercut the veracity of this video."

His grandfather rubbed his scalp hard enough to create a dandruff storm. "You can't do that kind of thing! Not with this Jericho group moving at will through these computer systems. You probably left a trail the size of an eight-lane highway."

"No, sir. I did not. I know people from school who are into that kind of thing and are the experts that other experts call. It turns out the Dawson people have great security in their Tennessee office where they're handling all the donations. In their Manchester field office, the firewalls are pitiful. And too many of them have been lazy, using the hotel's wireless rather than the dedicated broadband. Quite careless, really. I could have hacked into their accounts in my sleep."

"You didn't. That's what you said."

Tuck grinned. "You taught me never to get my own hands dirty. Instead, I paid cash and took the report in person, in a very public and noisy place. Because who knows where the NSA is lurking?"

"Are we secure here?" His grandfather glanced at the windows. The Capitol's lights gleamed like jewels.

No. Not that he'd tell the old man that, especially since he hacked into *The Journal Online* so he could protect sources and the like from his competitors on staff. Amazing to think he was doing a good enough job that he was a threat to other political reporters. Those snobs used to view him as a joke.

Now that he had another notch in his belt, would it soothe that familiar emptiness? Probably not. If he kept digging, investigating, and listening, maybe he'd see a way out. Or, as Dave Dawson and his crew might say—the *way*.

"Technology evolves constantly and security always hustles to keep up," Tuck said. "I'll take another look at where we are, what needs to be improved."

"You think I'm a relic." J.L. held up his hand. "Don't deny it, Tucker. I would think less of you if you didn't understand that I am way past my expiration point. I just . . . gaze at the world and think, where did the human touch go? Working sources, building trust, understanding where and *why* the bodies are buried.

"Your generation believes entirely and unreservedly in words and images that float through the air or buzz along the wires. Surely you see how hard it is for old-timers like me to trust what can't be seen or held or tasted. And yet, you and your contemporaries don't blink at embracing the virtual as more real than what can be smelled or heard or witnessed. You young people have eschewed faith in anything divine for hope in something as ephemeral as a bit or byte."

"Grandfather, it's all just tools. It's no different than going from film to digital recording."

"Perhaps." J.L. shook his head. "These past twenty years have convinced me of my own irrelevance."

"Don't say that." Tuck flushed to think he had thought—and too often said—the very same thing. "It's not all . . . you know."

"Not all about the Pulitzer." J.L. picked up his pen, fiddled with it. "What did your investigator find?"

"It's about what wasn't found. No emails or any references to the leaker by name or inference, or any link between Sanders and 'joking' or 'offensive' or the like. There was considerable angst in Dawson's inner circle regarding the Bowers/Todd attempted extortion, which said to me that the staffers weren't shy about using these email accounts."

"How do you know these communications weren't sanitized?"

"There were some . . . dismissive references to me and my inexperience."

"And your man was thorough?"

Tuck laughed. "Actually, my 'man' is a woman. Yes, she knows her stuff. She searched everything and scoured any trace of that search. So careless—there was only one staff member whose email was tightly protected, some lower-level assistant to Will Connors. They need to transfer that woman to their IT department. The ease with which they got into even the senator's emails was pathetic."

J.L. smiled. "Any dirt on Dark Ages Dave?"

"No, sir. I mean, I don't know because I programmed the search myself and instructed my friend to run it. I tried to maintain some integrity."

"Reading others' emails is integrity?"

"Oh, come on," Tuck said. "You never paid for information?"

"Of course I did. I just didn't break and enter to get it."

"Consider this a firewall for *The Journal*. Insurance that they weren't playing me. We don't want the paper to be embarrassed."

"Or worse," his grandfather said, punctuating his words with a firm fist to his desktop. "We don't want *The Journal* to be wrong. If I leave you with anything, remember that."

"That we need to get the truth."

J.L. pressed his palms on the desk and slowly stood up. "That you need to recognize the truth when you see it, Tucker."

Tuesday evening

Carrie and Dave stopped in the stairwell, the question about Jared hanging heavy between them. The senator had sent Jason Polke to pick up the car.

"So, why did you ask that?" she said. "About Jared O'Dea."

"Morning sickness is not easy to hide from a physician," he said. "And you've got a grand case of it."

"Senator, I—"

He held up his hand. "I'm Dave right now. When we get back to the work, I'll be the senator again. Hey . . . remember when you and Destiny used to call me Uncle D? Miranda and I didn't have a clue about kids and Will would drop the two of you off for an overnight. The next day we couldn't even find the energy to fry an egg so we'd have to point you toward the cold cereal. That time when you were, what . . . eight? Destiny decided to paint a mural in our powder room and you provided a defense that would have been worthy of Alan Dershowitz."

Carrie laughed. "Imagine if Dez had stayed in Tennessee instead of scurrying out to Hollywood. The two of us would either have you in the White House now or at a rehab center for a long, long rest."

Dave smiled, holding her gaze.

He's so good at being the stable center, not wilting under anything. "We'd better get back before they send the feds to look for us."

"In a minute. Caroline, I'm not going to say much about this. Just two things. The first is that you will always be special to me and Miranda. That is without reservation. You're family and always will be."

"I know." She fought tears. "And the second thing?"

"Consider how important Destiny is to Will and Melanie,

how important she has been to you. Think what could have been if her birth mother had made a different choice. And remember how blessed we all are because of the choice Julia Whittaker did make."

Carrie wanted to slap him. Not because she was offended but because she was touched by his gentle tone and by the truth of what he was saying.

"Two things, Senator." Carrie pinched the palm of her hand, trying to muster a cold detachment. "The first is that Jared O'Dea and I are friends. It's an odd friendship, to be sure, but it's nothing that compromises either national security or this campaign."

"Okay." Dave's expression didn't change. "And the second?"

"I appreciate that you rescued me from the agents and their pet nerd. But we are not in a doctor-patient relationship—"

"Of course not," Dave said. "Though I hope you're glad they called me to help."

"Sure. Of course I am." Carrie twisted her skin so hard she almost gasped. She couldn't give in to the sudden desire to want to cry on a sympathetic shoulder. Not with the feds and this pregnancy and the Sanders video bearing down on her. "Dave . . . Senator. It is in your best interest that I remind you that federal law prohibits us from having a conversation about a pregnancy, imagined or otherwise."

"I'm sorry. I am not prying. I'm just . . . Dave right now."

"No." She opened the door and took one step into the hallway. "You are Senator David Dawson, you are a presidential candidate, you are the best man for the job, and nothing—personal or otherwise—is going to get in my way to help you get there."

"If you need anything . . ."

"I need you to get back to the Radisson before Will comes storming after both of us. I have to stop at my room for a few minutes and freshen up."

Dave gave her a ready-for-the-camera smile. She knew him well enough to see the sadness in his eyes. "Let's pray right now," he said.

Carrie took his hands and bowed her head, his prayer for their safety and their work and her well-being and God's glory making her want to go to her knees and weep. No time for emotion. *Dear God, can't You see that this is the man our country needs in office?*

Dave said "amen" and kissed her forehead. They went through the lobby and outside where Jason had the car waiting for them.

The ride back to the Radisson was silent.

Carrie tried to clear her head. Should she call Jared and warn him about Terrio's and Bowse's questions? He couldn't possibly be involved with Jericho. She was superb at reading people. She would know if he was anything other than a bleeding-heart, sweet-tempered, too-sexy protest leader.

Think. What about the other options? Tuck made no sense as a Jericho sympathizer. Beltway friends who traveled in his circles always had the same assessment. Good guy who was too shallow in college and too addicted to the good life to be taken seriously, and wasn't that a shame?

Victoria Peters couldn't be the mole. No way she would bite the hand—Will's—that she was trying to get to feed her.

This threat-matrix talk was ridiculous. If there was someone inside, it had to be one of the volunteers. Any one of the folks who had been there from the day they opened the call center could easily have provided a list of names to someone in Jericho.

How hard would it be to backtrack names to get to addresses? Carrie suspected first and last name would be suitable to drill into the health records and release enough information to cause a panic. In the case of generic names like Art Smith or Mary White—two of her favorite volunteers—perhaps they weren't even part of the hacked records. Carrie had checked all Manchester staff and the interns before the feds cracked down. She could have downloaded all the records but even she wouldn't risk that kind of federal crime.

What a mess.

The government had vouched for the security of everyone's health records and had failed miserably. Who knew if their encryption was as stout as they claimed? Maybe Jericho was a group of teenagers living in their mothers' basements and stocking up on Twinkies and delusions of power.

And maybe Jericho was a major international enemy playing cat-and-mouse with the mighty United States of America.

Carrie slowly climbed the stairs. A hot bath was in order before going back to work. She felt like garbage.

If she couldn't take the physical stress now, how could she carry a baby to term? No way would she sit on the sidelines. Will needed her, Dave needed Will, and the country needed Dave. It was simple, straightforward logic.

It would be over on Monday. Until then, she would allow no time for emotion.

twenty-two

Thursday afternoon

BETH KICKED HER SHOES OFF AND PLOPPED INTO the leather armchair. She wore red socks with candy canes.

Melanie burst into tears. If only joy could be so easy as festive socks.

"You didn't tell him," Beth said. "I can see it on your face. Am I right?"

"I don't know how."

"Just like you told me."

"I can't. I mean, I accept intellectually that Carl was the predator and I was the victim. But I don't know how to go from mind to heart. Not on this."

"That's because your abuser worked on both your heart and mind," Beth said. "Remember when we talked about punishing the wrong people?"

"You said that instead of punishing my adult abuser—who knew better than to touch a child—I've been punishing Will. That I withhold intimacy out of fear." Melanie took a long breath, pain stabbing her ribs as if the emotion was steel and not ingrained habit. "I've been punishing Sophie, trying to lock her under my watchful eye."

Beth straightened up in her chair, took Melanie's hand. "But most of all, you've been punishing the hurting little girl trapped inside this grown woman's body. That yoke of self-blame doesn't fit you anymore. Before you can stop punishing anyone else, you have to stop punishing yourself. It *has* to start with you."

"I don't see how that's possible." Melanie clutched the arms of her chair. *Don't run. Jesus, don't let me run from this.*

"Do you trust me?"

"I'm learning to. Yes. I do."

"Come sit in this chair."

Beth slid two chairs out from the table, motioned Melanie into one and placed the empty chair across from her.

"I want you to pretend that there's a fifteen-year-old girl sitting in that empty chair. The fifteen-year-old girl whom Carl told was so special and so mature. The girl who touched his leg and yearned to be held close by him because he was attractive and made her feel so special while her own daddy and momma were too busy to notice.

"Go ahead, Melanie. Yell at her. Scream at her. Tell her what a bad girl she is. How she brought this on. Go ahead!"

Melanie sat there, gasping for breath. She couldn't envision being that cruel to anyone.

So why had she been so cruel to *herself*? She had easily said these words before, over and over—*you were bad to do what you did and that's why he left*. She had said these words to the fifteen-year-old girl in the mirror.

And to the young woman who married a fine Christian man whom she didn't deserve.

And to the woman in the mirror at the Radisson who had to grit her teeth this morning to make herself leave the safety of a rented condo and come to see Beth Sierra.

Each time she looked in the mirror, year after year, Melanie

Connors pointed an accusing finger back to the teenage Melanie Fallon.

No more. Melanie shook her head. That innocent teenage girl was *not* to blame. Seduced into thinking she was the seducer when she was the victim all along.

"It's not her fault," Melanie said.

"If she's *not* to blame, then tell her," Beth said. "Let her know she doesn't have to wallow in guilt any longer. Help her stand back up again so she can move on with her life."

Silence. Only tears.

"If your tears could talk, Melanie, what would they say? Would they say that this girl *can't* move on, or that she deserves to be free from all this?"

"The latter . . . ," Melanie whispered. "She deserves to be free."

"Tell her, Lanie! Say it aloud!"

"What do I say?"

"You know what to say. You minister to families with children this age all the time."

Melanie closed her eyes and saw herself as a teenager. "You had no idea what kind of fire you were playing with, and you got burned . . . and I'm so sorry for how you've walked around so scarred and so scared all these years!"

"Tell her she's free," Beth whispered. "Tell her she's free to continue growing up . . . free to blossom sexually, without guilt or inhibition. Tell her it's okay to feel good and to make her husband feel good someday."

Melanie reached out to her inner child. "It's okay. You don't have to be a prisoner of shame. No more. It's time. We're doing this together. It's okay."

"Remind her that natural desires are a gift, not a curse. Give her permission to be her sexual self."

"Carl was a jerk," Melanie said. "We thought he was the

sun and moon and that we were just dirt so he left. We know better now. Right, Melanie Fallon? Just because you had a false start with Carl back then doesn't mean we can't love Will now. Passionately and completely, just the way God intended."

Melanie stood slowly and crossed to the empty chair. A journey of two steps and three decades. She sat in the chair and wrapped her arms around Melanie Fallon and all the Melanies who had come since. Comforting her. Reclaiming her. Scooping her up and bringing her where she belonged. She would no longer deny *herself*—nor her pain, nor her passion. They would all become cherished gifts.

"Thank You, Father," she whispered. "Thank you."

Thursday evening

"Maybe we should wait until tomorrow," Melanie said. What had seemed so clear in Beth's office now was a rock caught in her throat.

"No. I'm here now," Will said. "You said you needed to talk."

They sat on the bed, fully dressed, like two strangers on a city bus. Sophie was in her bedroom on the other side of the living area, a kid on campaign time who said she couldn't sleep until she had a piece of pizza and a handful of M&M's. Melanie's diet had been the same in the old days with Bobby Joe. With no cell phones or computers, she'd lie on her bed and relive every moment with Carl in her fevered mind.

What she had experienced with Carl was molestation. She had invited his attentions and, no matter what Beth said about taking the shame off her, it would take time to trudge through that morass.

I forgive you, Melanie Fallon.

Will shouldn't have to pay for any of that. Melanie knelt, untied Will's shoes.

"You don't need to do that," he said.

"You've had a long day." She rolled off his socks, then kneaded the arch of his right foot. Even the smallest muscles were tense. She massaged each foot in silence. Will leaned back on the bed, too weary to protest. An occasional "*mmm*" told her this was at least a portion of comfort.

When she finished, she kissed the tops of his feet and sat down next to him. He stretched out on the bed, arms wide and eyes closed. Melanie could walk away, and he would bear her leaving.

Or she could slip into those arms, and he would bear her staying.

She curled into his side, arm over his chest so she could hold him close. "We need to talk," she whispered.

"Before you say a word—" Will took her face in his hands. "Do you know I love you?"

"I'm learning it all over again. Do you know I love *you*?"

"You're here," he said. "Here in this moment. That tells me you do."

Melanie clutched his hands, forced herself to hold his stare. "I had another pregnancy. Eight years ago."

"I know. The medical records . . . we had to vet all of them while they were still public. Why did you keep it secret from me? And the whole tubal ligation . . . I just don't understand."

Her heart pounded. Because he hadn't said anything, she assumed the records had been secured before anyone read hers. "You were only home enough that year to get me pregnant. But not home enough so I could tell you face-to-face. And then a week before Christmas when I planned to surprise you with a new ornament on the tree—the bleeding started. It was quick, it was very sad, and I decided never to go through that again.

"Because I felt so alone."

"I am so sorry." Will laced his fingers with hers. "I chose Washington over you and Sophie, and I don't know how I'll ever apologize enough for that. And I'm no angel, Lanie. Not by a long shot."

Melanie tightened her arms around him. "We work through things. Starting tonight. Starting right now. We spend whatever days or months or even years it takes to shed the dead skin. If you want to."

"Of course I want to."

Will relaxed, and she held him. She had never trusted herself in his arms because she had been terrified that melding into him as God intended would set loose the girl who threw her body at a man in hopes of a crumb of affection.

None of that mattered now. None of it because Jesus is the one who tears the curtain. Jesus is the one who pours His grace on their embrace.

Will stirred in her arms. "Lanie."

She stroked his hair and said hush because she had more to say. She told her story in reverse chronological order. From the moment they married, Melanie was certain he would leave because that's what Carl did. Will was the first and only man with whom sexual intimacy was so much more than two bodies entwined. So she drew to a safer place—safer for *him*—and left him in the cold.

Melanie let her tears speak for a few minutes. Then she told Will what it had been like, this demeaning of herself with Carl, and how he had just left without a word. And how she still felt *she* was the seducer, but she trusted Beth now, and if Beth said it had been abuse, Melanie would sift through that.

"Lanie, I . . ."

"Hush," she said, and she unbuttoned his shirt because she felt a stirring.

She wanted Will. Her heart and now her body chose Will.

"Not yet," he whispered.

"Why not?"

"Lanie, I want you to be sure," Will said. "Sure that there is nothing more holding you back. So I'd like to give you the time you need."

"Don't make me wait too long," Melanie said.

He laughed, nuzzled her hair. "I won't. I promise."

—

Friday morning

Carrie had a bounce in her step as she left the pool bathroom. She had taken to vomiting there instead of in her room or the situation room. She didn't want any more questions from Victoria and certainly didn't dare risk Will noticing her persistent morning sickness.

Dave hadn't said another word about the *possible* pregnancy and hadn't told Miranda. Carrie would have seen it in her eyes.

She found it hard to look either of them in the eye. She watched the Dawsons interact with Hannah and Will and Melanie with Sophie. What would it be like to have someone with a total claim on her heart? Dave Dawson had earned her loyalty, her friendship, her hard work.

Watching the pride, joy, and worry in Will's and Melanie's eyes only made Carrie sicker. The scrap of cells in her womb was half her. The other half a lone traveler, a onetime visitor named Jeremy Wainwright. It felt like shame instead of pride, joy, and worry. Every few hours she'd think *what if*—what if she let the pregnancy continue? And then she'd get a wave of nausea or a bout of light-headedness and she would put that out of her mind.

No time for emotion. Focus.

This morning's poll numbers showed that Dave had not only survived the Paige Bowers thing but picked up some momentum. The senior staff would meet in a few minutes to confirm strategy for next week. Who did they need to visit? What issues did they need to bring forward? Where could they chip away at Sheryl Bresler?

Sanders was a nonissue. The governor was still at the top of the polls, but Monday he'd fall. Imagine—Tucker Keyes taking down a party's front-runner.

Carrie's throat clenched. So much for a bounce in her step.

She hadn't told Will or Dave that she had passed Tucker the iPod. As far as Dave was concerned, the plan was to meet with Sanders right before Christmas and gently nudge him out of the race.

If she told them, they'd make her take the story back from *The Journal*. Not that she could. It was a done deed, scheduled for Monday. Just like her procedure.

She met Sophie and Hannah coming in through the lobby. They had been promoted this morning and would now act as her assistants. Their cheeks shone with the new responsibilities.

Even so, they had not been relieved of pizza duty. And suddenly Carrie was ravenous.

"Hey, guys," Carrie said. "Hope you got the order right this time."

"Don't abuse the free labor," Sophie said.

The two girls balanced pizza boxes and grocery bags filled with soda and snack cakes as they waited for the elevator. Their chatter was rapid-fire, almost incomprehensible—even to Carrie. How amazing that the girls understood each other perfectly.

"Oh no," Sophie said. "Mom's here."

Hannah turned and said, "Hi, Mrs. Melanie."

"Busy day, ladies?" Melanie smiled warmly.

"The best," Sophie said. "Mike said the senator got a bump in the polls."

Melanie winced. *What was that about?* Carrie wondered. Was her sister-in-law hoping for Dave to have to bow out so things could go back to her version of normal?

"Don't get too close to Mike," Melanie said.

"Huh?" Sophie glanced at Carrie, eyebrows raised.

"I'm sorry," Carrie said. "What does that mean?"

"It's not proper," Melanie said, "for a man his age to hug girls their age."

"They know that. I trained them myself in campaign etiquette."

The elevator binged, then opened.

Hannah glanced at the floor. Sophie's face reddened. She opened her mouth, shook her head, and grabbed Hannah's arm. "Take the soda upstairs," Sophie said. "It's getting warm."

"The pizza's getting cold," Hannah said.

"Just go on up. I'll be right there."

Hannah stepped by Melanie, mumbled a quick "Excuse me," and went into the elevator.

Sophie stared at her mother. "What is your problem?"

"Honey, I just want to remind you that there are boundaries that protect you from folks older than you. Like Mike."

Good grief, Carrie should have gotten on the elevator with Hannah. And she would have, if Sophie hadn't been clutching her arm.

"Why do you think everyone is so . . . so dirty?" Sophie said.

"Don't get dramatic," Melanie said. "Just remember that things move fast in this environment."

Carrie cringed at her sister-in-law's tone. She was delivering common sense with a huge helping of panic. No wonder Sophie didn't buy it.

"Is that what I am to you, Mom? A thing? Something to be

set on a shelf somewhere and dusted once a week?" Sophie shifted her armful of pizza boxes, grimaced.

"Let me take those," Carrie said. "They must be hot."

"Tell my mother to leave me be. And tell her to stop saying mean things about people."

"I'm not saying mean things," Melanie said, but Sophie was already in the other elevator, pushing the buttons with her elbow. The door closed before Melanie could follow.

"What was that about?" Carrie said. "Mike's just . . . like everyone else. We're close. We hug. I hug Sophie all the time."

"Because she's family. And that's why, Caroline, some of this is on you."

"Some of what? Are you saying Mike is . . . no, you're just being paranoid." Carrie couldn't envision anyone messing around with the girls. Maybe some of the younger college guys—the mild flirtations were normal. And it didn't go beyond that. She had made the guidelines doubly clear to them. Everyone was too busy.

Then again, she had managed to get pregnant in the middle of all this busyness. The thought of Sophie and some guy—especially an older man—made her nauseated all over again.

"What I'm saying is that Will is too caught up in everything," Melanie said, "to keep a clear eye out for her. I know Sophie sees me as a gargoyle perched in angry watch over her happiness. But she's a child. Don't forget that she's just a child."

People were moving through the lobby, heading to the main desk or the valet station. Someone could hear Melanie's imaginary dirty laundry and fling it at Dave. Carrie grabbed Melanie's arm. "Let's take this upstairs before someone hears you."

"*You* hear me, Caroline. It makes me nervous to have Sophie in this environment. I have good reason for that."

"Really?" Carrie whispered. "What is it? Oh, wait—you're

the mother and you know everything and the rest of us don't know a thing."

"That's right. I'm the mother, and I'm so glad you are not." Melanie ripped away from Carrie. "You'd make a terrible mother."

Melanie stomped into the stairwell, leaving Carrie among the ashes of what had been a good morning.

Was Carrie blind to Sophie's welfare? She thought she'd done a good job, teaching her the ropes, giving her more and more responsibility. Either Melanie was doing her usual helicoptering—or Carrie was too self-focused to see what might be in front of her.

Her sister-in-law was right about one thing. Carrie would make a terrible mother.

That clinched the deal.

Third Week of December

Presidential Primary Season

twenty-three

Monday before dawn

"I SWEAR, PEANUT. I DIDN'T WANT TO HAVE TO BRING you," Carrie said. "They won't let me do this unless I have a licensed driver with me."

"Yeah. Whatever." Sophie leaned her face against the glass. She had slept in Carrie's room last night so they could make this 6 a.m. appointment in Somerville. The sun was still over an hour from breaking the horizon. In Boston traffic, four miles could take an hour. She had built that into her schedule. If they arrived early, they could sit in the car.

"All you have to do is come in with me, show them your license, and then you can wait in the car," Carrie said. "Sleep. Or text your friends."

"At this hour of the morning? I don't think so. Why couldn't we do this at . . . a reasonable hour?"

Carrie was in no mood to explain fasting to her niece. Plus, early morning meant more cover from curious eyes.

Will and Melanie were booked solid through lunch. Donor meeting, the schedule said. Counseling—Dave and Miranda knew, Carrie knew, and no one else. At least, no one else spoke it aloud.

Sophie straightened in her seat. "Carrie, you don't have to do this."

"We'll be back in New Hampshire before you know it. Way before lunch."

Her niece clutched her arm. "Will there be protestors?"

"It's Massachusetts. The bluest of blue states. They're more likely to have people outside with signs that say 'God bless abortion providers.' "

"That is so sad." Sophie slumped back into her seat. "How far along is this baby?"

"Not far along enough to call it a baby. It's still a bundle of cells."

"You have to be honest with me, Carrie. Or I won't do this."

"Fine. Seven to eight weeks."

"Shoot. That's when the baby begins to differentiate fingers and stuff."

The girl didn't know how to tip in a restaurant but she knew every second of fetal development. She was definitely Melanie Connors's offspring.

"Do you think this is easy for me?" Carrie said.

"Easier for you than the baby."

"You owe me this, Soph. I've been fighting for you since September. Getting you access to all areas of the campaign. Training you. Helping you and Dillon do your thing. If it wasn't for me, your dad would have had to send you home. I was there for you, every day. I'm just asking you to be here for me."

"I'm here for you. I'm just not happy about it."

I'm not either, she wanted to say. Why bring Sophie into her sadness? She had to make this procedure as incidental as popular culture said it was so Sophie wouldn't freak and Carrie wouldn't wilt from shame.

Up ahead—the exit for Somerville. Carrie inched into the right-hand lane, using her blond hair and best smile to get a male driver to relent. The exit ramp was packed solid from a stoplight. It would probably take three cycles before they got to the service road.

"That's what life is about. We make compromises, we work things out, and we're often not *happy* about it. We prove our loyalty by swallowing our own happiness. Do you understand that, Sophie?"

"Did you at least tell the father?" Sophie asked.

"What father? There is no father."

Sophie laughed. "I may be naïve but you're not going to convince me that this is a virgin birth."

Birth. No, Carrie couldn't even think about that word. She probably should have told Jeremy Wainwright and made him drive her. She couldn't do that. He was a stranger. And she was ashamed, couldn't bear the thought of seeing him again.

This delay was Melanie's fault. She had persuaded Mike McGregor that switching Carrie for Victoria on the Iowa trip was essential. Clearly, she wanted Victoria to stay in New Hampshire so she couldn't barnacle onto Will in Iowa.

Carrie wasn't sure if anything was there or not. It was the type of question she and her brother did not ask. Maybe if she had asked him about his personal life, she wouldn't have had to pass that video to Tuck.

Today was the day that a man's world would explode. And she had provided the detonator. Blow up one man to save another. Not really Christian, but Carrie had given up trying to apply faith to politics. She trusted Dave and Miranda, followed their lead—unless family was imperiled.

"I'm praying for you," Sophie said. "Right now."

"Thanks." And she was grateful, given that she'd found it hard to look heavenward these last few weeks.

"Praying that you'll turn around."

"Sophie, cut it out." Carrie's head pounded. The crackers she had forced down with a Coke crawled up the back of her throat. This scrap of tissue in her uterus was a parasite, sucking the health out of her. She couldn't go another day with the morning sickness and fatigue and wearing compression socks to keep her blood pressure up.

"You can't stop me from praying."

"Oh, for Pete's sake, grow up. You claim to be an adult but you don't have a gnat of a notion how the world works. You should have gone out to visit Destiny in September instead of coming with us. Your sister is a realist. She knows how to make hard choices, stand on her own. You could have learned something from her. Since you insist on not learning a blessed thing from me."

"Really? Maybe we should ask Destiny what she'd do in this situation."

"Wake her up in the middle of the night Los Angeles time and she'll tell you a lot of things. Most of which will be directed at telling you to go to blazes without passing Go."

"Wanna bet?"

"I don't believe in betting."

"Because you know what she'll say."

"She'll say to mind your own business. And add some choice adjectives."

Sophie laughed. "That was the old Destiny. Now she's got Jesus—"

"Just shut up, will you? Shut up about Destiny and this thing I've got and Jesus and just . . . I'm begging you, Sophie. Please, my head is splitting."

Finally they got to the stoplight. It was red. No Turn on Red, the sign said. Carrie didn't care. She had to get to the clinic while she still had some semblance of control over Sophie. And some semblance of control over her own soul.

What was happening to her? She had pleaded, *Please, Jesus, please, Father, I need to duck out for a minute but I promise I'll be back.*

A curious peace surrounded her, even as the ground fog wrapped around the car and the rain drizzled and Sophie cried into a tissue.

I don't want Your peace, Jesus. In an hour or so. Not now, please not now.

Carrie pulled into traffic, plenty of room to make the right-hand turn because the oncoming traffic had sputtered, giving her an opening. Instead, she turned left—away from the clinic—and gunned the car forward.

An insane warmth flooded her. Every cell in her body seemed to be crying out "amen" to the whispers in that warmth. *I can take care of you. If you'd only let Me.*

She wiped her own tears away, swerved just a sliver into the wrong lane. She straightened the car and went faster so Sophie wouldn't jump out and abandon her. A police car pulled out from a parking lot, blue lights flashing. Her heart sank as the cop pointed at her and then pointed to the curb.

"It's God," Sophie said with a sniffle. "Telling you not to go."

"Really?" Carrie said, jamming on the brakes. "So where was He two months ago when the leaves were rustling and some guy I don't even know kissed me like he'd mean it forever and ever? Where was God then, telling me not to go?"

Sophie stared at her. Finally speechless.

"Yeah. That's what I thought," Carrie said and reached for her license.

Monday morning

NBC. Thirty Rockefeller Center. Tucker Reynolds Keyes, waiting to be interviewed by Matt Lauer.

It was hard to believe that a month ago Tuck had been a movie guy, in steady pursuit of nothing more than a good high and someone to share his bed.

This was a high—the breaking of national news. The game changer.

Tuck was about to live up to the Keyes name. He smiled at himself in the mirror and raised his hand in an imaginary toast to Caroline Connors. Like a finely aged bourbon, that's what this Sanders story was. He held it until it was perfect, dotted all the i's, crossed the t's, and vetted the man who had filmed the video.

Shane Ortiz was first-generation American. Of Mexican descent, he had worked for Hal Sanders for twelve years. Ortiz told Tuck he was "sick of Hal's ugly mouth," that he'd tried for years to raise the governor's consciousness about being culturally sensitive.

The irony of the situation was that the governor was colorblind enough to tell his racist jokes with Ortiz present. Though the number of women and minorities in his administration was impressive, that wouldn't save him. Not with a video made for Instagram and YouTube.

Tuck had roused his old computing skills to set the release for 8:18 a.m., during his appearance on NBC. The *Today Show* and *The Journal* would show the expletive-deleted video but he had rigged it so the world could see the governor in all his crude glory. By the time the car took Tuck over to FOX, the video would have made it around the world. And ruined Hal Sanders's breakfast.

Folks would think the "three men go into a bar" was pretty rank and might forgive Sanders that one. But the joke about the "retard with a lisp" would bring out all the interest groups. The governor would pull out of the race and go on an apology tour. Maybe he'd go into rehab. As if there actually was a rehab for bottom-feeding humor.

"It would have sunk him eventually," Ortiz had told Tuck. "He's been in power so long, thought he could insult anyone he wanted and have his team laugh. It's sad that most of us did."

Shane Ortiz had landed a job with a big investment firm that just *happened* to be a hefty contributor to Sheryl Bresler's campaign. The congresswoman was the typical financial conservative-social liberal who thought she could sweep up the Sanders voters and the independents if she won the nomination.

The Bresler camp had shuffled Ortiz and his cell phone video to the Dawson people—to Carrie Connors—so Sheryl Bresler could enjoy clean hands and righteous indignation.

Tuck had promised not to reveal any of his sources. Dawson would say, "We're praying for the family," and leave it at that. He'd make a show of respecting Sanders's privacy but there would be planted questions in his events to remind people of how almost squeaky clean the senator was.

Carrie and her people had timed this well to wash Dave Dawson's prostitute story into ancient history. Bresler's people would be caught by surprise and kicking themselves not to be in control of the release. Apparently Dawson and Bresler—through intermediaries—had made a gentlemen's agreement to force Sanders out without embarrassing him or the party.

Did Bresler's people, Will Connors, and Mike McGregor really think they'd *not* go to air with this? Or were they using Carrie as a pawn in this game? That would make Tuck a pawn, but he wouldn't go there. That spoiled the narrative he had built for his new career.

Where would Sanders supporters go? Bresler probably thought she had them sewn up. She had been solidly in second place in the polls. A chunk of them bristled at the congresswoman's acerbic nature and another chunk liked her feistiness.

Dawson would sweep in and grab them. That was J.L.'s

theory and, even in his dotage, his grandfather was keen on this kind of thing.

Rancic was a nonstarter. Carrie said he got into the race because he was bored. Sure, he had a vigorous intellect. No one actually liked the guy. He was best at writing laws and making policy and leaving the voters to candidates who actually had personalities.

Iowa and New Hampshire would become free-for-alls. Tuck was right in the middle of it all. It felt good. Almost healthy in a strange way, as if the sordidness of politics outflanked his personal shortcomings. Besides, Tuck had vowed to stop his drinking and partying. Get healthy. Lead a better life.

He'd cut way down on the pharmaceuticals already. By the time Thanksgiving rolled around, he'd been in psychological withdrawal. Fortunately, he had always eschewed the stuff that was physically addictive. Heroin, for sure, and he kept the coke way down. Wouldn't touch meth. The party favors were his preference.

He couldn't go cold turkey but he was close. And he'd stopped picking up chicks. They were there for the taking but it didn't seem right. Not with Carrie around.

Caroline Connors and Tucker Reynolds Keyes.

They were like sitcom stars who would eventually get together. Not too soon or the show would be over. Grandfather surely would approve of her, as would Mother. He and Carrie had a lot in common. Both raised in the Beltway with strong mothers and dead fathers, Tuck's from a reckless accident and Carrie's from heart disease. Each had substitute fathers. Tuck would have preferred an older brother like Will to a grandfather, but wow—who could possibly complain about being the scion of a legend?

What separated Tuck and Carrie was that he liked kicking back and she surged like a strong current. He admired her ambition and drive when it didn't intimidate him.

Stop it. Self-reflection was the purgatory of sobriety and the rocky road to self-doubt. He'd be on air shortly. This was his moment and he was going to shine.

The producer came into the green room to escort him onto the set. "By the way," she said, "your grandfather will be joining us from Washington."

Tuck stopped short. "What?"

"He knows Governor Sanders pretty well. He'll express his disappointment, and you'll lay out how you got the video."

"I'm not revealing my sources."

The producer waved her hand as if brushing away a fly. "Matt will ask for that but you know he doesn't mean it. It'll be a good opportunity to show your journalistic integrity. The video speaks for itself, though we've had to bleep the *bleep* out of it. What a potty mouth."

"I don't understand why J.L. has to join us," Tuck said. "This is my story."

She patted his arm. "We just wanted to inject some gravitas into the appearance. Who better than John Larter Keyes? You don't want to be seen as *TMZ* paparazzi, do you?"

"Of course not. But—"

"It'll be fine. You'll be great." She steered past the cameras. "The paired appearance makes for a good narrative. Your grandfather as the legend and you as the heir. He's the old way of pounding the beat and the typewriter keys. You're the new generation, fresh and good-looking and hip. It's pretty cool."

Cool? He was not cool, not one bit. This was his story—his scoop—so why did they think he needed his grandfather to present it?

Tuck needed a drink.

Monday morning

The police officer was broad shouldered, steely glared, and adamant. "I'm not arresting Ms. Connors," he had told Melanie on the phone. "She's dizzy and vomiting. I don't want her driving home, and your daughter is too young and unsettled to drive in Boston traffic."

Carrie sat in the backseat of the cop car, head in hands. When Melanie asked her what had happened, she just said, "Bad luck," and "I can take care of myself so go away."

Melanie was tempted to grab Sophie, head north, and leave Victoria to drive Carrie to Manchester. Sophie was white faced and red eyed, with nothing more to say than, "Carrie drove too fast in traffic," and "God protected us."

"Where were you going?" Melanie had asked.

"No clue, she just needed me to come with her, maybe to carry stuff or something."

Her voice quivered on the edge of a lie, and Melanie stopped. She didn't want to elicit perjury from her daughter. She and Will would get the story out of her tonight.

"Please take her to the condo," Melanie told Victoria. She glared at Sophie. "You stay there. No visitors—"

"Can't I go downstairs?" Sophie said. "I can help Dad."

You can help Mike McGregor. While he helps himself to you. Will might think she was unbalanced—okay, insane—but clearly, their daughter's judgment was shortsighted.

"No. You stay home until I get there." Melanie turned back to Victoria. "And you make sure you see her go inside."

Victoria took Melanie's keys, made sure Sophie was buckled in, and pulled out of the deli parking lot. She took the ramp onto Route 93 North. Midday traffic was light heading out of the city. They'd all be back in New Hampshire in an hour. Without rush hour clogging up the roads, Boston to New Hampshire was a quick forty-five miles north.

Carrie leaned against the police car, nodding as the state trooper lectured her.

Melanie started Carrie's car, held her hands over the heater. No warmth yet—it had taken almost two hours to get to Somerville with the inbound snarl of cars. Carrie's time was scheduled as a trip to Keane State, a college west of Manchester. A lie on the itinerary.

What did her sister-in-law need to hide?

Melanie brought up the last programmed address on the GPS. It didn't tell her anything beyond street name and number. She thumbed her phone to an online reverse phone book. When she typed in the address, it brought up Women's Wellness Center. She followed the link to the center's website and found the affiliation.

Planned Parenthood.

Oh God. Dear heavenly Father, not Sophie. Please, not Sophie.

Melanie phoned the number. The receptionist answered the phone. "Hi," Melanie said. "I'm calling for . . ." At the last second, she couldn't bring herself to say Sophie's name. "I'm calling for Caroline Connors."

"Yes?"

"She was scheduled for a procedure today, but she's been detained. Could you reschedule her, please?"

"Give me a minute," the receptionist said. Melanie heard the keyboard *tap-tap-tapping.* "Okay, I've got her canceled. Could you have her call me to reschedule? And please remind her that time is of the essence. My records show we've rescheduled her more than once."

"Sure. I'll let her know."

Her heart felt like lead. A member of the family would do this? And *dear God, oh dear God,* she dragged Sophie along?

Carrie got into the passenger side, slammed the door shut. The trooper touched the bill of his cap in greeting to Melanie. She waved, her arm like stone.

"Sorry to put you through all this," Carrie said. "I got light-headed, and Sophie panicked. I would have been totally fine to drive us both home."

Melanie couldn't find her voice. It took all her willpower just to nod.

"There's a cab stand across the street," Carrie said as she dug her phone out of her bag. "After he leaves, please let me off there. I'll take a cab to . . . wherever."

"There is no appointment. I canceled it."

"What?" Carrie turned to face her. "Sophie—"

"She didn't spill your secret. Though I plan to speak with her about misplaced loyalty. How could you, Caroline?"

"How could I what? Have sex? Oh, I forgot, Lanie. *You* don't remember how it's done."

"Don't deflect," Melanie said. "You know our position on abortion, Dave's position."

Carrie folded her arms across her chest. "This is not Dave's body. It's mine."

"What about the father?" Melanie said.

"There is no father. He's a guy I met in passing. Does that make you happy—I had a one-afternoon stand? That should make it even easier for you to write me off."

"What if her birth mother had aborted Destiny instead of giving her up? She's my heart, Carrie."

"She left home the minute she could. It's a wonder you finally got it together enough with my poor brother to have sex and make one of your own."

Carrie's low blow cut like a dull razor. "What Will and I do in our bedroom is none of your business."

"You mean, what you and Will *don't* do. Period." Carrie slapped the window. "Why doesn't that cop leave already?"

"How can you kill your child, Caroline?"

"How can you kill my brother?"

"What are you talking about?"

"I practically had to sell my soul to kill—yes, *kill*—a story about your precious husband. And you're the one who put him in that situation." Carrie opened her window, gulped in fresh air. "You're killing him. You realize that, don't you? When he needs a woman or a companion . . . when he needs a wife, and you're not there, it chips away at him."

"That's hyperbolic nonsense."

"You don't know the truth. You don't even have a clue."

"Are you talking about Will and Victoria?" Melanie said.

Carrie threw up her hands. "Like I said—no clue."

"Then give me a clue, Caroline. If you have something to say, then say it."

"You write these books that people purchase by the bushel and your readers and listeners think you've got it all figured out. Meanwhile, you and Sophie are shrink-wrapped in Nashville as if you'd never cut the umbilical cord. She's a good kid, but you want to keep her as your possession forever instead of letting her grow up in a healthy way."

The cold air from Carrie's window wrapped around Melanie like a cloak. She could smell diesel from the traffic, salt in the air because the harbors and piers were less than a mile away. And she could smell Carrie's anger as if it were a living beast.

Melanie was desperate to stay home, to view the world through an iPad or cable television. She wasn't agoraphobic; she was wise to the ways of this culture because she had been at the forefront of those ways and knew how sordid life could be.

How sordid *she* could be.

"What story did you sell your soul for?" Melanie said.

"Forget it. Just drive me down the block and I'll find my own way home."

"No. I'll get you home."

"Should I call that trooper over and tell him you're holding me against my will?"

"It's either me or jail." Melanie forced a smile. "Your choice."

Carrie leaned over the center console so she was almost in Melanie's face. "You, jail—what's the difference?"

"Shut up."

"Fine."

"What story did you get killed?"

"You said to shut up," Carrie said. "So I'll shut up."

"I want to know."

"No," Carrie said. "You don't. You really don't. I shouldn't have said anything. Trust me on this—you don't want to know."

"How can I trust you on anything now?" Melanie squeezed Carrie's forearm. "You tell me the story. Or I'll tell Dave and Will that you were on your way to an abortion clinic when the police stopped you. You think you'll be their golden girl then?"

"Get your bloody hand off me. There is no story."

"Tell me, Caroline, or I swear, I'll tell that cop that you held Sophie against her will. You want a slice of *real* life? Try sitting in a Boston jail overnight and then see if you don't want a little bit of shrink-wrap."

Carrie gave her an odd smile. "You really want to know?"

"I'm waiting."

"My brother is a good man. And you have tormented him with this sham of a marriage you've got him trapped in."

"He's not trapped into anything. We've got some things we're working out, and we're doing that because that is what adults do."

Carrie opened her door. "I'm getting out. If that cop stops me, I'll tell him I needed fresh air."

Melanie leaned over her and pulled the door shut. She clicked on the child-lock button on her left armrest. The locks engaged with a hard clunk.

"This is pathetic," Carrie said. "But *so* your modus operandi. Locking up Sophie, now me. No wonder Will . . ." She took a deep breath. "Forget it. Let's just get back to Manchester."

"No wonder Will—what?"

"Nothing."

Melanie dug her fingernails into Carrie's arm. "No wonder Will . . . ? Tell me."

"No wonder Will had himself a hooker problem."

"What?" All heat drained from Melanie.

"Paige Bowers confirmed Dave just asked for a ride home. But Will? Turns out he used her services, and more than once."

"Don't."

"You wanted the truth? You got it, sister. Paige Bowers told Tucker Keyes that your husband—the one you can't bother to live with—your husband had a relationship with her. And you know what she said about it? That Billy used her like a pressure valve."

"Shut up." Melanie pressed her hands to her ears. "Just shut up."

"She did what she could to help a lonely, stressed guy. How do you like that, Melanie? A hooker was a better wife to Will than you. And when he needed someone to defend him, I was there. Not you. I'm the one who stepped in and killed the story. And you didn't even have a clue."

Melanie covered her face, pressing her eyes shut. Like a baby, but nothing else would stop the tears. "How did you kill the story?"

"I bartered Tucker Keyes with a video of a drunk Hal Sanders spewing racist jokes. Foul, disgusting jokes. We were not going to expose it. Just use it to gently push Hal out of the race. But

I needed a bargaining chip to bury the Will story. *The Journal* is breaking the story and Tuck is giving interviews to network people. Right now, breaking news, Melanie."

"That can't be true. Dave wouldn't allow this."

"Dave doesn't know I gave it away," Carrie said. "Will doesn't either. We've had the video in our back pockets for a month now, waiting for a good time. I don't have the cold feet they have."

"Sanders will be destroyed when this goes public. He's got a family, Caroline."

"He's got a filthy mouth and he deserves whatever he gets. This is on you, Melanie. If you had either stepped up as a wife or divorced him, Will would be enjoying a healthy life right now. So stop pretending and just let him go."

Carrie reached across her and released the child lock. Then she got out, slamming the door so hard that the windows rattled.

twenty-four

Monday midday

Carrie took the commuter train from Boston to Lowell, a city about twenty-five miles south of Manchester. Jared O'Dea picked her up there.

"How did you know I had a car?" he said.

"All those propane tanks and five-gallon water bottles? You're not carrying them into camp in your backpack."

"And how did you know my phone number?"

"That night in the hotel with my drunk buddy. I got it then."

He still hadn't taken the car out of park. "Did I give it to you?"

Carrie grabbed his face and kissed him. He smelled musty and sweaty, tasted like chocolate.

Jared pulled away. "I'll take that as a 'No, you didn't give it to me, I took it.'"

"Do you need to get back?" Carrie swallowed, trying to keep her voice from breaking. "I mean, right away?"

"You know us MoveIn people. We don't *move* until midafternoon. And we've got nothing scheduled today while the steering committee tries to absorb this Sanders mess. Did you have something in mind?"

"A hike."

"Isn't it too cold?"

She smiled. "You live outside, remember."

"Where do you want to go?"

"There's a place in Hollis. Ten miles southwest of Manchester. When we first got started up here, I used to go there almost every day. Just to breathe clean air and get exercise. It's not a long hike, but it's a place where you can see the world without anything in the way."

"So what's going on?" Jared asked. "Why did you call me instead of your people?"

"I didn't want to get trapped in a car with any of them. Not today."

"I would think your people would be happy about this latest development with Governor Sanders."

"You would think. But someone had to do the dirty work so the candidate could have credible deniability."

"That's what stole the bloom from your cheeks. You're the leaker."

"It's more complicated than that. Mostly, I've got this . . . blood pressure thing going on. It drops, and I get woozy. I was on my way to Boston when I got mixed up on my turns. A cop saw me, wouldn't let me drive myself home."

He trailed his fingers down her cheek. "Are you okay or should we be going to an Urgent Care somewhere?"

She smiled. "You are my Urgent Care."

"Then tell me—what's really going on?"

He'd know in a couple months anyway. Assuming Dave or Will didn't kick her backside back to the Washington office. "I'm pregnant."

"Oh." Jared put the car in reverse. "We are *so* going for that hike."

Jared didn't say much on the way up Route 93, other than to

ask for directions. Every few miles he would squeeze her hand or touch her hair. Carrie wanted to ask about his family, his friends, if he'd ever been in love.

If he'd ever done something stupid.

Melanie had already told her *this* was stupid—this friendship or flirtation or whatever it was with the enemy. Her sister-in-law considered most of the world the enemy. Not that Carrie had the right to judge. She was standoffish as well, in her own sort of way. Drawing just close enough to make people think they knew her and liked her.

Freud would say it was because her father died when Carrie was young. Her brother had his own family and had to balance her needs with theirs. Her mother instilled in her the natural shields of being a political appointee.

If Melanie had only asked gently instead of jumping down her throat, Carrie could have asked her about what all of this meant and what she should do.

"Jared," she finally said. "Did the FBI come after you?"

He laughed. "Do you know how many times I've been grilled by police, FBI, even the ATF? I hold a sign, I talk to crowds, I hope for something better—and so I'm a suspect. It's okay, Carrie."

"I didn't tell them. They had a picture of us kissing. You've got a mole in the camp."

"I know. Doesn't matter—we don't have anything to do with Jericho. We don't get involved with wackos. It gains us nothing but contempt. Like your candidate."

"Dave Dawson is not a wacko."

"I know, I know. What I'm saying is that his opponents try to paint him into a corner so they can put the extremist label on him. He's pretty good at dodging those obvious ploys."

"Yes, he is. Can we count on your vote?"

Jared laughed. "I'm considering all my options."

Carrie loved being in the car with him. The cheap subcompact rental felt like a self-contained world where they could be warm and together without any of the shrapnel of politics tripping them up.

"What do you think about this Jericho thing?" she asked.

"I think it's very dangerous," Jared said. "Remember, I used to work in finance. I know how important those systems are to a healthy economy. And how devastated this country would be if a group of hackers took a bunch of them down at once."

"So you think it's hackers? The FBI asked about anarchists."

"The thing about anarchists," Jared said, "is that they're contrary to systems. I can't imagine that they could organize at this high level to do something as sophisticated as getting into the databanks and selectively releasing medical records. Between you, me, and the windshield, I think it's an attack from outside—China, Russia, Iran—take your pick. And I think whoever it is planted sleepers years ago. Maybe talented teenagers who then moved through Stanford and MIT."

"Wow," Carrie said. "I thought I was good at being suspicious."

He smiled. "I have a lot of time to think while we're waiting in the camp. And we have a lot of time to talk as well. You scurry everywhere. Do you ever want to just slow down?"

"I'm slowed down now." She leaned against the window, watched the world of brown lawns and houses with Christmas lights.

They stopped at a convenience store. Carrie went to the Dunkin' Donuts next door where she bought a smoothie for herself and a coffee for Jared. Just a guess on the one cream and two sugars. He was ecstatic when she handed it to him. Or maybe he was brilliant at seeming to be something he wasn't.

Would Melanie tell Will that Carrie was pregnant? Would she tell Dave that Carrie had been intercepted on the way to have an abortion? Perhaps the inner sanctum was so delirious with the

Sanders's video that her absence wasn't even noticed. Will would miss her and look for her and come unglued on her. Maybe even fire her.

She had muted the phone. No texts, no emails, no voice mails meant no recriminations.

When they arrived at the Hollis trailhead, Jared gave her a hat and down mittens from a pile in the backseat. He said he kept them for new arrivals to camp who didn't understand how *outside* worked. The temperature was near freezing and the sun bashful. The open air was invigorating. As they hiked deeper into the woods, a strange peace enveloped Carrie.

Exhaustion? Or maybe God was speaking to her now that she acknowledged the life inside her.

Her legs ached by the time they reached the rocky ridge. Jared's cheeks were pink, and he glowed with his own peace. Carrie could see it in his gaze as he searched the horizon, that for a few hours they both had surrendered their causes and yielded to the stark beauty of the barren woods.

The ridge gave them an almost one-eighty-degree view of the mountains.

"I thought you had to go north to see mountains," Jared said. "What am I looking at?"

"To the left is Mount Wachusett in Massachusetts. There's a ski area there. Straight ahead is Mount Watatic, and the big one to our right is—I think—Mount Monadnock."

He smiled, took her hand. "I thought you were a city girl."

"I am. But this . . . you need this sometimes. Don't you?"

Carrie sat down on a large rock, fatigue bearing down like a heavy hand. Jared sat next to her. She snuggled into his chest, listening to him breathe, wishing she could feel his heart beat through his sweater.

"What are you going to do about the baby?" he said.

"Let it be born. And then . . . I don't know."

"What does the father want?"

"He doesn't know. He was a one-night stand and . . . I'm ashamed."

"Okay. It's okay. Sleep," he said. "We'll worry about this later."

Carrie let the warmth of his arms and the hum of the wind lure her into slumber.

—

Monday afternoon

Carrie woke up to a splendid campfire and a ravenous hunger. She plowed through two snack bags of pretzels and a bottle of Coke before saying anything other than "Pass the cupcakes." Jared laughed and picked at some string cheese.

When she finally took a breath, he said, "Do you want to talk about it?"

"Let's watch the fire," she said.

The cold wind stung Carrie's cheeks. A bird squawked from the trees. Somewhere below the ridge, the brush rustled.

"I hope that's not a coyote," she said.

Jared laughed. "Ah, the city girl's back. We're bigger than them, you know."

"It's almost winter," she said. "Why are they still around?"

"The woods are full of life. Even now. Squirrels and blue jays and rabbits."

"And coyotes," Carrie said.

"Owls and turkeys and cardinals."

"Wolves."

"Chipmunks and deer," he said.

"'Lions and tigers and bears—oh my.'" She laughed and snuggled into him.

"You don't want to see it, do you?" Jared's grin vanished. "Right in front of you and all around you, and you refuse to acknowledge the truth."

"Don't give me a lecture on global warming. I'm not in the mood."

Jared slid his arm around her. His cheeks were a bright red, the wind biting into his fair skin. "I'm not talking about the receding ice caps or the rise in atmospheric carbon dioxide. I'm talking about the miracle right around us. Even with the trees stripped of leaves and the brooks forming ice—life abounds."

"That kind of life is dangerous," Carrie said. "The squirrel pops out for a look around, and a coyote munches him like a pretzel."

"Do you believe in God, Carrie?"

"Me? I work for Dave Dawson, for Pete's sake. What do you think?"

"Where were you going today when you got stranded?"

She kissed him and he kissed back for a moment before pulling away. "Surely you don't use sex to deflect," Jared said. "That's so . . ."

"Ungodly?"

He laughed. "Bourgeois."

"Do *you* believe in God, Jared?"

"I believe in the Jesus who said that whatever we do for the least of them, we do for Him. And so I believe—like His followers—that the guy who has two coats should share with anyone who has none. And if you've got food, you share the same way."

Carrie wrapped her arms around her knees. "I just assumed you were an atheist."

"Why? Because Christians are obedient souls who don't protest callous government and rapacious business?"

"Why are we talking existentialism? That's a little deep for two people who barely know each other," Carrie said.

"And yet, we have a fire. I don't know why. To be honest, this flame you lit in me is a bit frightening. Distracting—and neither of us can have that right now." Jared traced her lip with his finger. "You didn't tell me."

"Tell you what?"

"Do you believe in God?"

"Faith was what I was born into. No one ever gave me a choice. Faith was a fact of life." She tapped his nose. "Like your freckles."

"And if you were free of all that?"

Carrie turned away so he wouldn't see her well up. One tear—she'd allow that and no more. "I'm free of all that now."

"What happened in Boston?"

"None of your business," she said without moving an inch away.

"You were going to get an abortion."

"Now you know," Carrie said. "I'm a hypocrite."

"You didn't do it."

"Really? What happened to my right of privacy?"

"You said, 'I am pregnant.' Not, 'I was pregnant.' You chose life."

"I made a split-second, unreasoned, impulsive decision. I had one choice, then made another and got arrested for making the wrong turn."

"Choosing life is usually the messiest thing you can do," he said. "So what now?"

"You want me to figure out my future?" Carrie said. "I'm still trying to figure *you* out."

"What are we going to do about us?" Jared asked.

"Honey, I don't even know what I'm going to do for dinner. *Us* isn't even on the menu. Besides, did you forget that I come with a side of baby?" Carrie had turned left instead of right. And for her trouble she got lectured and almost arrested—and held. Held in a man's arms and fed pretzels and comforted.

Maybe life wasn't as complicated as she made it out to be.

twenty-five

Monday afternoon

A GOOD CHRISTIAN WOMAN DOES NOT MEET A MAN alone in his hotel room. At the moment, Melanie was not a good Christian woman. She was a wife tied in knots.

She stood in the hall outside Tucker Keyes's room. He must be riding high. Breaking the Sanders story. Fielding calls from the networks and cable outlets. Eli DuPont had said *Rolling Stone* wanted to do a feature on him. "We didn't release this story," Eli said, "but we're going to make the best of it."

When she had left the situation room, Will, Mike, and Dave were talking high-level strategy. Eli was in and out of the room because the media was going crazy. Nothing like a video that needed to be *bleep-bleeped* to make the story zing.

A politician with a dirty mouth wasn't news. Bringing down a presidential front-runner in the lagging news cycles of December was priceless.

The story that *hadn't* made the news had set Melanie ablaze. Will and Paige Bowers? She needed to confront him. She would confront him. But not until she was able to shake the story out of Paige Bowers.

She knocked so hard her knuckles hurt. That felt good, as if she could beat her anger into the door.

Tucker Keyes opened his door, room phone to his ear, his cell phone in his other hand. He squinted, clearly not recognizing who she was. This was the guy who had planned to make a public spectacle—and a name for himself—out of Will's indiscretion. He could have at least had the courtesy to understand what was at stake.

"I need to talk to you," she said.

"I'm sorry. Ms . . . ?"

"Melanie Connors. Mrs. William Connors."

"Oh." His eyes flicked left and right.

"One minute, please," he said, motioning her into his suite.

Tucker's accommodations were on the same floor as their condo. Ironic how he had booked himself into the presidential suite with its luxurious furniture, a four-poster bed, and a marble bathroom while the good man who should be president slept two floors down in a standard suite.

What did Carrie think about all this? She had complained about having to share a room with Victoria because the finance team took care to manage campaign money well.

Dear God, what should I do about Carrie? After leaving her on that Somerville street, Melanie had called her sister-in-law several times. She wasn't picking up. Had she found a cab and gone to the clinic as planned? Will would never forgive Melanie if anything happened to Carrie.

He would never forgive Carrie if he knew she had planned to have Sophie drive her home from her abortion. Melanie could only pray that bringing her along was Carrie's foolishness and not some sick attempt to normalize abortion in Sophie's mind.

And what about the baby? Was there still a baby? Either way, going forward, Carrie would need support and care. She was too pigheaded to realize that she'd need family beyond just Will.

Tucker Keyes kept her waiting while he fielded another phone call. Melanie clenched her fists, fingernails biting into her palms. She wanted to punch Keyes in the jaw and slap Paige Bowers and shake Will.

She should be looking for God in all this, be willing to surrender this fury that made her safe because she was the wronged one. Anger felt good, but God's smallest touch would be the cool water that could still her fury.

She could have that if she asked. *God, make me willing.*

He clicked off and faced her. "Sorry about that. What can I help you with?"

Melanie stood up, shaking her fingers loose. "I need to get in touch with Paige Bowers."

"You're kidding, right?"

"No. I understand you've got her latest contact info."

"What about 'ongoing investigation' don't you understand? Not to mention maintaining the privacy of my sources."

"This has nothing to do with whatever happened between the Bowers woman and Dave Dawson."

Keyes studied her. "Ask your hubby for her number."

"Don't play games with me."

"Seems like you're the one playing games, Mrs. Connors."

"Please." Tears burned her eyes. "I need to talk to her."

"Call her lawyer. That's how I got her number."

"That and how much cash? You bought her rights, didn't you? That's what J.L. would have advised."

"Fine. Then call my lawyer," he said.

"We made you, Mr. Keyes." Melanie poked him in the chest—what a cliché—and then poked him again. "You were lazy and trivial and cruising on your family name until Dave brought you on board."

"Oh, that's rich. Carrie got me up here because they needed someone to break a story the way they needed it broken. They were counting on my family name for gravitas and on my inexperience so they could control the fallout. They didn't count on my actually investigating further. And my goodness—look what I turned up under the rocks."

Do not cry in front of him. Do not beg. "Please. I need to ask her a simple question."

Keyes scratched his nose. He wore a yellow dress shirt and blue jeans. His feet were bare. He was an attractive young man, strongly built with the bone structure that comes from generations of upper-class breeding.

And he was thinking. Melanie knew that look. He was trying to figure out what he could get from her. Scuttlebutt was that he drank too much, worked too little, but was very smart. It was probably not a good decision for the campaign to stir him from his stupor.

"Tell you what," he said. "I'll call Paige for you. On one condition. I want to listen in on the call."

"You're kidding," Melanie said. Wouldn't he love that? She could see the headline "Lord's Heritage Founder Shakes Down Prostitute."

He smiled. "Absolutely serious."

"You cannot write anything about me," she said. "If you listen, it is all so far off the record, it might as well be on the moon."

"I have no interest in your personal story. I'm just curious about . . . the nature of relationships. And how people get through things like this."

His eyes looked wounded. Bobby Joe and J.L. used to be respectful adversaries. Melanie knew the history of J.L.'s son, how Tucker Keyes had grown up without a father. No wonder he and Carrie had a bond.

"Have you ever been in a committed relationship?" Melanie asked. "Been in love?"

"I haven't seen the point," he said. "So if you'd care to let me have a glimpse of *the point*, I'd like to see how this works."

"Fine." She couldn't wait much longer. Her resolve was eroding. "Make the call."

Tuck dialed, left a message, and then went back to work. Melanie sat on the sofa and tried to pray. Keyes took more phone calls. He glanced at the minibar more than once.

He needs a drink.

Lord, I don't feel like praying for him or for anyone right now, but he's here, I'm here, and oh God, I desperately need You here. So shower Your grace on him, on this Tucker Keyes. And forgive me because I am so angry with You too.

The phone rang. Tuck answered it, his tone courteous and charming, as if he were speaking to the first lady instead of a whore.

"Mrs. Connors is with me. Yes, his wife. No, I know you don't want anything to do with this. She has one question for you. No, you don't have to. I think it would be a kindness. Okay. Hold on." He nodded at Melanie. "She says you get one question. And that's—sorry, she said I have to say this—that's only because your husband gave her so much business."

Melanie took the phone. "This thing with you and my husband . . . are you telling the truth? Was he a client?"

"Yes."

"Did it seem—"

"Hold on there. I said I would answer one question. Do you not grasp the concept of one?"

"Please." Melanie fought tears.

Paige sighed dramatically. "Make it quick or I'll charge you for my time."

"Did my husband's . . . relationship with you seem to mean anything? Beyond the obvious?"

"Not one stinkin' thing—other than the obvious," Paige

Bowers said. "Now get off the phone, and if you try to contact me again, I'll sue you."

"You've told me all I need to know. Thank you." Melanie handed the phone back to Keyes.

"Did it?" he asked. "Did it mean anything to him?"

"I'll tell you her answer if you let me ask you one question."

He shrugged. "Sure. You can ask. I'm not going to promise an answer."

"Which do you think is worse: if it meant something to my husband or if it didn't?"

"Okay, I'll play. If it didn't mean anything to him, then he dehumanized Paige Bowers by treating her like a living blow-up doll. If it did mean something to him, that means he has dehumanized you by connecting intimately with another woman."

"You do get it." Melanie smiled.

"You didn't answer my question. What did Paige say?"

"She said it didn't mean anything to him."

"So, what does that mean to you?" Keyes asked.

"Honestly, I don't know. Can I ask you another question?"

"If you make it fast. I have a deadline."

Melanie took his hands in hers. "Do you know Jesus?"

—

Monday evening

It had been a hectic day, a horrible day. Melanie had her own part in it, the rush to Boston, the rush to Tucker Keyes, and—*God, please forgive me*—the rush to judgment.

Carrie was still among the missing. Will was in the maelstrom that was the aftermath of the Sanders exposé. When she had last seen him, he flitted like a raw nerve in the situation room, hopping from the governor's people to media response to instructing the Tennessee office to pick off Sanders's donors.

A prostitute. Will had used a prostitute for what Melanie should have been giving him. The guilt and rage and fear strangled her. Just like they always had. Guilt, rage, fear. What a toxic mix.

Now sorrow. Mourning for what she and Will should have been, were it not for her guilt, rage, fear. Sorrow and compassion came in surges, like labor pains on a pregnant woman.

All this emotional energy—and she overlooked the life right before her. Carrie was missing and needed to be found. Smart, energetic, bold Carrie. Tell her what to do, and it's done. Had they really never stopped to ask her what she might need?

Melanie was ashamed of her own hypocrisy, promoting family values while ignoring the needs of her husband and daughter and sister-in-law.

She knew where Carrie must be, and who the father of her child must be.

A big part of her was saying, "So what?" Why should she care where Carrie was? Her sister-in-law had betrayed Will in an angry moment.

Why should Carrie get to indulge her anger when it was Melanie whose fire was righteous and justified? Yes, indeed—anger felt good. It gave her the rationale she needed for piling the anger on top of herself so nothing else could get in. Scripture said perfect love drives out fear.

Anger also drives out fear.

So, that was one choice—indulging the fury surging through her every cell.

Melanie had other choices. She could go back to Nashville. Paige Bowers gave her the way out of this marriage and the way to seize custody from Will. That was the obvious choice.

God usually was found in the less obvious.

Option two was to move forward as if nothing happened. She couldn't take that into consideration, not with anger searing her throat.

Narrow the choices, then. Find Carrie. Find Will. And do what? Pile anger on them like burning coals? Or shrug off the anger, swim through the sorrow, and grasp hold of compassion.

Choices were terrifying. It was far easier to hide in a safe place and blockade that safe place with justifiable rage. She made that choice too readily and too often.

Simplify. Find Carrie. Find Will, tell him Carrie needed him. Tell him that she needed him too. Or hold on to the anger so she wouldn't be scared.

Life scared Melanie. Faith scared Melanie. Understanding Will scared Melanie. She was so sick of being scared and so scared of letting anger be her crutch.

Choose, she told herself. *Father God, help me choose.*

Choose faith. Choose life. Choose Will.

twenty-six

Monday evening

Carrie texted her brother. She should tell him face-to-face but she didn't have the energy.

> Lanie knows about Paige Bowers. I told her. I am so sorry. Please . . .

"Put that phone down," Jared said.

Carrie sat on a camp chair in his tent, hands shaking though she was toasty warm. She had to tell Will. She couldn't let him be blindsided by Melanie. It was done, and she'd wait and take her medicine—later. For now, she'd sit with Jared and enjoy being snug.

No doubt the propane heater was illegal, especially on public property. The Movers were as snug as that proverbial bug because the mayor refused to enforce laws regarding habitation of public property.

This tent was worthy of any military general. Why were so many computers needed when the MoveIn strategy seemed to be a mirror of Dave Dawson's? Show yourself for what you believe. That simple.

Carrie ran away from an abortion. Did that show her as cowardly or as obedient? When had her own life slipped out of her control? Choosing life—choosing faith—was beyond unsettling.

Admit it, she told herself. *You're shaking in your Ugg boots.*

Jared had heated a mug of tomato soup for her, with chunks of American cheese in it. She plowed through the soup and eyed the Oreos next to his computer. If she kept this up, she'd be big as a house. Then again, with a pregnancy brewing, she didn't need refined sugar and trans fats to blow up like a balloon.

"All hell is breaking loose," Carrie said. "Sanders is bringing in minority buddies to vouch for his fairness and tolerance. The nets are going bonkers, running the video and bleeping the crap out of it. The talking heads are spending time trying to figure out who recorded the thing so they can scandalize the whistle-blower."

"Scurrying rats," Jared said.

Carrie laughed. "That's what we—I mean, *they*—say about you guys."

"Some guy telling jokes should not qualify for 'all hell breaking loose.'"

"Easy to pronounce from under the canvas," Carrie said. "Try being out there."

"I have been out there. All hell breaking loose is genocide and famine in Africa. Civil war and atrocities in Syria and Libya. The carnage unleashed by cartels in Mexico. Earthquake devastation in Haiti. Kids killing kids in Chicago."

Carrie wanted to snap at him but the tenderness in his eyes was as clear as the night sky. "So what are you doing here? Doesn't this tent sitting and sign holding become meaningless in the face of a fallen creation?"

"'The creation waits in eager expectation for the children of God to be revealed.'"

"That's just words."

"No, it's a call to action," Jared said. "'If God is for us, who can be against us?' We do the work God puts before us and trust Him to reveal His grace."

"Good grief! You were easier to digest when you were just a run-of-the-mill remnant of the sixties. I still come back to *why*—why camp out instead of reach out?"

The tent was high enough for Jared to stand up straight and long enough to let him pace. "Senator Dawson and the others have position papers, platforms, policies. They diagnose and prescribe action for recovery without understanding what part they have in the disease. We want to be the agenda item that they cannot ignore. 'Look at us,' we say and—if they finally do—we say, 'Okay, this is the real world where we all need to pitch in and do a whole lot better.'"

Carrie laughed. "Occupy was ready to rip the throats out of anyone who worked their tail off and became successful. Their wail was 'Goodie for you, now we're going to suck you dry because we want what you have.' Vampires in ski caps and sweaters."

"Occupy Twilight, eh?" Jared stopped midstep, pivoted toward her. "We are not Occupy."

"You sure look like you are."

"Occupy was a frustrated tangle of causes. They began with righteous indignation and, in their desire to be inclusive, muddied the message—and the messengers. MoveIn is peaceful. The stone in your shoe. You feel the nudge, take it off, see what's there."

Carrie's phone vibrated. She ignored it for the first time in eight years. "I get a stone in my shoe, I don't bother looking. I just shake it out. So you've gained nothing except a hop on one foot."

"You're listening, and you're thinking. That's a start."

Carrie stood up, grabbed his sweatshirt, and kissed him. "So *this* thing between us is just a lobbying move?"

Jared snuggled his nose into her hair. "You are not a *this*, Caroline Connors."

A commotion outside the tent stopped her from kissing him again.

"Am I supposed to . . . I guess one doesn't knock on a tent," Melanie said on the other side of the canvas. "Carrie? Are you in there?"

"Are you up for receiving visitors?" Jared whispered.

Carrie sighed. She was about to go from Jared's creamy tomato soup to Melanie's bitter coffee.

"Let her in," she said. Jared got up and untied the flap.

Melanie ducked in, looked around. "Wow. It's warm in here. I didn't expect that."

"WiFi too. We draw the line at cable, however," Jared said. "How are you, Mrs. Connors?"

"Sorry to intrude. I need to speak to Carrie."

Jared unfolded a camp stool, motioned for her to sit. "I need to make a trash run. If you'll excuse me . . ."

"No. Stay," Carrie said.

He leaned over her, kissed the top of her head. "You've got this."

Carrie watched him leave, then turned to Melanie. "I know the first question out of your mouth. And no, unfortunately, he's not the father."

"That would have been my second question. I tracked you down to ask if you were all right. Are you?"

"After the abortion? Did you come to measure how much sin I've heaped on myself?"

Melanie twisted her wedding ring. "Of course not."

"Stop that with the ring," Carrie said. "If that's some sort of subliminal metaphor, just say it."

"I was worried about you." She folded her hands, stared at

Carrie. "I left you on a street in the city after yelling at you. I didn't even go after you. I shouldn't have left you. I am so sorry."

"Yeah, well. Jared picked me up. So I didn't need you."

Could she trust Melanie's tears? And what about Jared, with his suffering world and his unspoken agenda? Yes, Carrie was cynical. Anyone would be, given the world she moved in. But all those calamities and horrors—she was one person, one voice, one soul—what could she do about any of them?

"Is there anything I can do for you?" Melanie said.

"Like what? Refer me to a link on your website for counseling?"

"Maybe walk you back to the hotel. You might want a hot bath or a nap."

"Am I fired yet?" Carrie said.

"Will doesn't know about the procedure. Or the pregnancy."

"I'm talking about the Sanders tape. Will told me not to release it, and I did anyway." Her chest tightened. She had traded stories so Melanie and Sophie wouldn't find out about her brother's hooker issue. And Carrie had thrown Paige Bowers right in Melanie's face.

"It's all positioning right now, and trying to poach donors," Melanie said. "You know that political rule—your scandal is my opportunity."

"I'm sorry," Carrie said.

"For the Sanders tape? Something like that needs to be exposed."

"I'm sorry I threw Will and that woman in your face. I killed the story to keep it from you, to give you the chance to make a go at counseling. And now . . ."

"This won't stop me from trying," Melanie said. "I have things I need to work on. I hope—*I pray*—my husband will stick with me. And that you will too, Caroline."

"Stick with you? Don't you understand why that confounds

me? You haven't been a part of our lives for years. And don't say that goes both ways. I know it does. But the . . ."

Carrie couldn't find the words. It wasn't her business what was wrong in her brother's marriage. Melanie had no right to lump her into the stew, as if making a half-baked apology fixed everything.

"Communication?" Melanie said. "Is that the word you're searching for?"

Exhaustion flooded Carrie. How lovely it would be to curl up next to Jared, put her head on his shoulder, and just sleep. Asking him to step away from his path would be asking him to lessen who he was.

"What do you want, Lanie. I mean, really. Why are you here?"

"You're tired. Get some rest. Here or at the hotel. Just get some rest. We can talk again tomorrow." Melanie stood, hands aflutter as if she didn't dare hug Carrie or even touch her shoulder. "That's all I wanted. For you to know how sorry I was that I left you."

Carrie grabbed her wrist. "I didn't do it. When it came time, I panicked. That's why I turned the car into traffic. I'm sorry. I could have gotten Sophie hurt, and I am so sorry."

"Oh. Okay." Melanie nodded. "Why don't you come back with me? If you want me to sit with you and Will, I can. If that would help?"

Carrie forced herself to stand up. "Yeah, okay. I'll walk back with you."

Melanie offered her arm. They left the tent, Carrie fastening the flap to keep in the heat. Jared stood on a bench, backlit by spotlights as he spoke. A small crowd had gathered around him.

She smiled at the thought that tonight, when she stood on her balcony and brushed her hair, they would see each other in the darkness.

Yes. That was the metaphor she'd hold on to.

Monday evening

Melanie left Carrie in her hotel room, then returned to the condo. Will was there, stretched out in the recliner. He had changed into a T-shirt and sweatpants. His back must hurt. She hated the thought of adding anything to his burden. No, it was time to understand that confronting the past could be the bearing of another's burden—and a sweet release.

"Are you okay?" she said.

He stared at the ceiling. "Carrie shouldn't have told you about Paige Bowers. It's none of her business."

Melanie sat on the arm of the chair. "No, no. It's really not her fault. I hounded her about . . ." She couldn't say. The pregnancy was Carrie's story to tell. "I berated her about something else, and I was so wrong in how I handled it. I was an absolute banshee, to be honest, and drove her to tell me about how she had killed the story. How she had released the Sanders tape to Tucker Keyes to protect you."

Will set the recliner up, brought the footrest down with a bang. "She shouldn't have. I told her not to."

"She killed the story for us—you, me, the girls, Dave."

"I can't . . . I don't even know what to say. I'm embarrassed, ashamed, and so . . . worried that this will derail all the progress we've made."

"You're worried that I won't forgive you."

"How can you?" Will asked.

"I will forgive you in this moment and if the next moment makes me think about her and you, I'll find a way to forgive you all over again. The question is, Will—can you forgive yourself?"

"I can't compartmentalize this like I do everything else. I have no idea how to nix this." He hid his face with his hands. "Maybe we should hold this discussion until we can see Beth."

"No. She's given us tools to get through things like this." Melanie wedged into the seat next to him. All these years of marriage and only now did she understand Will's modus operandi. Something goes wrong, he gets up and fixes it. Was that the confused message she had gotten from him in those early days? Too much getting up, going to do something—anything—that would keep him busy so he didn't see how desperately she wanted him to stay.

"Lanie, I am so sorry. But sorry doesn't cut it."

"I spoke to Paige," Melanie said.

"What! Why?" Will said. "Why would you ever talk to that woman?"

"I had a question for her. And she answered it."

"What question?"

"I asked if there was more than just . . . your body in the relationship."

"Either way, I was a pig." He tried to gently push her up and off the chair.

"Hey!" Melanie curled her leg over his. "Stop trying to get away. We work through these things. Starting right now. We let Jesus wash over us and spend whatever days or months or even years we need in shedding the dead skin."

Will groaned, turned his face away. "Can you forgive me? How could you possibly?"

Melanie slid her arm under his head and turned him to face her. "How could Jesus possibly, Will? If He had the audacity to forgive all of mankind for every sin ever committed, shouldn't we exercise the same mercy and grace toward ourselves?"

"I thought you'd be furious, Lanie. Carrie texted me a heads-up, and I thought—she's gone. Melanie's gone, and it'll be for good because now she knows. And yet here you are. Where is this coming from?"

"Oh, I was. Furious and hurt and, I'll confess, somewhat relieved to have a reason to pull the shell back over me. That's not what I want. Not anymore."

After working through her own past, Melanie felt as if she'd been given a looking glass into her heart and, God willing, her husband's.

There was no use beating him up any longer, because Melanie didn't want to beat herself up any longer, or Paige Bowers for that matter.

She held him so tightly that he let out a little *oomph.* "From now on, we do it all together," she said. "We work through anger, pain, betrayal—and my fear—and anything else. Will, I don't want to be alone anymore."

Will kissed her. Kissed her for a long time.

twenty-seven

Tuesday before dawn

Carrie had a horrid night. She would roll one way and see Melanie, the other way and see Jared. Every time she captured a moment of sleep, she'd see her brother. "Billy," she would say, "I'm sorry," and he'd just turn away.

She'd wake up, toss again, find no escape.

At three in the morning, Carrie became ravenous. The calm before the storm of morning sickness. Victoria wasn't in bed. She was strict about her nighttime routine, the application of beauty products and the last *tap tap* on the iPad before she climbed into bed.

Strange to think that Carrie had slept more soundly with Victoria in the next bed.

She got up, dug through her dresser drawers. Usually she kept packets of crackers gleaned from downstairs. Nothing.

Maybe Victoria had something. Carrie had never snooped through the woman's belongings—except for that one time when she had her head on the edge of the shower and found the pill bottles in the trash can.

Victoria had a sweet tooth and seemed to have an unlimited supply of candy bars and cookies. How she stayed so slim was a mystery. Carrie had no right to open her drawers. She was lightheaded and couldn't make it to the vending machines. The top drawer had all Victoria's silky underwear. Neatly folded, coordinating panties and bras. Other drawers had jeans, T-shirts, and the like.

Under the sweaters—*thank You, Jesus*—a package of peanut butter cups. Carrie would pay her back with a whole bag of them. She unwrapped the candy, shoved it into her mouth, and felt the sugar rush through her body.

Victoria's pills were hidden with her candy. Carrie shouldn't look. She had invaded enough people's privacy with the Sanders video and the scouring of medical records. But why weren't these prescriptions listed in Victoria's record?

She grabbed her phone and flashed a picture of the bottles with Victoria's name clearly showing. She turned the bottles slowly to capture the name of the medication and the prescribing doctor, Marissa Tomlin. Vicodin, prescription-strength ibuprofen, Gabapentin, and another one. Tramadol. Carrie Googled it, not surprised to find that it was another painkiller. Searching for the doctor, Carrie found Marissa Tomlin in Baltimore. She was indeed a pain management specialist.

Victoria must have serious chronic pain. Maybe when she swung her backside in high heels it wasn't to be alluring, but to relieve some lower back pain. Carrie should muster some sympathy for the woman—campaigns were tough when you were perfectly healthy, but to run all day and half the night with chronic pain had to be horrible.

"What are you doing?"

Carrie startled, dropped her phone. "I didn't hear you come in."

Victoria lunged at her. "You have no right going through my stuff."

"I was . . . just looking for peanut butter cups. I saw your pills.

You must have some serious pain. Why haven't you told anyone? We could have made things easier for you."

"Have I ever asked for help?"

"Eventually secrets come out." Carrie took a step back. "For example, why did you lie on your résumé?"

"Why do you think, you idiot? Because of perception. Women are supposed to be good at communicating. Not computing. I wanted to be part of government where I could make a difference. Not stuck in some room, tapping out code with nerds who don't even know what day it is."

Carrie couldn't argue with that. She rammed into the fabled glass ceiling often in her career. You just had to lower your shoulder and keep pushing. And yet—there was something in Victoria's eyes that implied there was more to the story.

"Why didn't your condition show in your health records?"

The woman smiled. "Oh, you are so cruising for a lawsuit. You want to keep Dave and your precious brother out of the courts, you will stop asking questions. Right now."

Carrie held up her hands. "I'm sorry. I just needed something to eat. I didn't mean to cause any problems."

"Keep your mouth shut and there won't be any." Victoria left, slamming the door.

Sure, Carrie would keep her mouth shut. For now.

—

Tuesday dawn

After a quick shower Carrie slipped on a sweatshirt and flip-flops and went down the four flights to the breakfast nook. It wasn't officially open but the staff set out bread and cereal before they left for the night. She'd find something approximating real food and not vending-machine cardboard. Carrie ate four pieces of toast and drowsily laid her head on the table, trying to remember what Jeremy Wainwright looked like.

Trying to remember what Jesus looked like.

Mother had taken her to church because that's what one does. It had to be the right church, of course, and one must be seen amiably chatting with one's peers. Carrie had gone to a private girls' school that required chapel every morning. It was Will—*oh Jesus, of course it was Will*—who explained what it all really meant. And she said yes and she meant it for years until Jesus became a talking point, and she became too busy to reclaim Him.

Her chef friend poked his head out of the kitchen and held up a pot of coffee. Carrie shook her head sheepishly and went upstairs to find Will. Eli DuPont was already in the situation room, bleary eyed and jumpy. "Up all night," he said. "Working through Sanders talking points for today. Dave needs to be on perfect pitch. Compassionate, forgiving, and appalled."

"Stop worrying," Carrie said. "Even the Paige Bowers thing came out like a symphony. I need to talk to Will."

"He's usually up by now. I had to make my own coffee."

She laughed. "Let me make the next pot. Yours is sludge, and that's at its best."

Making coffee. Cracking jokes with Eli. Waiting for New Hampshire to wake up so they could get on with the business of wooing voters. And Carrie still wasn't sick. *Dear God, did something happen to the . . . fetus?*

It's a baby. Yesterday it was a product of conception, and today it was a baby. She wasn't sure *whose* baby it would become.

She and Jeremy had come together in an unthinking moment. Now there was a tiny soul to be thought about, worried about, prayed about. Maybe given up, maybe held tight. Who knew?

After a quick trip to the bathroom in what used to be Sophie's room, Carrie knew one thing. She was still pregnant.

She wandered back through the main room, not surprised to see a couple other staffers frantically at work. She traded small talk and then knocked on Will's door. No answer.

She peered into the bedroom. "Will?" His bed hadn't been slept in.

Eli peered up from his laptop. "Not staying, Carrie?"

She smiled at his balding head and jowly cheeks and remembered being in absolute love with him when she was fourteen. If he suspected she crushed on him, he never said a word or even gave her more than a passing pat on the shoulder.

"I've got to get dressed." Carrie rode the elevator past her floor, up to the top floor. She could stop in on Tuck, sack out on his sofa so she wouldn't be alone. That would give him the wrong message, and hadn't she been doing that for the past ten years?

She took a left down the hall and knocked lightly on Melanie's door.

Will answered. It took a moment to sink in. Since Melanie rented this condo, he'd had meals up here, spent family time, and then always wandered back to the situation room and bunked down there.

"Hey, pumpkin," he said, his eyes bright. "What's up?"

"I'm sorry. I know you probably want to rip my head off—"

"Shush." Will gave her a quick hug. "We'll figure this out."

Melanie wandered out of the kitchen and slipped her arm around Will's waist. "Are you okay, Caroline?"

She hadn't seen them fit together so comfortably since Sophie was born. They were *together.*

"I'm pregnant," she said. The blank look on his face told her that Melanie hadn't said anything to him.

"Wow. You'd better come in," he said.

Carrie's feet wouldn't move. The impetus of her whole life was forward movement, and now she couldn't budge.

Melanie tucked her arm around Carrie's waist and steered her into the condo. She didn't let go until she had settled Carrie into a recliner and draped a soft throw over her legs. Will stood by, a faraway look in his eyes. Processing.

"Are you up for some breakfast?" Melanie said. "Maybe Cheerios or some toast?"

"I'm just so tired," she said, her eyes drifting shut on the image of Will with one hand on her shoulder and the other on Melanie's as he bowed in unspoken prayer.

Bright sunlight woke her up three hours later. Will was in corporate dress, gray suit, power tie, phone in hand. Everyone needed to be sharp today.

Sophie sat at the table, rubbing sleep from her eyes. Melanie sat on the sofa, scribbling on a legal pad. Likely writing a comment on the Sanders tape for Lord's Heritage. She glanced up at Carrie and said, "Can I get you something?"

"Coke," Carrie said. "It's all I can take this time of day."

She expected Melanie to tell her that Coke was bad for the baby. All she said was, "I'll run down to the vending machine."

Carrie got up, blanket wrapped tight around her. "Will," she said. "Sophie and I have something to tell you."

Sophie glared at Carrie, wouldn't look at her father.

Carrie told him about bullying her niece into silence about the pregnancy and the trip to Somerville. Will was renowned for his control. Carrie and Dave Dawson might be the only people alive who knew how to read the subtle changes in his jaw and eyes.

"You're furious," Carrie said. "I never should have involved her. I am so sorry, Will."

"You were scared, Carrie," Sophie said from between her fingers. "You didn't say it, but I knew you were afraid."

Will sat down at the table, muted his phone. "Why didn't you come to me? Both of you?"

"It was an epic screwup," Carrie said, "and you'd be so disappointed in me."

"Dad, she turned the wrong way," Sophie said. "When we went to the appointment, she turned the wrong way."

"You knew that?" Carrie said. "That I turned away from the clinic?"

"I prayed it. Every second that I was not praying some insane Boston driver wouldn't kill us, I prayed you'd change your mind."

"I didn't change my mind," Carrie said. "I just got confused."

Sophie sat up, face blotchy but eyes triumphant. "You did. You just didn't know it. And you're keeping it, aren't you. I prayed that too."

Carrie leaned back in her chair. "I'm having it. Keeping it? Wow, I can't go there. Not yet."

Melanie came in with three cans of Coke. She set one in front of Carrie and put the other two in the fridge. No one spoke until she sat down and said, "Looks like we're having a family discussion."

"Caroline," Will said. "Who's the father?"

Carrie popped the tab on the Coke, took a slow swallow, then burped. Sophie burst out laughing.

"One of our donors," Carrie said. "Jeremy Wainwright from Exeter."

"You have to tell him," Melanie said.

Carrie sighed. "I know."

"Caroline. No matter what," Will said, "we're going to be here for you."

"You're not going to fire me?"

"Because you're pregnant? Of course not."

"Because of the video."

Will frowned. "You're a bloody hero to Eli, the rest of the crew. That doesn't matter. I can't protect you if Dave wants you gone."

"Sophie," Melanie said. "Go to your room."

"What the heck?" Sophie said. "I thought this was a family discussion."

"Go. Now."

Sophie left the table muttering.

Melanie leaned across the table. "You know why Carrie did it," she whispered. "She had to stop the story about you and Paige Bowers."

"I told her not to, and she did it anyway," Will whispered back. "So why are you taking her side?"

"We have to start being more honest so there isn't a mess that we'd have to send our daughter out of the room to discuss."

"Listen, guys," Carrie said. "It's done. You both have stuff to work through and I have consequences to bear. So we probably should . . . pray? Pray and move on."

Sophie came back out, took her seat. Will raised his eyebrow at her. "What?" she said. "You thought I wasn't going to eavesdrop? I did, I'm here, and let's pray, guys.

"And then you can tell me what all the whispering is about."

Tuesday late morning

Have you met Jesus?

Melanie Connors asked that last week as if she were asking if Tuck had ever tried grilled broccoli. Tuck rolled over in bed, those words drumming inside his head. "Sure," he should have said. "Jesus is coming for a round of golf, and then we'll party."

After she asked the question, Melanie and he had danced a short jig until his patience ran out. He began taking phone calls as if she wasn't in the room. She finally left. A minute later she texted him.

Just ask. Jesus, if You're real, just show me.

He texted back thx just because relationships were vital in this business, and he didn't want to tick off Will Connors's wife. Three hours later he was in a Nashua bar where he'd picked up a chick with pink cheeks, blond hair, and a decent vocabulary. He went back to her place, drank vodka and cranberry juice, had careful and courteous sex, and then left before she finished her shower.

He remembered this one's name because he had her put it into his phone. When Tuck got back to his hotel, he ordered a bouquet of roses to be delivered later that day.

If he could have sent Jesus a bouquet, he would have. Hey, man, let's have a sit-down. If You've got nothing to hide, then why are You hiding?

Nothing there—other than this itch. Like that time when he was eleven and broke his leg skiing. Italian Alps, Mother was off somewhere else, so the nanny took him to the hospital. Mother arrived in a flourish, and they spent the winter in Italy while his leg recovered. The plaster cast went over his knee. As the healing began, the itch was like a locust, never satisfied. He tried to get at it with a wire clothes hanger. It was too deep and too encased in that hard shell.

Perhaps Jesus was the same way—Jesus could itch but Tuck couldn't scratch because he was like that plaster cast. Maybe more like an oyster shell, the hard layers of his psyche formed from Dad's quick departure from his life, J.L.'s constant disapproval, and Mother's latest boarding school.

Excuses. Booze and drugs, women and more women, activities and adventures. No pearl forming there. Not with excuses flowing so freely.

Was it hardened ambition or Jesus that made it possible for Miranda Dawson to forgive her husband? Carrie had risked her career to save her brother from public embarrassment. She didn't say that but Tuck knew how these things worked. Someone lower-level gets fired so the upper-level guy can float above it.

The Beltway was wired on ambition.

The Dawson people had a different air to them. They were bound by a rare loyalty. Was it because they were good ol' folks from Tennessee, aligned against the bitter forces of federal government? Or maybe it was because Connors ran a tight ship, and Dawson inspired people to keep in line.

Tuck knew almost no Bible but he did know "render unto Caesar." The Dawson people fooled themselves when they mixed politics with faith. How could Tuck even begin to approach that question?

Jesus. It couldn't be that simple.

Someone knocked on his door. Blast it all—he hadn't even showered yet. He sat up, searched for the alarm clock, and saw it was an unholy 7:12 a.m. The campaign rose before the sun but media slept off hangovers until Dawson or his surrogates were on the bus, off to kiss up to some random bunch of New Hampshire folks.

More knocking. He put his pillow over his head. And then his cell thrummed with a text. Tuck blinked, tried to focus.

Let me in. Carrie

"Coming," he shouted. He grabbed a piece of gum from his bedside table. He chewed it enough to wash out the morning breath and then lumbered to the door.

Carrie stood there in jeans and a bright red Patriots shirt. No makeup, and she didn't need it because she was much more beautiful in raw form.

"Please tell me the world is exploding," Tuck said. "Otherwise, I'm heading back to bed."

She pushed past him into his suite, worrying her hands as if she were trying to wring out some prophecy of doom. "I have some news. Bad news, I'm afraid. Can we sit?" She didn't wait for permission, just pushed his jacket aside and sat on the sofa.

Tuck sat with her, a sinking feeling because her eyes were so sad. "What?" he said.

"It's your grandfather." Carrie took his hands, squeezed them. "It's all over the news. I'm sorry, Tuck. They think it was a heart attack. Last night. The housekeeper found him in his library."

"A heart attack." Just yesterday Tuck almost jumped a shuttle because he'd wanted to strangle the old bird for horning in on the *Today Show* interview.

"I slept late," he said numbly. "I haven't seen the news or anything yet."

"Check your messages," Carrie said. "Some people tried to call you."

"I muted the phone."

Tuck grabbed his phone, scanned the voice and text messages he had ignored last night. The housekeeper, panic in her voice as she said his grandfather was being taken off in an ambulance, "but he's a bad color, Mr. Keyes, a strange blue and please call me." Other messages, one from Mother and one from *The Journal*'s editorial director.

"Go ahead," Carrie said. "Call them back. I'll stay with you."

He made the calls with only enough energy to thank the people on the ground in DC and tell them he would get back to them about arrangements. "What am I supposed to do now?" he asked Carrie.

"He must have an obituary ready," she said. "Everyone does. Call his secretary, get it emailed to you, and then you finish it."

"He's been chipping at it for the last five years. It's probably perfect."

"It won't be. Not until some who loved him takes it to the finish line."

Love? Had Tuck ever really loved John Larter Keyes? He respected him for the long career and integrity. Mocked him for his inability to move into the new millennium. Feared him because his grandfather called him a "pinball" and was completely right.

Love never entered into the equation with J.L. It was all about who Tuck was and who he was supposed to be. The grand inheritance—a dying newspaper. The sacred heritage—following the story, learning the truth.

And then what? Write political exposés that were more soap opera than studious reporting. Carrie had used him, and they both knew it. No secrets there. Throw the dog a bone and watch him run through the neighborhood in triumph.

"What does it all mean?" Tuck said.

Carrie circled him with her arms. "We've got time to figure that out."

"I don't even have a church for the memorial service," he said, face in her hair. She smelled sweaty, and for some reason, that comforted him.

"I'll help you with that," she said. "For now, make them send you the official statement before it's released. Get the obituary, make sure everyone knows that you're taking charge because you'll have lawyers and *Journal* people all scrambling to be the public face. You're family. You need to do this."

The sob came from under his breastbone, just one gasp before he swallowed it back. Carrie tightened her grip on him. "Tucker," she whispered. "Would you mind if I said a little prayer?"

"Go for it," Tuck said. She did, and he felt Jesus skulking somewhere around the edges of her prayer and the edges of his life, and he thought, *Go for it.*

Someone—God? Give me strength.

Christmas Week

Presidential Primary Season

twenty-eight

Wednesday morning

"THE UGLY WORK IS BEHIND YOU," BETH SAID. "THE hard work is still ahead."

"We'll be gone the first week of February," Melanie said. "To Florida and South Carolina if things go well. Or to DC if Dave's out. Leaving you is like a bird falling out of the nest. I know I'm going to flutter and tumble."

"We can't pretend," Will said, "that none of this stuff happened. There's forgiveness—and then there's dealing with consequences."

"Agreed," Beth said. "We can try some long-distance coaching. If that doesn't work out, we'll find you someone on home turf."

"Home turf?" Will said, staring at Melanie.

She smiled. "Virginia, right? We'll buy something near the Dawsons. Unless, of course, Dave is in the White House."

"You would do that?" Beth said. "Leave Nashville behind?"

"I've been thinking," Melanie said. "About the woman in Scripture who lost the coin and swept her house clean until she found it. You and I are like that lost coin, Will. We've been sweeping the house clean and yeah—we can celebrate. And we understand that more dust will be raised between us. That's natural. Right, Beth?"

"Yes. Don't stop sweeping."

"The question is—how?" Will said. "The pressure of our lives is only going to increase if Dave can squeak out something in New Hampshire. So how do we maintain our equilibrium when the wind blows up the dust cloud?"

"Oh, come on," Melanie said, laughing. "All this talk about dust makes me feel like I need to get back to the condo and vacuum."

"There's a variety of approaches we can take," Beth said. "First, both of you keep going with your individual sessions. Second, we make sure you continue with the shared sessions. If we can't maintain good progress long distance, I know several therapists on this coast who could step in. People you can trust, and you would like."

"Beth," Melanie said. "I am going to miss you."

Beth smiled. "Likewise. But this isn't about me. It's about you two continuing to work hard to get this marriage and family back on track. There're some exercises I can share with you, things that will provide excellent communication tools. Based on the splendid progress you're reporting, I have one that you can try this week."

Splendid progress. What a funny way to describe this reawakening in her body, this new and honest hunger for her husband. *Splendid blessing* was the better term, the casting of gratitude to the loving Father who had brought them back together.

That was the sunny side of what happened last week.

And now this—more work. When Beth said "exercise," Melanie heard "exertion." It was one thing to rest in the arms of the husband she had abandoned. It was quite another to keep picking at the wounds, especially ones that were so heavily scarred. They had exposed the past, offered forgiveness, loved each other through that moment. *Loved* each other in every way. Why not just bury it all again, now that they had acknowledged the truth—and the staggering guilt.

Will had been lonely and lost. Melanie had been young and stupid. No, not stupid. She had to stop thinking of herself in those terms. Beth was right—the very essence of her youth made her a victim. For many years she had prosecuted Will in place of her abuser.

No longer.

"I'm game if Will is," Melanie said.

"Anything that keeps us moving forward," he said.

Beth went to the closet, took out two small whiteboards. She unwrapped them and passed them to Will and Melanie. "When something comes up and doesn't leave," Beth said, "some way that you think your spouse has injured you, write it on your whiteboard. Or draw a picture or write a poem. Be creative and be intentional. Then go to your loved one—peacefully and honestly—and show it to him or her. Acknowledge it and then erase it. Slowly and with determination. Be honest, say it, and then wipe it out. If it's a third party who has injured you, let your spouse help you in wiping it away."

"I don't want to," Melanie said with a minor panic in her chest. "I don't want to go back to those ugly places."

"And why should we?" Will asked. "Why should we bring that bad stuff back up?"

"You're human," Beth said. "You think the past isn't going to intrude? It's there, it's part of who you are. Now you can learn how to manage it. Let's try it."

"I'm in such an upbeat mood," Will said. "Do you have to ruin that?"

Beth smiled and held out two markers. "Just offering you something to help. Is there anything close to the surface that you want to wipe away?"

Melanie scooted away from Will and wrote the one thing that she'd been suppressing all weekend. She was ashamed to even think such a thing, but Beth was right—so much percolated under the surface.

Will glanced at her, eyebrows raised. Then he got to work.

When they were both finished, Beth asked which of them wanted to go first.

"Not me," Will and Melanie said in unison. The laughter that came felt good. Cleansing.

Melanie turned her board to Will so he could see what she had written.

> You didn't come to Sophie's first birthday party because Dave had a town-hall meeting two nights later and you chose to work with him over celebrating with us.

"I am so sorry, Lanie. I knew I had to get home but the days just piled up. I am so sorry I wasn't there for any of that. I put too much importance on myself and ignored how you might need me."

"Now what?" Melanie asked, wiping tears with the back of her hand.

"Can you forgive me?" Will said.

"I already did."

"Then wipe it away," Beth said, holding out a tissue. "Slowly, carefully. Intentionally."

Melanie rubbed the words away, leaving a black smear. She took another tissue from the box on the table and rubbed and rubbed until no speck remained.

"How do you feel?" Will asked.

She glanced at Beth. "It's not how I feel, right? It's what I determined to do and then did. But it feels . . . pretty good." Melanie liked the symbolism and the notion of Jesus using His hand to blot out her sins in His book.

Beth nodded at Will, and he turned his board to Melanie. She squinted at the picture he had drawn. It was a crude rendition of their home in Nashville with a giant lock on the front door. "That

Thanksgiving when Sophie was two," Will said. "You changed the locks and never told me or gave me a new key."

"I changed them the week before Halloween," Melanie said. "I said I'd give you a key that weekend, but you didn't come home."

"You could have mailed me one."

"I wanted you to come home. So I could tell you," Melanie said, "that I was scared. We'd had two break-ins on the street, and I told you I was scared and wanted a dog. And you said no because dogs needed training, especially big dogs, and Sophie was just a little girl. So I bought a stronger lock instead. But I shouldn't have done that without considering how it would make you feel—no doubt shut out of your own home—and even out of our lives."

"Are you willing to wipe it away?" Beth asked.

"Of course," Will said and reached for the tissues.

"Wait," Melanie said. "Can we do it together?"

He took her hand in his and together they dabbed away his picture. "It's good this way," he said.

Melanie breathed a silent *amen.*

—

Thursday afternoon

Carrie couldn't stop fidgeting. Melanie smiled and said, "I know you've had a gynecological exam before."

"Not with a baby looking out the other side," Carrie said. "Can you come in the examining room with me?"

"Of course. If you're really sure?"

"Not about a blessed thing. But I'm not facing that speculum alone."

Thirty minutes later Carrie had seen an ultrasound of her

baby, was told to buy prenatal vitamins and iron pills, and listened to a lecture on not standing up too fast because, "my dear, you do have low blood pressure and probably anemia, so stress less and sleep more."

She'd gotten through her first visit with an obstetrician. And tonight she had a date—sort of—with Jared. The encampment was hosting a pig roast for holiday shoppers. "Who can resist that aroma?" he had said. "We'll have a chance to chat them up while we're feeding them."

Riots and arrests were starting in the Seattle MoveIn. How long would Jared be able to keep his people peaceful? If there wasn't any excitement, most would leave when bitter January came. He would too. Would he get a job, join the Peace Corp, travel to a Florida MoveIn site?

Could she and Jared work something out where they found common ground? Time would tell and maybe God would too.

After getting dressed, Carrie found Melanie in the waiting room.

"Let's go," Melanie said. "He's waiting."

He was Jeremy Wainwright. Active volunteer in Dave's Concord group. Architect, deacon at his church, father of Carrie's baby. She had made the appointment yesterday to meet him at his office. No doubt he thought she wanted to see him and fish for another donation.

He couldn't imagine this, and didn't. Carrie could tell by the look on his face when she was escorted into his office. He hadn't connected the name to the face—or in her case, the body. Strongly built, he had sandy hair, elfin eyes, and a quick smile to cover his surprise that Ms. Connors was the woman he had bedded in a nest of golden leaves and warm sunshine two months ago.

"Um, I'm sorry I didn't call you," he said, holding her hand between his. "I feel like a jerk."

"Hey. Neither of us promised to do anything. However, we did do one thing together." Carrie pressed her hand to her abdomen.

"No." Jeremy leaned against his desk. "I used—"

"Not correctly, apparently."

"What can I do for you . . . uh."

"I don't need you to do anything for me. Or the baby. I needed you to know that he or she exists. I haven't decided yet on adoption or keeping it."

"Do you need money? Medical bills or child support?"

Carrie laughed. "Can we sit down? You look like you're about to keel over."

"That day up in Hooksett was a mistake. A huge moment of weakness."

"I know. For me too. I am sorry."

He shook his head. "No, I'm the one who should be sorry. I knew better."

"I debated not telling you, more from embarrassment than anything else. That would have been wrong. So . . . now you know."

"What can I do?" Jeremy asked. "I don't want you to have to deal with this alone. I can't . . . wrap my head around this."

"Trust me, I understand," Carrie said. "For now, I'll make sure you have my contact information. I want to think through what's best for the child. You get to be part of any decision if you want. If not, I'm okay with moving forward on my own. That may mean adoption."

Jeremy shrank back in his chair. It was hitting him hard. She'd had days to consider the pregnancy when her period was late and she'd had to work up courage to buy a pregnancy test. This was a sixty-second dump on this poor guy's head.

"I don't know how to think about this," Jeremy said. "I don't know where to begin."

"Maybe you could touch base with me every month or so?

And please understand that I don't need anything from you. I have family support and I have means. If I keep this child, he or she will have a father figure."

"A boyfriend?"

"My brother." Will had already volunteered. He wanted to redeem the name Billy. Melanie was on board if Carrie wanted to give it a go, and Sophie was already thinking of baby names for her cousin.

Carrie had to slow them down. Pray about this. Let Jeremy have his say. Do what was best for the child.

Her Lord's heritage.

Thursday evening

Will surprised Melanie with his request to visit the Donegan farm and see Dillon's film. "I shouldn't have thrown away the stills," he said. "I should have taken a better look."

"Have you seen something?" she asked, clutching his collar in a sudden panic.

"No. We've been scheduling the girls pretty tightly. We use that Jericho group as an excuse. It's just . . . I owe it to you to have really listened."

"I was irrational," Melanie said. "In expressing myself."

"Sure. But that doesn't mean that you weren't picking up on something."

"Or just projecting. Now I'm not sure." She trailed her finger along his jaw. "I never told you the real reason I wanted to see all of Dillon Whittaker's film."

"You thought I was screwing around," Will said. "I may be

single-focused most of the time, but that was a pretty obvious ploy. Why haven't we discussed this in therapy?"

Melanie laughed. "We haven't gotten that far yet. Should we discuss it now?"

"Say the words, Lanie. Tell me what *it* is."

"Victoria Peters."

"Yeah. I figured that out with your request that Carrie make the Iowa trip and Victoria stay with you. What did you see on film?"

"A beautiful woman who commands attention from every man she encounters. That includes you. The exception is Dave—and that's probably because he's so disciplined."

"I'll admit, I thought about it," Will said, his voice breaking. "This spring and summer were so lonely. Carrie, me, a skeleton staff. I needed Carrie to take on more so we brought Victoria up. She's brilliant, you know. It's not always easy to see the brains under that fine packaging. And being in a quieter environment early on and all the monotony—it was tough for me."

"I'm sorry," Melanie said. "I'm the one who put you in that position."

"Yeah, well . . . we don't have the whiteboards with us, so let's just hold that thought for later. It's both of us and thank God—*oh, thank You, Jesus*—it's both of us going forward. In a way, we can thank Victoria for me going to see Beth. I realized that I couldn't take marital limbo anymore. And if you say 'I'm sorry,' I'm going to—"

"What?"

Will grinned. "Kiss you so you'll shut up about being sorry."

"I'm sorry," Melanie said. "I'm sorry sorry sorry."

He kissed her. After a long moment, he said, "Let's call Jeanne, see if we can go there tonight."

An hour later they were at the Donegans' farm, scanning the latest batch of raw film. At one point, Melanie stepped out to use the bathroom. Jeanne met her in the hall. "I know this isn't about campaign stuff," she said. "And you don't need to tell me. I just want you to know . . . I'm praying for you."

Melanie hugged her and went back into the den Dillon used for his editing. Will stared up at her with a stricken look. "What?" she said.

He showed her a session filmed four days earlier. It was the situation room, where Dillon was allowed when nonvital matters were being discussed. He had likely set up the camera at the front of the room and left it running. The room was almost empty.

Eli DuPont and his assistant huddled over photos for brochures at the front of the room. Sophie was at the back, working at her laptop. Mike McGregor sat next to her at a discreet distance, picking at his laptop with one hand.

"It's the look on her face," Will said. "I've never seen her smile like that. As if she has a secret."

He zoomed the image. Melanie's head spun because she knew what Will must have already seen, and she knew how it had been with Carl. And all she could do was watch the fuzzy image of Mike's hand coming to rest on Sophie's knee.

Sophie just sat there, holding her breath.

Melanie knelt next to Will because she couldn't stand, couldn't even keep her head up. She didn't know what to pray because guilt strangled her with a noose of regrets and what-ifs.

If she hadn't tumbled into this herself, maybe Sophie wouldn't have. If she had only been honest with herself and with Beth, they could have been more alert. If she had just fought to bring Sophie home or come up to New Hampshire weeks earlier, her daughter would have been protected.

If. If. Like a gun firing, each *if* finding a mark.

She groaned and remembered that Jeanne was praying, and that was the only light in what had become a very dark world.

"I'll kill him," Will said.

Melanie made herself stand because she couldn't let him do anything in this moment. She wrapped her arms around him and squeezed. "She's safe," she said. "She's with Dave and Miranda in North Conway. And Mike's in Iowa, right?"

Will yanked away, dialed Sophie's number. Melanie took the phone from him. "You're too upset," she said. "I'll check on her."

What miracle had given her this control of her voice, this clear head? Sophie answered with a cheerful, "What's up?"

"How's North Conway?" Melanie said. Will paced like a wild beast. She grabbed his right arm before he could put it through Dillon's editing screen.

"Awesome. Hannah and I did some trail work in the National Forest. I actually like hiking, it turns out. Who knew, right? We got the photo op, of course. And the trail volunteers are so cool. Maybe I'll go to college up here and get a forestry degree."

"Where are you now, honey?"

"In the ballroom of the Mount Washington Hotel. It's beautiful, so stately. But I was a little creeped out when we drove up because it's like that hotel in *The Shining*."

She's fine, Melanie mouthed to Will. She listened to four more minutes of Sophie's excitement—what they had eaten for dinner, what she was wearing to the black-tie fund-raiser for White Mountain National Forest, what Hollywood actor was rumored to be there in support of the park system. "And if he's also here in support of the senator, we'll get a picture, and Eli said he'd make sure I was in the photo."

"It sounds marvelous," Melanie said. "Don't wander too far from Hannah, okay?"

"Oh, Mother," Sophie said. "Why do you have to ruin everything?"

"Oh, Daughter," Melanie said, holding back her emotion, "it's my job. Because I love you."

"Love you too, and now I have to go. Bye."

"This is all my fault," Will said. "You told me, and I thought you were coming from a warped perspective."

"First of all, it's not your fault. These guys . . . they're devious. And I've been seeing shadows everywhere so my judgment was unreliable." Melanie tightened her arms around his waist. "We'll check in with Beth first thing in the morning. She'll help us."

"I want to get up to North Conway tonight," Will said. "I need to see with my own eyes that she is safe."

"That's a two-hour trip from here."

"I don't care."

Melanie texted Jason Polke.

Can you have someone keep an extra eye on Sophie? This is her first big event without Will or Carrie.

Jason's reply was prompt.

Already on it. She has instructions to stay in sight.

"I still want to go," Will said.

"Of course," Melanie said. She was desperate to go too, and grateful that she wasn't the one to have to say it. They hugged Jeanne and went out into the cold night to find their daughter.

twenty-nine

Thursday night

AS THE DAUGHTER OF PROMINENT PEOPLE, CARRIE had been to elegant state dinners. Mother had started her when Carrie was five and Daddy had just died. She had thrown an Oscar-worthy tantrum at being left with the nanny. Her mother finally washed her face, dressed her, and brought her as her escort to the state dinner for the prime minister of India.

Mother went in black and pearls. Carrie remembered wearing a creamy blue dress. Legend said she had been a captivating dinner partner, but Will said she'd simply been a good reason for Mother not to break down in tears.

She'd dined in Paris and London and Japan at Mother's side and, for these past five years or so, been Will's dinner partner in DC in Melanie's absence. She had never dressed as carefully as she did tonight.

Her jeans were getting tight. This was really happening. What would Jared think when she sprouted a belly instead of a six-pack? Did it even matter? Snow was forecasted for next week, perhaps a Nor'easter that could drive MoveIn out of the public square and back to whatever dorm rooms, eco-huts, or homeless shelters they came from.

She settled on a pair of woolen slacks that had a little give at the waist. She slipped on a white turtleneck and a red sweater because she felt in a holiday mood. What a relief to have everything out in the open and to think rationally about the future.

If Carrie were to keep this child, she would have to curtail her career and rely on Will and his family. If Jeremy Wainwright wanted to be in this sprout's life, he had the right. On the other hand, there was adoption. Melanie was so right—the world would be at a loss if Julia Whittaker had aborted Destiny instead of surrendering her for adoption.

Decisions like these were tricky, even when one had family and money. What must a single woman with no means go through? Carrie had ignored the reality of some women, working the mechanics of her job and letting Dave ooze the empathy.

She now had an inkling of what Jared meant when he said *see us*. Religion was a matter of tradition, rules, causes. Faith had a human face and Carrie suspected if she looked, she might *see* that face.

See us, Jared had said. *See Me first*, Jesus said.

"Don't expect perfection." Carrie grabbed her jacket.

She took the stairs to the ground floor because she had the energy and could go faster than the elevator. At the bottom, the door opened, giving her a heart attack. Tuck, looking drained. Carrie kissed his cheek and then hugged him. "You're back?"

He smiled. "You disappointed?"

"Are you staying? I don't see any luggage."

"I sent it up with the bellhop. I decided to take the stairs so I wouldn't have to make polite conversation."

"Here, sit. Tell me about it." She sat on the bottom step, patted the spot next to her.

"Hey. Thank you for flying down for the service. You and your brother. I know how busy you are."

"I just wanted you . . . to have a friend. How did the rest go?"

"You know what's odd? The board of directors thinks I've got a good face for the camera. They want me to be the public face while they restructure."

"What do you want, Tuck? You must own a majority share, or you will when probate clears."

"I own J.L.'s share. My mother still owns my father's share. She's kept it all this time, in case I ever needed leverage."

Carrie smiled. This was a different side of Tuck—someone who actually thought past the next pub crawl. "I have a feeling you used that leverage."

"The board wants to sell off some of the physical resources and the contracts for our best writers. I fought them because I want *The Journal* to go into this millennium, not Chapter 11 bankruptcy." He grinned, stretched his legs out. "I had already been talking to some Amazon people I'd done some hacking around with. They have big ideas about how to deliver information faster without losing accuracy and integrity of content. I've been back and forth with them for the past year in case my grandfather actually admitted we needed to make a change. I didn't expect this change, of course."

"You thought he'd live forever?" Carrie said.

"He always had. A legend, right?"

"So . . . you staying or going?"

Tuck shrugged. "The paper is going to lumber on for the next month or so while my buddies design a business plan for the tech side. I'm in New Hampshire until the primary. Then I'll decide what I want to do. The point is, Carrie—I want to do something. Something that counts."

"And journalism doesn't?"

"There's one thing I know about good reporting." Tuck helped her stand up. "It isn't about the Pulitzer."

"I don't understand."

"I don't either. But I will. Where are you off to?"

"The pig roast. I'm meeting some people across the street. I've got to run. Maybe we can have lunch tomorrow, if you're still in Manchester."

"Sure." He kissed her forehead. "Be safe."

He seems happy, Carrie thought as his footsteps echoed in the hallway. For all their making merry in college and the occasional socializing in DC, had he never been happy? He'd been high and giddy and funny. Contentment was a new fit on him. She liked it.

Carrie smelled the roasting pig as soon as she left the Radisson. The valet parking crew was positively salivating. She'd ask Jared to send them over a couple plates of food.

The night was overcast, keeping the temperatures from plunging. The air buzzed with holiday excitement. Shoppers crowded the sidewalk, many of them carrying bulky shopping bags. The smartest thing this city had done was to convert empty buildings on this street into outlet shopping. The name stores like Banana Republic and L.L. Bean were in one of the big brick complexes. The older department stores—some empty since the eighties—had offered less expensive options to local craftspeople or bargain sellers. This night had been advertised for a month as twenty-percent night where all stores offered deep discounts.

Because Jared planned well, MoveIn had the permits to offer food. Will's local liaison was still kicking herself for not pulling the permits first. "We just want to talk to people," he had told Carrie. "And listen to them."

Dawson volunteers would be passing out balloons marked with "Common Sense." They didn't add the name Dawson so no one could accuse them of using kids as pawns.

Politicians did that all the time. Children in need made the best pawns. No, Carrie would not be cynical. Not this night when the smell of roasting pig and now apple crisp made her believe everyone could sit at the same table.

The Movers had folded up about half their tents to make room for the pig roasters and tables of corn bread and baked beans. Carrie saw about six health violations that would make Massachusetts bring back the death penalty if this were fifteen miles south. New Hampshire proclaimed "Live free or die" and didn't try to pass off gluten-free soy patties as roast pig.

As long as no one died from trichinosis, they should all be just fine.

Jared paced the perimeter of the crowd, his hair tied back in a knot. He wore a light blue sweater, black jeans, and motorcycle boots. He could fit in with the shoppers or the protestors or even the staffers who went to the black-tie with Dave and Miranda. An *everyman* with freckles and a deep fire.

Maybe someday he would be president.

Jared spotted her and waved. She headed his way, then stopped when her phone buzzed. Being available by phone was Will's condition for giving her this night off.

"Jared," she said and then yelled, "Jared!"

He ran to her and pulled her close. "Are you okay?"

"No. That blasted Joshua is trying to ruin Christmas." She instinctively pressed her hand to her belly. Together they watched the screen flood with red—even as the Christmas lights sparkled around them.

—

Thursday night

Melanie and Will were almost to the highway when he said, "What is Sophie wearing tonight?"

"What does that matter? Slow down, Will. I want to get there in one piece."

"You said you started dressing differently. For Carl. I should have noticed—"

"Stop, Will. Just stop. Recriminations won't get us there faster."

"Check Mike's itinerary again."

"It'll still say Iowa like it did fifteen minutes ago." And the five minutes after that when Melanie had checked it without telling him.

Will slammed on the brakes, took a hard right into a liquor store parking lot. "I need to check something." He tapped his way through a series of screens on his phone.

Sophie did wear her black dress, didn't she? Melanie had bought her a modest one with a high front and slight scoop to the back neckline. She looked mature in it, attractive but not flashy. What if Sophie had raided Carrie's closet? Her sister-in-law dressed with an elegance but also a bit of a zing that was appropriate for a career woman but not a teenager.

Why was she obsessing on this? Because obsession was the only protection she could provide her daughter when they were a hundred miles apart.

"Come on, come on," Will muttered, shaking his phone. "Our account at the airline is so slow."

"Holiday ticket-buyers," Melanie said, logging onto Facebook. Sophie had posted some pictures of tonight's fund-raiser. She did wear her black dress. The heels were new, rhinestone-encrusted platforms with ribbon laced around Sophie's calves. With the heavy eye makeup, her daughter looked like one of those foolish women on those endless Housewives of Rich Means and Poor Taste shows.

"Oh no," Will said. "McGregor's got an open ticket between Manchester and Iowa."

"That doesn't mean anything," Melanie said. "Don't you all have that? If you don't, someone's wasting your— Oh no. No.

Look." She showed him Sophie's latest photo on Facebook. She and Hannah waved for the camera at the fund-raiser.

"Is that Mike?" Will said.

"I can't tell." She zoomed in on the photo. The background images were fuzzy, but the man stood with Mike's confident posture.

"Call her. I'll call him."

Melanie dialed. Sophie's phone went to voice mail. Melanie's screen flashed red. "Will. Will!"

"I've got it too."

Please, Father in heaven—all we want to do is make sure our daughter's safe. And now this?

"It is midnight in America." The Joshua marionette wore his skeletal face and the Uncle Sam costume. This image had been ridiculed on editorial pages and blogs for the past month. The hacking of the Health and Human Services database of medical records was no joke. Nor was the chill in Melanie's spine.

"Dude can't tell time," Will said. "Let's just go."

"No, wait," Melanie said.

"We the people of the United States in order to form a more perfect union, establish justice, ensure domestic tranquility—" Joshua tipped his head back and laughed in that jaw-clacking way that sent skitters up Melanie's spine.

She glanced at the two guys in front of the liquor store. Both held phones, the red glow reflecting off their faces.

Joshua shook his finger at the screen. "How's that justice and peace treating you? Oh, how you love your neighbors, eh? I waste time with such absurd questions. The answers are self-evident. Look at who you are."

The screen dissolved into rapid cut-ins from the news. Historical moments—the shooting of John Kennedy, Lyndon Johnson being sworn in with a blood-splattered Jacqueline Kennedy at his side, fire hoses used against civil rights protestors, the Klan lynching a black man, napalm being dropped in Southeast Asia, the beating of Rodney King, the *Challenger* explosion. The cut-ins advanced to rallies. Gay rights, pro-life, pro-choice, SEIU, Tea Party, Occupy Wall Street.

Will took deep breaths. "We're that . . . but so much more."

Joshua was touting the shame of America as if nothing good or right had ever come of the nation. Melanie felt rage coalescing because that which was good and lovely—like Sophie—was prey for vultures. You could plug a hole one place and a minute later the vultures ripped the veil elsewhere and let the light trickle out and the poison rush in.

"I can't bear it," Melanie said.

"Don't watch. We need to get moving." Will glanced over at the liquor store. The two young men in hoodies stared at their car.

She couldn't help herself, watched the grainy film of drones exploding homes and shops. The drones became planes that plowed into the towers, first one, and as that billowed smoke, the second plane hit, followed by the collapse and the unending dust of this generation's innocence.

The Joshua character emerged from the dust, morphing to flesh and blood, his face shadowed by a black hoodie. He wore black jeans and carried a club. "'Hypocrites! How is it you know how to interpret the appearance of the earth and the sky?'

"'How is it that you don't know how to interpret this present time?'

"It is midnight in America. Are you sheep—content to be herded and sheared? Or are you men and women who are ready to march? If you've had enough, then listen to the Lord Almighty inside your head, because there is no other God but you. You alone determine fate. You become your own destiny if you are willing to raise your arm—"

Melanie gasped as Joshua raised the bat over his head and

swung. The image on the screen shattered, shooting spikes of lightning in a sea of blood.

If Sophie sees this, she'll be scared, and whose arms will she run to?

Joshua reappeared, now with a black executioner's mask. The image doubled and then increased exponentially into an army. "'Behold! A mighty storm is rising from the ends of the earth.'"

"That's from Jeremiah," Will said.

"Our only salvation," Joshua said, "is in the reboot. Turn it all off, tear it all down, and those who are not sheep will rise from the ashes. The rest we simply grind underfoot. You will shine in the darkness. Jericho must fall. And I must . . ."

What followed wasn't a shout or a scream or even a shriek. Coyotes, Melanie realized. It was like the howl of the pack when the prey is brought down. The screech of bloodlust when coyotes gorge on their prey's innards.

As suddenly as it came, the video disappeared.

Melanie stared again at Facebook. "What now?" she said.

"Now that we've seen the latest cartoon, let's be grown-ups and go check on our daughter. This isn't the best place to linger."

The world went black.

Streetlights, storefronts, security lights, windows of homes across the street—all went out. And Melanie's phone, *please, God, not the phone.* The only light came from their headlights, shining on the pavement.

Will put the car into drive but he was too late because a hulking shadow in a hoodie slammed a trash can against the driver's-side window. The glass held, Melanie screamed, and Will fumbled with the gearshift. The trash can came down again. Though it wouldn't be able to break the safety glass, the sound was nearly unbearable.

"Drive," Melanie said.

"I can't." The other hooded man blocked the path of the car.

Melanie fumbled in her purse for pepper spray and thought how stupid—it wasn't like she'd roll down the window to use it. At least she had it if they broke through the safety glass.

Will inched the car forward as the man with the trash can bashed it against the car. *Bang! Bang!* Melanie prayed, *Dear God, please don't let them have guns.*

"Move!" Will bellowed. The other man in front of the car just stood there. Will turned his steering wheel to the right to get around him. The man jumped, landing on the hood of their car, his face on their windshield. Melanie cried out because they were trapped—she and Will in the car—and these two young men, playing parts in Joshua's drama.

"Use the windshield wipers," she said. "With the washing fluid."

"What?"

"Just do it, please, Will, do it and get ready to drive."

Will fumbled for the controls. "Blasted rentals," he said and suddenly the wiper fluid squirted up and the guy on the hood pulled back, startled. Will peeled hard to the right and the guy let go, tumbling to the pavement. The other guy flung the trash can at the car and stood silhouetted in the red from the brake lights.

The war that the hackers had waged in cyberspace had come to the streets.

thirty

Thursday night

MANCHESTER SEEMED TO HAVE HELD ITS COLLECTIVE breath while shoppers, storekeepers, and protestors viewed the latest video from Joshua and his Jericho group. When it was finished and her phone resumed, Carrie laughed. "What an idiot."

"I don't know what all that accomplishes," Jared said. "Other than to close people's minds to things that really—"

Darkness fell with a thud.

Streetlamps and stores blacked out. Carrie's phone service died so that the only light was from the reddish glow of emergency boxes and the orange glow of the coals in the pig cookers.

She was more angry than frightened because it was fine if some hackers wanted to play games, but did they have to take the Christmas lights away from what had been a magical night?

"Come on," Jared said. "I've got flashlights."

"Of course you do." Holding on to his sleeve, Carrie followed him to the main tent. Jared led the way with a penlight. Prepared for this, her cynical side wondered—or just marvelously prepared in general?

He unlocked a trunk and showed her piles of flashlights and boxes of batteries. "We've got to load batteries in quickly," he said, "before a panic starts."

"Right. Because who besides you carries a penlight? Where did all these come from?"

"FEMA," he said. "Left over from Hurricane Sandy. We bought them last year at pennies per unit. All the encampments have them."

"Why?" Carrie didn't bother to hide the sharpness in her tone. "Did you expect this?"

Jared held his penlight under his chin like a child telling a ghost story. "What do you think?"

Suspect everyone. That was the lesson drilled into her by Mother and Will. She was a good student, and she *had* suspected everyone—even God. Because no one has pure motives. Jared would be the first to acknowledge that.

"This is what I think," she said and kissed him. He laughed, kissed her back—twice—before they got to the business of loading batteries into flashlights.

When they had an armful ready, they went out to the street. Enterprising people had turned on their car headlights. Traffic jammed the main roads because the stoplights weren't functioning.

"Be selective. Give them to elderly folks or people with young kids," Jared said. "I've got about a hundred total. In this crowd, that won't last. You're okay, right?"

"Sure. Just . . . as long as you stay near." Light flashed behind her. *They're coming back on,* but when she turned, she saw it was the Radisson. The generators must have kicked in. The lamps on the sidewalk and the dimly lit lobby looked like an oasis from a block away.

"Why don't I walk you back to the hotel?" Jared said. "Things could get ugly out here."

Carrie tugged his ear. "I just got here. You're not making me leave."

He laughed and pulled her in for another kiss. The elderly

woman they had just given a flashlight to shined it on them. People hooted and clapped. *Okay—maybe there's Christmas spirit here after all.*

And then a woman screamed. Someone shouted and another person screamed and Jared said, "They've been shopping. It's the shopping."

Carrie couldn't comprehend what he was saying until someone in a hoodie pushed by, clutching a boxed laptop. A man chased him, yelling, "Stop him, he's a mugger!" The chaser tripped over something and sprawled into a shadow. Someone slammed into Carrie. She went down hard, her face scraping pavement.

She lay there, trying to catch her breath. Then someone kicked her. Pain ripped through her side. *My baby, dear God, save my baby!*

She tried to get up. Jared found her, pulled her up, asked if she was okay. Sirens split the night. Police cars—three cars, *thank You, Jesus*—worked their way past the parked cars and the terrified shoppers, lighting the night with flashing blue.

She took a shallow sigh of relief and winced at pain from what had to be a broken rib. She leaned against Jared and heard him shout, "No, no, stop it!" She looked at the line of cop cars and saw a crowd of kids rocking the police car from side to side.

The first car went over with a clunk, the lights now upside down and cops getting out of their cars, weapons drawn.

Carrie heard a *pop*. One of the policemen spun sideways, grasping his arm.

"Get down," Jared said.

"No, I'll get trampled. Why—"

"Get down!" He pushed her to her knees and wrapped his body around hers.

Carrie wanted to scream at his stupidity until she heard a *pop pop pop*, and Jared yelling, "Stay down," and he pushed her face into the ground he had just helped her up from. "They're shooting, they're shooting, stay low."

People started running away from the shots, and Jared got up, hands in the air, shouting, "You're okay, everyone, please just stop. Please stop, and it'll be okay." Though Carrie believed him, no one else apparently did, because someone crashed into him and he landed on top of her.

Something exploded, a thundering boom that brought a breath of silence and then more screaming. Carrie peered out from under Jared's arms and saw a fist of flame rising into the air.

"God, please don't let anyone be hurt," she said. Jared just moaned and she realized he was wounded.

A window shattered somewhere and then another one. This was Joshua's army, anyone who would grab a stick or rock and bring havoc onto a peaceful street of holiday shoppers. She had worried about votes and money and policy positions and forgotten that governing was the product of the goodwill and trust of people.

There was only one law that could ensure tranquility.

In the chaos and pain, fear and darkness, there would be hell to pay. And could someone please turn the Christmas lights back on?

Thursday night

Tuck watched from his luxury suite on the top floor of the Radisson as darkness and light battled on the street below. Light strobed out of alleys and side streets, police vehicles unable to get onto the main road because of the crowd and a tangle of traffic. The headlights illuminated terrified people, many with little children.

Youths in hoods ran through the crowd, mugging people for their shopping bags, smashing windows on storefronts, creating havoc because they could.

Tuck shut his blackout drapes against the madness. Television and his phone were out but he could listen to his iPod, maybe some classical music, get into bed, and pretend nothing was happening. Pull up the covers, hope the locks on his door held, pray that no one set the hotel on fire.

Wait out the blackout until order was restored.

He tabbed up some music, had forgotten that he had an FM radio. He found a good signal and heard the deep tones of a news reporter. He listened, absorbing pieces, making little sense of it.

"Two massive blackouts . . . The Northeast from Montreal to New York City . . . The West Coast from San Diego to Seattle . . . Simultaneous loss of power . . . Switching stations crashed, cell communications and satellite transmissions blocked. Hacker group Jericho hijacked airwaves with threats . . . Massive act of terrorism. White House statement, 'Stay calm. Power should be restored shortly. Shelter in place.'"

Tuck would obey and hide under the covers. When it was all over, he'd go back to movie reviews because it was stupid to think being involved in politics could give his life meaning.

And yet the clamor of the world—the chaos of the street—filtered in. "Jesus," he said, halfway between a curse and a prayer. He flipped his iPod onto the bed, went back to the windows and saw the pig roaster in Veteran's Park explode.

Carrie was down there somewhere. He said "Jesus" again, this time feeling the desperation that turned it from curse to prayer.

He slipped on his sneakers, pulled on a sweatshirt, and went out.

The elevator wasn't working. He took the stairs. Eight flights, dark closing in, his heart pounding, sweat pouring down his back, wanting a drink.

No. No drink. He was a journalist now and it was his duty to get out there, observe and report.

The lobby was lit—they must have some generator power—and surprisingly empty. Two men guarded the main entrance, iron bars jamming the frames so the door couldn't be pried open.

The only thing Tuck could see in the window was his own reflection. He heard the shouts and screaming from outside. Somewhere farther away, the *pop pop* of what had to be gunfire.

He pressed his face to the glass. Observe and report. That didn't mean he had to actually go out there. He could go back to his suite—high above the insanity—and take notes from up there. Or he could even do it from one of the first-floor conference rooms where no one could see him.

Observe and report. He saw people searching for a way out of the madness. It wasn't his problem and yet he heard himself say, "Open the door."

"Can't," one of the guards said.

"People are scared. We've got light. Let them in." And there it was—the metaphor for this presidential campaign, the message of Dave Dawson and many others, including MoveIn.

This Jericho movement was antithetical to people drawing together as a nation. Joshua's cry for anarchy was the greatest enemy America could face.

Tuck wanted to run upstairs and hide from this madness and this realization. Instead, as if his feet had a life of their own, he ran to the main desk and said to the night manager, "We've got to let them in."

"Liability," the man said. His face was shadowed in the lesser light. "Can't."

"There're kids out there, for heaven's sake!" Tuck slammed his hand on the counter. "I'll cover any liability. Just please open the door, and let the people in."

"I'll lose my job."

"I'll get you another one."

"You can't do that."

Tuck pulled out his wallet, showed the night manager his license. "Have you watched the news? They've been reporting for two days about the death of John Larter Keyes."

The manager squinted at the license and then Tuck. "You're related to that Keyes?"

"And now I own his newspaper," Tuck said. "So open the door and we'll worry about the rest later."

The manager stared at Tuck, then waved one of the security guards to the counter. "I'll open the door, Mr. Keyes. But it's on you if any of those punks get in. You understand what I'm saying?"

Tuck nodded, went back to the main door, and waited while the guards unlocked the iron bars. He took the arm of an elderly woman whose face was tight with terror and helped her in. The security guards stood on either side of the door and herded people into the lobby.

Sirens continued to wail. Some stores and houses had light, running on generators. What would happen when the gas or diesel ran out? The Jericho group that took down the grid probably built in firewalls to keep the power company or the feds from bringing it back up quickly.

Would Joshua give back the lights like he did in the arena? Or would this be a cyberbattle with real casualties?

Tuck spotted Carrie in the crowd, arms wrapped around Jared O'Dea. They were both bloodied. Carrie was clear eyed but O'Dea seemed loopy. Tuck ran to help them. The three staggered into the hotel.

The lobby was emptying, the manager telling Tuck, "We're moving them into the ballroom."

Tuck steered Carrie and O'Dea into the breakfast nook, past a glaring maintenance man who stood guard at the stairs. He would have taken them to his room, but the elevator was out and neither could make the climb up eight flights.

They helped O'Dea lie on a bench. Carrie worked at the sleeves of his sweater, trying to get at his wounds. "Get me some napkins or towels," she told Tuck. "We need to look at his wound. We got trampled, got up, and then the windows were breaking and glass was flying."

"Shush," Tuck said. "It's okay now. What about you?"

"Ribs, cut, nothing much. I'm pregnant, by the way. And no, Jared's not the daddy."

"I'll congratulate you later. I'll be right back with some towels."

Tuck ran back to the lobby, got the manager to give him a card key for the laundry, ran to the basement to collect a bundle of towels, then to the maid's closet to get some bottled water, back to the lobby to ask if they had a first-aid kit.

The manager dug through his emergency supplies. "There's looting in Seattle and Philadelphia," the manager said. "It's only been a few minutes and already things are falling apart. They've got FEMA and troops and all this other heavy gear moving into the cities."

"It's quieted out here," Tuck said and saw the reason why. Armored SWAT troops moved through the main street, lit by floodlights and carrying automatic weapons and shields.

One group of hackers did all this. Both coasts of the United States brought to their knees because the nation was no longer strong enough to stand up for itself.

God, help us. It startled Tuck that he actually meant it.

Thursday night

Melanie listened in silent dismay to reports of riots, looting, fires. Already cities in the Northeast and out west were battling looters. Unthinkable.

At least the back roads in New Hampshire were quiet. Will drove, keeping his speed down because there was little light anywhere. The rare convenience store or gas station was closed. In this rural area houses were set back from the road and hidden by brush.

They had stopped at a police station, asked to make a call on their landline. The desk sergeant glared until Will flashed his Senate ID. They got the call to go through to the Mount Washington Hotel. The desk clerk said, "Yes, the blackout is up here too, but we've got some emergency lights, and the guests seem comfortable. The heating system is a priority for generator use because of the cold. Sorry, but we can't track down individual guests, but anyone in the hotel is quite safe, I can assure you."

Melanie wasn't assured at all. The best course of action was to drive safely, pray for Sophie, and oh—how the list went on and on.

"Did you know?" she asked.

"That this was possible?" Will said. "Of course. If a hacker or group got into a substation, they might be able to cripple the switching and transformer stations."

"How?"

"You're asking me? Victoria would know," Will said. "I think they could put programs into a loop so that human operators couldn't get real-time information. And there're viruses and the like to disturb communication between servers."

"Isn't there a defense good enough?"

"You think we don't do this too?" Will said. "Use cyberterrorism?"

"For good means. Taking out weapons systems. And the rumor about Iran's nuclear program."

"No comment on that. It is like the war waged against 'principalities and powers of the air.' Nations like China and Russia might be trading partners, but they still mess with us. And you've got Iran and various militant groups."

"So we don't know what this Jericho is?"

"Maybe Jericho is homegrown or maybe not—freedom of speech and of association make us vulnerable."

"It also makes us great," Melanie said. "There's no firewall to life. I've spent thirty years thinking I could make one."

Will reached for her hand. "We're through the worst part of it."

"No!" Melanie pulled away. "No, we're not. Not until we make sure Sophie is safe from Mike McGregor."

They traveled in silence for the next hour except for the occasional check-ins with the news. Reports were spotty because most cell phone carriers were down and old-fashioned landline phones were scarce.

Melanie felt a flutter as they reached North Conway. The hotel was still almost twenty miles west, but this was the last landmark. The trip past the town's outlet stores with generators was too quick and then they were back in darkness.

"If they're a nationally sponsored group, the answer is obvious," Will said. "If they're a group of hackers flexing their muscles, the answer is murkier. The nature of pure anarchy is not to worry about what comes next. They tear things down, just to watch what struggles out of the rubble."

"Entertainment."

"What? What are you talking about?"

"Will, they're bored. I just know it. This is all about pulling the strings and seeing how we jump. The whole marionette in the

Uncle Sam outfit is a sick joke. Social manipulation and civil collapse simply because the beast needs to be fed amusement."

"Dear God," Will said. "I bet you're right."

"It's sick. I can't bear it because it's so sick."

"Lanie." Will pulled the car over, put it in park. "Let's get out."

"Why? Is something wrong with the car?"

"Just for a minute." He turned off the headlights. "Wait for me. I'll come around for you."

He opened his door. In the dome light, she saw the tension in his neck. When he came to the passenger side, she saw a strange serenity in his eyes and his smile. Both couldn't exist simultaneously. And yet she knew—of course they could in Christ.

Will walked her carefully away from the car. "It's dark," she whispered. "It's never as dark as this."

"That's the point. Lanie, look."

Melanie tipped her head back and saw the stars. She'd never seen them like this because there was always too much light.

On this terrible night, this frightening night—before they had even found Sophie—she and her husband were immersed in an endless display of God's power and beauty and wonder.

"In Him," Will said, "all things hold together."

thirty-one

Thursday night

LARGE AND MAJESTIC IN THE DAYLIGHT, THE MOUNT Washington Hotel was a looming specter in the darkness. The lobby seemed well lit but guest rooms had patchy moments of illumination. "Flashlights," Will said. "They'd prioritize generator use for hallways and stairs."

The hotel was locked up for the night. Melanie pushed the buzzer before remembering it couldn't work. Will pounded on the door. "They hear us," he said. "They have to."

"They must have heard the news reports. They're scared," Melanie said.

"So am I. I want to find Sophie." He pounded for a full minute before a woman with sleepy eyes and a blue blazer came to the door. Will had to slip his license and Senate ID under the door before she unlocked it.

"What room is she in?" Melanie said. "They might be listed as Martha and Carrie Hill. That's the name for this week."

"First of all, I am not giving you any guest information. Second, even if I would, I can't. Not with the computer down. The only thing we've got power to are common areas."

"Your two-way radio," Will said. "You would have given our head of security one. Jason Polke."

"I have twenty frequencies," the woman said.

"So try them all. Or hand that to me, and I'll try them."

The woman sighed and systematically went through each channel. She got some cursing for her efforts. "Mostly no one's on the channels," she said. "Electrician, kitchen manager, housekeeping manager—they're all at home."

"Try again. Please," Melanie said. *Please, God.*

The two-way buzzed. The woman tabbed it on. "Yeah, I was looking for you. Do you know a William and Melanie Connors?" She glanced at them. "Could you come down and escort them to your suite of rooms? Okay, thanks."

Two minutes later Jason Polke met them in the lobby. "Are you okay? What is this about?"

Melanie glanced at Will. "Sophie has been involved with someone. We want to make sure that person hasn't taken advantage of her being up here without us."

Jason frowned. "She's with Hannah. I can't imagine . . ."

"You've got three boys," Will said. "Trust me, I *can* imagine. We just want to lay eyes on her."

"Sure. Okay, here's what we'll do. Lanie, I'll let you into the suite and point you to Hannah's room. We'll see if we can do this without waking up Dave and Miranda."

"Been listening to the news?" Will asked as they climbed the stairs.

"I'm not surprised," Jason said. "We spend money on frivolities and pretend we're not vulnerable in key locations. The senator started to draft a new speech about thirty seconds into the blackout. He looked like Abe Lincoln, paper and pen and candlelight."

They went down a long hallway. A security guard sat on a

folding chair, reading a book. They would need Secret Service guys on all the campaigns after this event. What a sad notion.

Jason unlocked the suite, closed the door quietly behind them. The living area was cluttered with the usual campaign stuff. Eli DuPont snored on the sofa, his tablet on his chest.

"That's Hannah's room." Jason pointed to the left.

Melanie knocked softly on the door. No answer. The girls had probably stayed up late and then crashed. She cracked the door a bit. "Sophie?"

"Hmm. What?" Hannah's voice. "Who's there!"

"It's Lanie. I'm looking for Sophie." Melanie swept the room with Will's penlight, spotted Hannah trying to open her eyes. A teddy bear sat on the end of her bed. For all the girls' intelligence and campaign savvy, their parents couldn't forget that Hannah and Sophie were still children.

The other bed in the room was empty.

"Where is Sophie?" Melanie said.

Will came into the room with Jason close behind. "She's not here?"

"She was," Hannah said, rubbing her eyes. "Is she in the bathroom?"

Jason peered in. "No, she's not. Hannah, if she's gone somewhere, we need to know."

"I don't know! Please don't ask me because I don't know."

She did know. Melanie could see it in her face. Maybe she didn't know with whom, but she knew something.

"She wouldn't have gotten by my man," Jason said.

Will pulled the curtains aside. The slider to the veranda was unlocked.

Miranda Dawson came in. "What is going on? Good grief, did someone die?"

My daughter's innocence, Melanie thought. "Tell her, Hannah."

"Tell me what?"

Hannah lay down, pulled the covers over her head. "Nothing."

"Sophie's gone," Will said.

Melanie stared at Miranda, her usual loveliness obscured by dim lighting and lack of sleep. She gently pulled the cover off her daughter. "We need to know where Sophie is."

"I don't know. I swear I don't," Hannah said. "I only know that she's been, like . . . talking to someone with the campaign. About personal stuff. She wouldn't say who, said it was a sweet secret and even I couldn't know. She must have sneaked out after I fell asleep."

"Is that all you know?" Miranda said.

Dave came into the room wearing sweats and thick glasses. "Hannah. If you know something, tell them."

"I swear. That's all I know. Let me get dressed. I'll help look for her."

"Honey, no," Will said. "You just wait here and say a prayer."

Thursday night

Jason took them to Mike's room. It was empty.

"We'll knock on every door until we find her," Dave said.

Will was already heading down the hall. "No," Melanie said.

"Give me one good reason," Will said.

"Two," she said. Her own calm amazed her, as if she could warm her emotional hands by the Spirit's fire. "I don't care about ruining Mike McGregor, but this could bounce back on Dave."

"None of that matters," Dave said, with Miranda nodding.

"And it would devastate Sophie," Melanie said. "I know.

From experience, I know. She's not thinking clearly now, and if we make this public . . . please, trust me."

Will took her arm. "Okay, let's think this through, then."

"We took the van up here," Jason said. "I've got the keys so there's no way to leave this place. We're out in the wildnerness, it's not like they could go on foot. Listen, I'm going to shake the front desk silly until I get a list of guests. He may have booked a second room. Why don't you all check public spaces? Conference rooms and the like."

The skies outside lightened—the full moon coming up. Power remained off. Melanie prayed as they walked every hall, checked the corner of every conference room. This was a huge hotel and lots of real estate to cover.

Dave and Miranda took turns saying, "I am so sorry," and "How did I not know?" Everyone spoke in hushed tones, not wanting to drive Sophie and Mike—*dear Lord*—into hiding. Melanie knew the cost of recriminations because she'd lived them for three decades. She sneaked in prayers for the Dawsons and Will among all her prayers for Sophie.

Please, don't let us be too late. Please be in the flirtation stage and not seduction. Please, Father, have a parent's heart for my child.

Jason caught up to them on the first floor. "Half of the rooms are empty. It's low season until Christmas. Unless he swiped a housekeeping key, I don't think they're in a room."

"This is the last conference room," Will said. "We've got to find them."

Panic rippled through Melanie, waves of heat and cold, as if her body couldn't decide. Her calm was slipping and her fear rising. Each step took her closer to that empty chair—empty room, empty hallway, empty heart—to which she'd been shackled for too long.

Will scanned the corners of the room. "Nothing," he said.

How many meetings and conferences had Melanie helped set up? Tables and chairs had to be kept somewhere nearby. She pointed to what looked like a small closet where she suspected the racks of tables were stored.

Will opened the door, shined the flashlight full on Sophie, clinging to Mike. Will pulled Sophie away, shoved her at Melanie, and then leaped for Mike.

Dave got there first, connecting a solid punch to Mike's nose. Will pulled him off, held him until Miranda had him by the arms. Then he turned to Sophie.

She shook so violently that Melanie had to hold her up. "Shush," she said. "It's okay."

"I hate you, hate you, hate you—"

"That's okay too. We'll work through it." Melanie's fear wilted like a fern in the hot sun. She believed it. They'd work through this, no matter what.

"Just hold on," Will said, arms tight around Sophie and Melanie. "We'll be okay."

Jason helped Mike up, pressed Mike's forearm against his bloody nose.

"I'll sue," Mike said. "She was scared, and I found her, and she thought the voices were Jericho people coming, so I helped her hide."

Dave lunged again. Will caught him by one arm while keeping a grasp on Melanie and Sophie.

"No, that's what he wants," Melanie said.

Sophie had broken into a stream of *how could you*'s. Melanie pushed away the tightness under her ribs by thoughts of that empty chair and her own voice saying, "It's okay, we'll work through it, and we'll keep going."

Friday midday

"It's a nightmare," Will said. "We just need to go home."

Carrie's heart wept for her brother. Melanie had explained everything, including her own molestation thirty years ago.

"I was so stupid," Melanie had said.

Carrie had hugged her. "And I was smart—getting pregnant? We make mistakes."

And now Will sat at the kitchen table, trying to fix everything. Sophie barricaded herself in her room, refusing to do anything but scowl.

"We'll go to Nashville, find a therapist," Will said. "That's what our doc is recommending. Beth isn't the best option because we won't be staying past . . . well, February's off the table now."

"No." Sophie stood in the doorway to her room. Her eyes were so red, they looked painted.

"Hey, peanut," Carrie said.

Melanie rose to go to her. Sophie held out her hand to stop her. "We need to stay in the Dawson campaign. Here and then Florida or wherever we're needed."

"Honey," her mother said. "We've got stuff to work on and Nashville is the best place for all of us."

Sophie slowly walked to the table, sat in the empty chair. "He said that I was special, that no one else was like me. I believed him."

"I know," Melanie said. "I know."

Will rubbed his face. "Baby, I'm sorry. I should have protected you."

"I am not a baby. I just acted like one. It won't happen again."

"Soph," Carrie said, "we all make mistakes. That's when you need family. And we're here. We're all going home to Nashville."

Melanie gave her a sharp look. "What about . . . your friend?"

"Jared will be in the hospital for another day while they

monitor his wound." She cringed at the thought of that long gash in his side. The doctor wasn't clear on whether he had been stabbed or cut by flying glass. Jared only remembered the pain and Carrie only remembered the blood. Whatever it had been, it had just missed his liver.

"You can't leave him," Sophie said.

"I won't, not until he's out of danger. And then he's got to go someplace safe to recuperate."

"What about you . . . and him?" Melanie said.

"He's got his thing, and I've got the baby. I just don't know how to make any of it work."

"You work by not running. By staying." Sophie slowly laid her hands—palms down—on the table. She spread her fingers as if seeking wisdom in the space between. "The senator needs us," she said. "Just because you guys are freaked out about me—and I still kind of hate you guys a bit—that doesn't mean we abandon Dave."

"No," Will said. "We're going home to Nashville."

That would be the best thing, Carrie knew. Will had gotten so thin. This situation with Sophie and Mike was like whatever had ripped through Jared's side—except with her brother, the pain was coming from the inside out.

"No. We need to work this out. Not run away." Sophie turned to Melanie. "Right? We don't let my stupid mistake endanger all we've worked for. Promise me we'll stay until the primary. You promised to do whatever it takes to help me, and I am telling you that the worst thing any of us can do is run away."

Sophie turned her gaze to Carrie. "Right? We need to stay here, work things out, finish what we came for."

Oh God, how could I ever think I could be a mother? This is too hard. Carrie squeezed her eyes shut, searched somewhere for inspiration. She opened her eyes and spread her fingers, palms down, on the table so that her fingertips touched Sophie's.

"Why don't we do this," Carrie said. "Let's table this for today. Do whatever we can do that's useful. And then you can meet again this time tomorrow. The Connors situation room and all that."

Melanie gave her a teary smile. "*We* can meet again tomorrow, Caroline."

She realized that one day at a time would carry them through—not just for the next twenty-four hours but until the first Tuesday in February. If Sophie needed help, they'd get it. If word got out about Dave punching Mike, they'd deal with it.

If Jared O'Dea came up with some idea for them to get to know each other better, she'd listen to it.

New Year's Week

Presidential Primary Season

thirty-two

Wednesday morning

MELANIE OPENED THE DOOR TO CARRIE AND Tucker Keyes. What was he doing here? He'd left the Dawson bus to follow up on other stories. That's what he had told Eli. Why was he back—*dear God, please no more exposés.* Fortunately Sophie was in the Dawson suite, helping Hannah with her homework.

Melanie prayed every day that it had not been a mistake to stay in New Hampshire. Leaving the campaign would have been a load of guilt on Sophie's shoulders. The deal to stay and work for Dave had been contingent on Sophie's agreement to do therapy. Beth had connected them with a psychologist specializing in adolescents. Dr. Crisp reported great progress and didn't anticipate any more than three or four sessions to get Sophie on solid ground.

Will had offered to return to Nashville for good after this was all finished. Melanie was leaning toward DC. She'd hidden away for too many years, pretending that a website and a few books and speeches were sufficient to fulfill God's call on her life.

There was more to do—more she felt equipped to do. Hopefully Tucker Keyes wasn't here with something devastating.

"Tuck needs to talk to Will," Carrie said.

"He's eating breakfast. Can't it wait?"

Will came into the front hall, wiping his face with a napkin. "What do you need?"

"Tuck's been to Chicago," Carrie told them. "He's found something interesting."

"I talked to people on Mike McGregor's last campaign," Keyes said. "You'll want to hear this."

"You told him, Caroline?" Melanie said. "How could you?"

Will clenched his fist around the napkin. They dealt with Sophie calmly during the day, but he paced at night, admitting he wished he had been the one to punch McGregor.

"I didn't tell him anything," Carrie said. "Let us in, and he'll explain."

"I saw McGregor leave the hotel," Keyes said, "suitcases and all. His nose was obviously broken. I tried to ask him about it and he just shoved me. I assumed he had gotten injured in the blackout. He would have played that for all it was worth. When he didn't, I guessed something else had happened. No one here would comment on his departure other than the press release about differences in philosophy. So I made some calls . . ."

Carrie grinned. "He did what reporters do."

"I called around on his last campaign. Didn't get far. Eli DuPont called them and asked for a list of their volunteers."

"That blasted Eli," Will said. "He was told to 'no comment' this."

"I promised him a favor. A big one, whenever he needed it," Keyes said. "He got me the list, and I began calling. Not the professionals because I knew they wouldn't talk. I got a copy of their database and tracked down young people. I assumed they'd be unpaid volunteers. I was right.

"I found a father who was furious when he heard the name McGregor. So I flew out here with *The Journal*'s lawyer. And I was given copies of two sworn statements. The girls are in college now. Each one didn't know McGregor was messing with the other one. They were totally in love and each one thought it would last forever."

We always do, Melanie thought.

"They're arresting him tonight." Carrie beamed at Tucker Keyes like a proud parent. "We're going to see Dave next so he'll be ready with a statement."

"No!" Will said. "We can't."

"Eli DuPont will shade it as a minor who worked as a volunteer. Someone well known to the Dawson and Connors daughters. We won't lie, but he knows how to fix these things."

"It's going to come out because of the arrest," Keyes said. "The focus will be on what happened in that last campaign and not about what McGregor might or might not have done here."

"I'd be grateful if you would watch out for our . . . volunteers," Melanie said.

Keyes nodded at her, his cheeks flushing. "Absolutely."

"There's something else," Carrie said. "The FBI is coming in to interview Victoria Peters again."

"What?" A month ago Melanie would have been close to rejoicing. Now she was confused.

"I told Tuck about some prescriptions she has that didn't show up on her medical records."

"Carrie, you can't be blabbing stuff like that," Will said.

"Off the record," Keyes said. "I know the difference."

Melanie listened in amazement as Carrie told them about Victoria's prescriptions. Tucker Keyes had traveled to Baltimore to speak with a cousin of hers and learned Victoria had been in a brutal car accident as a teen. She had years of physical therapy and pain management that she still needed.

"The feds know there are moles in all the campaigns," Keyes said. "They're working overtime on all the interviews. And the best hackers in this country are working with the feds on Jericho. I know some of those guys so I passed them the photos that Carrie took of the medication bottles and also a copy of her sanitized medical record."

"I feel a little creepy," Carrie said. "Like a snitch. But this is national security. I'm glad connections are being made."

"Speaking of connections," Keyes said. "And this is a query on the record. One of my colleague's insiders with Zogbe says you're getting another bump in the polls. Care to comment, Mr. Connors?"

Melanie smiled as Will stepped into the hall in his bare feet. No politicking at home, they had decided. And this condo was home for the next twenty-four hours—or maybe five weeks.

No more pizza runs for Sophie or Hannah, though. Someone else would have to bring home the bacon.

Friday midday

Melanie and Carrie walked arm in arm through Veteran's Park on their way to the hospital. MoveIn had gone, its seasoned campers on to Maryland, Jared had told her. He stayed behind to recover.

Carrie knew that had something to do with her. They made a bizarre couple. Clearly she couldn't plan *everything*.

"I need to talk to you about the baby," Carrie said.

"What are you thinking?"

"No clue. Adopt. Parent. How do I know? I'm praying, Lanie. But I just don't know."

"We're with you, no matter what," Melanie said.

"Like that's a big help? It is and, at the same time, it's not."

"Carrie, if you decide you want to parent this child, then you need to parent him or her. One hundred percent. And it won't be easy, even though we'll be with you. I was a part-time single parent for Destiny and almost full-time single parent for Sophie. You know that."

"You always seemed to have it together. You made it look easy."

"It was anything but easy. If you decide to keep this baby, you have to be all in. Just like you are with Dave's campaign and with your brother. All in."

"I haven't got a clue about what 'all in' even is. It's not like I can internship in motherhood like I did in Dave's office when I was a teenager."

"It's tough," Melanie said. "I didn't have an inkling of how hard it must be to give up a child for adoption until I was pregnant with Sophie. The first time she kicked, I thought, Destiny's birth mother felt this. When she'd get hiccups in the womb—"

"Wait. Babies get hiccups in utero?"

"Pregnancy is one long miracle and one long burden. And motherhood? Wow. I know what it was like to have Destiny put in my arms for the first time. It wasn't until Sophie was born that I really cried for Destiny's birth mother because the thought of someone taking Sophie away from me was devastating. Adoption is such a gift."

"What about for the child?"

"Ask your niece." Melanie laughed. "Destiny will have an opinion."

"That she will," Carrie said.

"I'm hungry. Let's make a pizza run on our way back to the hotel."

"You still remember how? It gets complicated."

"Some things you never forget," Melanie said.

And other things just fade into the forgiveness that follows.

February

Presidential Primary Election

thirty-three

Tuesday night

"YOU'RE PREGNANT?" DESTINY SAID, EYES WIDE.

She and Luke had come east for a week of skiing in Maine with her birth father and his family. Perfect timing—they couldn't vote in the New Hampshire primary but they could come to headquarters and support the Dawsons.

Carrie stood up, modeled the swelling at her waistline. She and Destiny had come upstairs to her room to change into looser pants as they waited for votes to be counted.

It was close. Dave was nip and tuck with Sheryl Bresler. Vice President Haines had been declared his party's winner within twenty minutes and had already gone in front of the press.

"It's that guy in Dillon's video. The redhead, right?"

"What're you talking about?"

"Dillon sent me the interview. I saw the way he looked at you."

"No, he's not the guy. But he is important to me."

"Wow. Doesn't this make for a complicated courtship," Destiny said. "You're not expecting me and Luke to take the baby?"

Carrie laughed. "Nah. Your mother says you'll get payback when you give birth to someone with your genetic pigheadedness."

"So, the father?"

"He's not interested. He'll do whatever I ask except, like . . . get married. Not that I'd ask him. It was just a onetime thing."

Destiny shook her head. "You tramp, you."

"Yeah, that's about it."

"I like this redheaded guy."

Carrie laughed. "Yeah, you would."

"Are you going to keep at whatever it is that makes his eyes shine? You used to be a hard woman, Carrie. Now look at you. The glow and all that."

"I don't see how, Dez. I work for the senator and he's a protestor. I've got to be in DC if I keep the baby because I need Will and Melanie. Jared is a . . . do-gooding idealist."

"You make him sound like an ax murderer."

"He goes where his heart tells him."

Destiny tapped her knee. "I've seen the look his heart gives."

"I can't ask him to come to Washington so we can pursue whatever this is between us. That would dampen his fire."

"Don't give up so easily. Pregnancy must be softening your brain."

"And my waistline."

"Let's think about this. What did he do before he lived in a tent?"

"Finance. He was on the VP track but couldn't resolve that with where he felt God was leading him."

"Aha," Destiny said. "Ahhh!"

"Stop showing me your tonsils, Dez."

"Do you remember my sister from another mother?"

"Chloe, sure. We were bridesmaids together, or were you too deliriously happy at your wedding to notice us standing up for you?"

"So check it, dude. Her husband runs his family's foundation. The Deschene Trust. Its mission is to ensure currency integrity in developing economies."

"You memorized that, didn't you?" Carrie said, laughing.

Destiny shrugged. "Absolutely. I have no idea what it means. They're setting up an office in Washington and Chloe says he's really picky about who he brings on board. You have to have the experience in economic stuff and proven commitment to all that matters. And yes, I memorized that too. I could make a phone call?"

"Sure. Okay. No, wait. I guess I should ask him. I'm pretty much over doing things for people and then telling them what they did."

Destiny hugged her and said, "Hey. Do I get to be the godmother?"

"I'm not sure I'll keep—"

"Come on, Carrie. It's not often I volunteer to change diapers."

"Yeah. The whole diaper thing. I can't believe I envision myself as a mother—diapers, spit-up, the terrible twos."

"I suppose baby poop and power suits aren't a good mix."

"No kidding," Carrie said. "And yet I dream about rocking my baby until we both doze off. Talk about going mush! And other stuff too. Like cutting the crusts off of bread so we can feed the ducks at the park. Marking the door frame with a Sharpie every few months and making a big deal out of how fast he or she is growing up."

"That's what your dad used to do for me, Dez. Only he used to do it in his office and not in Mother's home because . . . well, you've seen her house."

"Historic registry and all that," Destiny said. "Intimidating."

"Mother didn't have anyone to . . . moderate her. I'm so afraid I'm too selfish and I'd do the same thing. Which is why I dream about my child having a father. That's not something my trust fund can buy, and I can't expect Will to drop everything and play Daddy on a daily basis."

"When he can make time for it," Destiny said, "he's good at it. He was always busy, but I knew he loved me—never doubted that one minute."

"And that is the security I want my baby to have. What a gift your birth mom gave to you when she handed you to *two* loving parents."

"Julia would've found the strength to do right by me either way—and so will you. You're *already* a great mother," Destiny said, "the way you are so carefully considering what's best for your baby."

There was a knock on the door. Carrie opened it. Melanie came in, gave Destiny a quick hug before turning to Carrie.

"Did we win?" Carrie said. "Tell me we won."

"No, they're calling this one for Representative Bresler," Melanie said. "But we're only a couple percentage points behind. And we've got donors contacting Will already about getting on board. They want Dave to keep going."

"So we're moving forward?" Carrie said.

Melanie smiled. "Dave is making a quick statement and then heading to Florida. Will's already on a plane to South Carolina. He said to tell you he'd call about Pennsylvania."

Carrie rubbed her belly, smiled at the thought of running the organization in a battleground state. Everything in her wanted to jump for joy.

But she had a baby to consider. "I was thinking, Lanie," she said, "that I should go back to DC and work in the Senate office. It's better, I think, to keep things quieter. And someone's got to have Dave's back there. I can check in on Tuck and"—she glanced at Destiny—"work on some other items."

Melanie wrapped her arms around Carrie, whispered, "I'll make sure I'm there when you need me. We won't leave you to do this alone."

"I know," Carrie said.

"Hey, can we stop with the hugging and get some food?" Destiny asked.

Carrie smiled, linked her arm through Destiny's. "Yeah, let's go eat pizza before there's nothing left."

"Because you're eating for two," Destiny said, laughing.

"Yeah, and I'll be needing maternity clothes soon. And have stretch marks. And good grief—can you imagine me in labor?"

Melanie took Carrie's other arm. "You've labored your whole life—just for other causes. Laboring to bring a new little life into the world—now *that* is a very worthy cause, Caroline Connors!"

"Amen to that," Destiny said.

Carrie smiled. "Amen, and let's eat!"

Reading Group Guide

1. As the story opens, what would you say is the "real deal" behind Melanie's desperation to reach and rescue her teenage daughter?
2. Why do women often feel the need to "rescue" someone else, when in fact, they are the ones in emotional peril? When we project our issues onto someone else, does it help them? Or simply hinder our own growth?
3. Stephen Arterburn says in his book *Healing Is a Choice*, "You do not bury pain dead. You bury it alive, and it must be fed every day." How were the following characters compelled to feed the pain they'd never learned to process? And what might they have done differently to keep from spiraling down into such desperate situations?
   Melanie? Will? Carrie? Tuck?
4. Why do you think Will turned to Paige Bowers in his season of weakness and loneliness? Is a wife (or husband) ever to blame for a spouse's infidelity? Why or why not?
5. Describe the power that every husband and wife possess to help their mate live with sexual and emotional integrity. If everyone took responsibility for sifting through their own sexual and emotional baggage to become an interested and motivated intimacy partner, what impact would that have on society?

6. Do you think Melanie could have responded so compassionately toward Will's indiscretion had she not learned to have compassion for her own shortcomings? Why or why not?
7. Why do we often find it so hard to apply God's unconditional love, endless mercies, and abounding grace to our own lives? Does receiving these gifts from God enable us to share them more readily with others?
8. What do you think were Melanie's and Will's most valuable takeaways from their counseling relationship with Beth? Do you think they could have learned to reconnect after all those years without the help of a neutral third party? Why or why not?
9. If Carrie decides to raise her child, what impact do you think motherhood will have on her personal life? Her professional life? Her spiritual life? If she decides to offer her child for adoption, what gifts will she be giving that child?
10. What long-term impact do you think this awkward and abusive experience with Mike McGregor will have on Sophie? How can she avoid letting this ruin her life and future relationships? What kind of choices can Sophie make that will foster continued growth and healing rather than let this ruin her life and future relationships (as her mother did for too long)?
11. Melanie finally managed to be honest with Will about her experiences as an attention-seeking teenager, and the impact all of her inappropriate relationships had on her own sexual development. Do you think Melanie should be as open and honest with Sophie? Why or why not?
12. How can parents most effectively guide their children toward a lifestyle of sexual and emotional integrity and healthy relationships? Does "helicopter parenting" work, or does it have the opposite effect we're aiming for?

Acknowledgments

We both wish to thank the hard-working team at Thomas Nelson—Amanda Bostic, Natalie Hanemann, Jodi Hughes, and so many others for their wise and loving guidance.

Shannon:

Joel Kneedler and Alive Communications—thank you for connecting me and Kathy on these fiction projects! We love being part of the Alive family, and you couldn't have paired me with a more delightful, creative soul to bring this vision to life!

Thanks to all of my readers for encouraging me over the past decade to go in this exciting new direction of developing fiction. YOU are why I delight in creating books and other ministry tools because of how YOU allow them to transform your lives, marriages, and families!

Special thanks to my own family and friends for so enthusiastically supporting my "ministry habit" for almost two decades. You know who you are, and so does God. May He bless you abundantly for the blessing you are to me.

Kathryn:

I add my gratitude to Shannon's in thanking Joel Kneedler of Alive Communications. I am so grateful that Joel is among all the legacies of blessings and love that Lee Hough passed on to me.

Many thanks to my husband, my writers' group, and my dear friends for their constancy and encouragement.

I give my love and appreciation to Shannon for her boldness and faithfulness in ministry. May the Lord multiply her fruitfulness in shining the light of Christ in a treacherous culture.

9781401688677-C

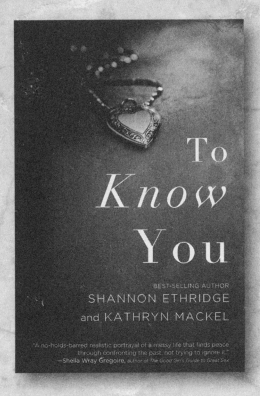

9781401688677-B

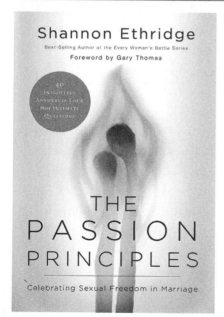

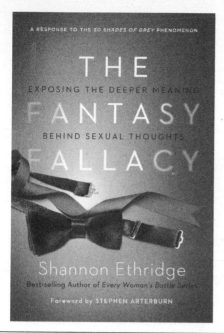

About the Authors

Photo by Rebecca Friedlander

Shannon Ethridge is a best-selling author, international speaker, and certified life coach with a master's degree in counseling/human relations from Liberty University. She has spoken to college students and adults since 1989 and is the author of twenty books, including the million-copy best-selling Every Woman's Battle series. She is a frequent guest on TV and radio programs and host the Sexy Marriage Radio Shoe. She also mentors aspiring writers and speakers through her online BLAST Program (Building Leaders, Authors, Speakers & Teachers).

Photo by Angela Hunt

Kathy Mackel is the acclaimed author of *Can of Worms* and other novels for middle readers from Putnam, HarperCollins, and Dial. Her latest book, *Boost*, tackles the thorny issue of steroids and girls' sports. Writing as Kathryn Mackel, she is the author of the YA fantasy series the Birthright Books and of supernatural thrillers including the Christy finalist *The Hidden*. She was the credited screenwriter for Disney's *Can of Worms* and for *Hangman's Curse*, and has worked for Disney, Fox, and Showtime.